T0100191

Build an Orchestrator in Go (From Scratch)

TIM BORING

MANNING

SHELTER ISLAND

Manning Publications Co.
20 Baldwin Road
PO Box 761
Shelter Island, NY 11964

Development editor:	Katie Sposato Johnson
Technical development editor:	Mike Shepard
Review editors:	Adriana Sabo and Dunja Nikitović
Production editor:	Keri Hales
Copy editor:	Alisa Larson
Proofreader:	Melody Dolab
Technical proofreader:	Mike Haller
Typesetter:	Dennis Dalinnik
Cover designer:	Marija Tudor

ISBN: 9781617299759
Printed in the United States of America

For Jennifer, who has always believed in me,
even when I didn't believe in myself.

brief contents

PART 1   INTRODUCTION 1

    1 ■ What is an orchestrator?   3

    2 ■ From mental model to skeleton code   22

    3 ■ Hanging some flesh on the task skeleton   36

PART 2   WORKER 53

    4 ■ Workers of the Cube, unite!   55

    5 ■ An API for the worker   71

    6 ■ Metrics   88

PART 3   MANAGER 103

    7 ■ The manager enters the room   105

    8 ■ An API for the manager   122

    9 ■ What could possibly go wrong?   138

PART 4   REFACTORINGS 161

          10 ■ Implementing a more sophisticated scheduler   163
          11 ■ Implementing persistent storage for tasks   188

PART 5   CLI...219

          12 ■ Building a command-line interface   221
          13 ■ Now what?   251

contents

preface xiii
acknowledgments xv
about this book xvi
about the author xix
about the cover illustration xx

PART 1 INTRODUCTION 1

1 What is an orchestrator? 3

1.1 Why implement an orchestrator from scratch? 4

1.2 The (not so) good ol' days 4

1.3 What is a container, and how is it different from a virtual machine? 6

1.4 What is an orchestrator? 7

1.5 The components of an orchestration system 8

The task 8 ▪ The job 9 ▪ The scheduler 10
The manager 10 ▪ The worker 10 ▪ The cluster 10
Command-line interface 11

1.6 Meet Cube 13

1.7 What tools will we use? 15

1.8 A word about hardware 16

1.9 What we won't be implementing or discussing 18

*Distributed computing 18 ▪ Service discovery 18
High availability 19 ▪ Load balancing 20 ▪ Security 21*

2 **From mental model to skeleton code 22**

2.1 The task skeleton 24

2.2 The worker skeleton 27

2.3 The manager skeleton 29

2.4 The scheduler skeleton 30

2.5 Other skeletons 31

2.6 Taking our skeletons for a spin 32

3 **Hanging some flesh on the task skeleton 36**

3.1 Docker: Starting, stopping, and inspecting containers from the command line 37

3.2 Docker: Starting, stopping, and inspecting containers from the API 40

3.3 Task configuration 41

3.4 Starting and stopping tasks 43

PART 2 WORKER 53

4 **Workers of the Cube, unite! 55**

4.1 The Cube worker 56

4.2 Tasks and Docker 58

4.3 The role of the queue 59

4.4 The role of the DB 60

4.5 Counting tasks 60

4.6 Implementing the worker's methods 60

*Implementing the StopTask method 60 ▪ Implementing the
StartTask method 61 ▪ An interlude on task state 63
Implementing the RunTask method 66*

4.7 Putting it all together 67

5 *An API for the worker 71*

   5.1   Overview of the worker API   72

   5.2   Data format, requests, and responses   74

   5.3   The API struct   76

   5.4   Handling requests   77

   5.5   Serving the API   80

   5.6   Putting it all together   81

6 *Metrics   88*

   6.1   What metrics should we collect?   89

   6.2   Metrics available from the /proc filesystem   90

   6.3   Collecting metrics with goprocinfo   93

   6.4   Exposing the metrics on the API   98

   6.5   Putting it all together   99

PART 3   MANAGER 103

7 *The manager enters the room   105*

   7.1   The Cube manager   106
         The components that make up the manager   107

   7.2   The Manager struct   108

   7.3   Implementing the manager's methods   109
         *Implementing the SelectWorker method   109 ▪ Implementing
         the SendWork method   110 ▪ Implementing the UpdateTasks
         method   112 ▪ Adding a task to the manager   114
         Creating a manager   115*

   7.4   An interlude on failures and resiliency   115

   7.5   Putting it all together   116

8 *An API for the manager   122*

   8.1   Overview of the manager API   123

   8.2   Routes   124

   8.3   Data format, requests, and responses   124

   8.4   The API struct   126

8.5   Handling requests   126

8.6   Serving the API   129

8.7   A few refactorings to make our lives easier   129

8.8   Putting it all together   131

9   What could possibly go wrong?   138

9.1   Overview of our new scenario   139

9.2   Failure scenarios   139

*Application startup failure   139 ▪ Application bugs   140
Task startup failures due to resource problems   140 ▪ Task failures
due to Docker daemon crashes and restarts   141 ▪ Task failures due
to machine crashes and restarts   141 ▪ Worker failures   141
Manager failures   142*

9.3   Recovery options   142

*Recovery from application failures   142 ▪ Recovering from
environmental failures   142 ▪ Recovering from task-level
failures   143 ▪ Recovering from worker failures   144
Recovering from manager failures   145*

9.4   Implementing health checks   145

*Inspecting a task on the worker   146 ▪ Implementing task updates
on the worker   148 ▪ Healthchecks and restarts   149*

9.5   Putting it all together   153

PART 4   REFACTORINGS 161

10   Implementing a more sophisticated scheduler   163

10.1   The scheduling problem   163

10.2   Scheduling considerations   164

10.3   Scheduler interface   165

10.4   Adapting the round-robin scheduler to the scheduler
interface   166

10.5   Using the new scheduler interface   169

*Adding new fields to the Manager struct   169 ▪ Modifying the
New helper function   170*

10.6   Did you notice the bug?   173

10.7   Putting it all together   175

10.8 The E-PVM scheduler 178

The theory 178 ▪ In practice 179

10.9 Completing the Node implementation 183

10.10 Using the E-PVM scheduler 186

 Implementing persistent storage for tasks 188

11.1 The storage problem 189

11.2 The Store interface 189

11.3 Implementing an in-memory store for tasks 191

11.4 Implementing an in-memory store for task events 195

11.5 Refactoring the manager to use the new in-memory stores 196

11.6 Refactoring the worker 201

11.7 Putting it all together 205

11.8 Introducing BoltDB 207

11.9 Implementing a persistent task store 208

11.10 Implementing a persistent task event store 212

11.11 Switching out the in-memory stores for permanent ones 215

PART 5 CLI 219

12 Building a command-line interface 221

12.1 The core components of CLIs 222

12.2 Introducing the Cobra framework 223

12.3 Setting up our Cobra application 224

12.4 Understanding the new main.go 224

12.5 Understanding root.go 225

12.6 Implementing the worker command 227

12.7 Implementing the manager command 233

12.8 Implementing the run command 236

12.9 Implementing the stop command 241

12.10 Implementing the status command 243

12.11 Implementing the node command 246

13 *Now what? 251*

   13.1 Working on Kubernetes and related tooling 252

   13.2 Manager–worker pattern and workflow systems 252

   13.3 Manager–worker pattern and integration systems 253

   13.4 In closing 253

   appendix Environment setup 255

                 index 257

preface

I was introduced to orchestrators when I started at Google in 2007. And my introduction was not to Borg but rather Ganeti. Ganeti was an internally developed cluster management system that operated on virtual machines. At the time, it was a basic wrapper around the open source version of Xen, and it provided a clustered solution that allowed us to provide virtual (instead of physical) machines to engineers.

We didn't refer to Ganeti as an orchestrator, nor did we talk about it in the same vein as Borg. In hindsight, I don't think it's too much of a stretch to consider Ganeti a kind of orchestrator. Instead of operating on tasks (in the form of containers), it operated on virtual machines. Internally at Google, Ganeti served as a bridge from a world where some engineers could run their applications on physical machines to a world where every engineer ran their applications on Borg.

Several years later, I got a proper introduction to Borg when we rewrote the life cycle management system we built to manage Ganeti clusters and virtual machines. We ran it on Borg. Fast-forward to 2020. The COVID pandemic hit, and like everyone else, I found myself working from home. Suddenly, I had three-plus extra hours per day as a result of not having to commute to a Manhattan office. What to do?

Of course, the obvious thing to do was to start a personal project of some kind. But what? After 13 years of working with orchestrators, I thought it might be fun to try to write one from scratch. How hard could it be?

I spent most of the summer of 2020 working on my orchestrator. I called it *Cube* in an effort to continue the Star Trek theme. Surprisingly, I got it working in less than 3,000 lines of code.

Around the same time, I read Thorsten Ball's *Writing an Interpreter in Go*. While I wasn't necessarily interested in interpreters or writing programming languages, I was interested in learning how they work. And then it hit me! I could do a book about writing an *orchestrator* in Go. It would be the book that I wish I'd had back in 2007! Thus was born the book you have in front of you now.

I realized early on in the writing process that orchestration is a big topic. It's easy to get distracted by secondary concerns when talking about orchestration systems. How do you handle service discovery? How do you handle DNS? What about consensus? I wanted to strip away all the stuff that gets piled on top of orchestration systems and present just the core, the foundation on which all that other stuff sits. Not that things like service discovery, DNS, and load balancing are unimportant. But in the context of an orchestration system, we talk about those things because they are tools in service to the core function of an orchestrator: scheduling applications to run on a pool of nodes and managing their life cycle.

So in a nutshell, that's what this book is about: taking a request from a user to run an application, identifying a machine that can run the application, and then sending a request to the chosen machine to start the application. It seems simple when you put it that way, doesn't it?

In addition to presenting the foundational concepts of an orchestration system, another goal in writing this book is to make the content approachable to a broad audience. So while I've chosen to write the Cube orchestrator in the Go programming language, my hope is that anyone can work through the book and get the code working, even if you've never written a line of Go in your life. All of the code uses basic Go features. While we do use goroutines to do some basic concurrency, we don't use channels (there are many great resources to learn about concurrency if you're interested). And we don't use generics. (Shortly after Go 1.18 was released, I did attempt to refactor the code and manuscript to use generics. While I got the code working, I realized it introduced unnecessary complexity to the book. It became one more thing to explain in an already long list of things to explain.)

I hope you have fun while you read this book. And in the process of having fun, I hope you learn as much from this book as I did writing it.

acknowledgments

With most things in life, we get a lot of help from others. And this book is no different.

I'd like to start by acknowledging all the folks at Manning who helped make this book a reality. I'd like to thank Andy Waldron for taking on my book and believing in it throughout its many shapes. Katie Sposato Johnson was instrumental in helping me navigate the Manning process. Without her help, this book would not exist. I'd also like to thank the many other folks at Manning who have worked on the production and marketing of the book.

I want to thank the reviewers who read the manuscript at various stages and provided thoughtful feedback: Alain Lompo, Alessandro Campeis, Andres Sacco, Becky Huett, Bobby Lin, Christopher Villanueva, Clifford Thurber, David Paccoud, Emanuele Piccinelli, Ernesto Bossi, Fernando Bernardino, Fernando Rodrigues, Geert Van Laethem, Gregory Reshetniak, Katia Patkin, Kosmas Chatzimichalis, Larry Cai, Lucian Enache, Madiha Khalid, Matthias Busch, Michael Bright, Muneeb Shaikh, Nathan B. Crocker, Nghia To, Richard Vaughan, Sanket Naik, Simone Sguazza, Thomas Dybdahl, Timothy R. J. Langford, Tim van Deurzen, and Vamsi Krishna.

Special thanks also go out to Mike Haller, technical proofreader, for his thorough review of the code shortly before the book went into production. It's quite challenging to keep the code presented in the book in sync with the source code, but Mike was invaluable in helping me clean up the many discrepancies.

about this book

Build an Orchestrator in Go (From Scratch) was written to help you better understand the fundamental components of orchestration systems. Whether you work as a DevOps engineer, site reliability engineer (SRE), or software engineer, much of today's technology can seem like a black box. You just deploy it to the cloud, and then magical "stuff" happens. As we all know, magical technology is great when it works! When it fails—and it will fail!—that magical aspect can be a barrier to quickly identifying problems and fixing them. As more developers move their applications to the cloud, they are running them (or will do so) on an orchestration system. Unless they work at a larger company that has a dedicated DevOps or SRE staff, they will likely need to deploy and manage their applications themselves. This includes handling problems when they arise. My hope is that this book will remove some of the magic from how applications run on an orchestrator.

Who should read this book

Build an Orchestrator in Go (From Scratch) is for anyone responsible for deploying and operating an orchestration system (i.e., DevOps engineers and SREs) and for anyone responsible for deploying and managing applications that run on an orchestration system (i.e., software engineers). If you want to learn how orchestrators work, you could read the source code for either Kubernetes or Nomad, both open source projects available on GitHub. Kubernetes has 5 million lines of Go code. Nomad has a considerably smaller codebase, but it's still 500,000-plus lines of Go. I don't know about you, but I would struggle to get much value from trying to make sense of half a million lines of code, let alone 5 million lines!

How this book is organized: A road map

The book has five parts that cover 13 chapters. Part 1 introduces the mental model for the Cube orchestrator and sets up the skeleton codebase that will be implemented throughout the rest of the book:

- Chapter 1 briefly explains the purpose of orchestration systems and then describes the mental model for Cube, the orchestrator implemented throughout the rest of the book.
- Chapter 2 uses the mental model from chapter 1 to create a skeleton codebase for the core concepts of the Cube orchestrator.
- Chapter 3 illustrates how we'll implement the codebase by taking the skeleton for the `Task` object and fleshing it out in detail.

Part 2 implements the concepts necessary for the worker component:

- Chapter 4 fleshes out the implementation details of the `Worker` object.
- Chapter 5 builds an API for the `Worker`.
- Chapter 6 creates a framework for the worker to expose metrics about its state and the state of the tasks it's running.

Part 3 implements the concepts necessary for the manager component:

- Chapter 7 fleshes out the implementation details of the `Manager` object.
- Chapter 8 builds an API for the `Manager`.
- Chapter 9 explores failure scenarios and implements solutions to handle them.

Part 4 walks the reader through refactoring two components from the initial implementation:

- Chapter 10 describes a scheduler interface and implements a more sophisticated scheduling algorithm.
- Chapter 11 designs and builds a storage interface that allows the manager and worker components to store their tasks in-memory or persistently in a database.

Part 5 implements a command-line interface (CLI) that allows the reader to operate the orchestrator:

- Chapter 12 builds a CLI that implements commands for starting the manager and worker, starting and stopping tasks, and getting the status of tasks in the system.
- Chapter 13 offers a summary of what we've accomplished and provides some suggestions for where to go from here.

About the code

This book contains many examples of source code both in numbered listings and in line with normal text. In both cases, source code is formatted in a `fixed-width font like this` to separate it from ordinary text. Sometimes code is also **in bold** to highlight code that has changed from previous steps in the chapter, such as when a new feature is added to an existing line of code.

In many cases, the original source code has been reformatted; we've added line breaks and reworked indentation to accommodate the available page space in the book. In rare cases, even this was not enough, and listings include line-continuation markers (➥). Additionally, comments in the source code have often been removed from the listings when the code is described in the text. Code annotations accompany many of the listings, highlighting important concepts.

You can get executable snippets of code from the liveBook (online) version of this book at https://livebook.manning.com/book/build-an-orchestrator-in-go-from-scratch. The complete code for the examples in the book is available for download from the Manning website at https://www.manning.com/books/build-an-orchestrator-in-go-from-scratch and from GitHub at https://github.com/buildorchestratoringo/code.

liveBook discussion forum

Purchase of *Build an Orchestrator in Go (From Scratch)* includes free access to a private web forum run by Manning Publications where you can make comments about the book, ask technical questions, and receive help from the author and from other users. To access the forum and subscribe to it, point your web browser to https://www.manning.com/books/build-an-orchestrator-in-go-from-scratch. This page provides information on how to get on the forum once you're registered, what kind of help is available, and the rules of conduct on the forum.

Manning's commitment to our readers is to provide a venue where a meaningful dialog between individual readers and between readers and the author can take place. It is not a commitment to any specific amount of participation on the part of the author, whose contributions to the forum remain voluntary (and unpaid). We suggest you ask the author challenging questions lest his interest stray!

about the author

TIM BORING is a software engineer with 20+ years of industry experience. For most of those years, he has been a user of orchestration systems, including Borg, Kubernetes, and Nomad.

about the cover illustration

The figure on the cover of *Build an Orchestrator in Go (From Scratch)* is "Femme Baschkirienne," or "Baschkirian woman," taken from a collection by Jacques Grasset de Saint-Sauveur, published in 1788. The illustration is finely drawn and colored by hand.

In those days, it was easy to identify where people lived and what their trade or station in life was just by their dress. Manning celebrates the inventiveness and initiative of the computer business with book covers based on the rich diversity of regional culture centuries ago, brought back to life by pictures from collections such as this one.

Part 1

Introduction

The first part of this book lays the groundwork for your journey to writing an orchestration system—from scratch!

In chapter 1, you will learn the core components that make up every orchestration system. From these core components, you will build a mental model for the Cube orchestrator, which we will implement together through the rest of the book.

Chapter 2 guides you through creating code skeletons from the mental model you learned in chapter 1.

In chapter 3, you will take the skeleton for the Task object and flesh it out in detail. This exercise will illustrate the process we'll use to implement the rest of Cube's codebase.

What is an orchestrator?

This chapter covers

- The evolution of application deployments
- Classifying the components of an orchestration system
- Introducing the mental model for the orchestrator
- Defining requirements for our orchestrator
- Identifying the scope of our work

Kubernetes. Kubernetes. Kubernetes. If you've worked in or near the tech industry in the last five years, you've at least heard the name. Perhaps you've used it in your day job. Or perhaps you've used other systems such as Apache Mesos or HashiCorp's Nomad.

In this book, we're going to build our own Kubernetes, writing the code ourselves to gain a better understanding of just what Kubernetes is. And what Kubernetes is—like Mesos and Nomad—is an orchestrator.

When you've finished the book, you will have learned the following:

- What components form the foundation of any orchestration system
- How those components interact
- How each component maintains its own state and why
- What tradeoffs are made in designing and implementing an orchestration system

1.1   Why implement an orchestrator from scratch?

Why bother writing an orchestrator from scratch? No, the answer is not to write a system that will replace Kubernetes, Mesos, or Nomad. The answer is more practical than that. If you're like me, you learn by doing. Learning by doing is easy when we're dealing with small things. How do I write a `for` loop in this new programming language I'm learning? How do I use the `curl` command to make a request to this new API I want to use? These things are easy to learn by doing them because they are small in scope and don't require too much effort.

When we want to learn larger systems, however, learning by doing becomes challenging. The obvious way to tackle this situation is to read the source code. The code for Kubernetes, Mesos, and Nomad is available on GitHub. So if the source code is available, why write an orchestrator from scratch? Couldn't we just look at the source code for them and get the same benefit?

Perhaps. Keep in mind, though, that these are large software projects. Kubernetes contains more than 2 million lines of source code. Mesos and Nomad clock in at just over 700,000 lines of code. While not impossible, learning a system by slogging around in codebases of this size may not be the best way.

Instead, we're going to roll up our sleeves and get our hands dirty. We'll implement our orchestrator in less than 3,000 lines of code.

To ensure we focus on the core bits of an orchestrator and don't get sidetracked, we are going to narrow the scope of our implementation. The orchestrator you write in the course of this project will be fully functional. You will be able to start and stop tasks and interact with those tasks.

It will not, however, be production ready. After all, our purpose is not to implement a system that will replace Kubernetes, Nomad, or Mesos. Instead, our purpose is to implement a minimal system that gives us deeper insight into how production-grade systems like Kubernetes and Nomad work.

1.2   The (not so) good ol' days

Let's take a journey back to 2002 and meet Michelle. Michelle is a system administrator for her company, and she is responsible for keeping her company's applications up and running around the clock. How does she accomplish this?

Like many other sysadmins, Michelle employs the common strategy of deploying applications on bare metal servers. A simplistic sketch of Michelle's world can be seen in figure 1.1. Each application typically runs on its own physical hardware. To make matters more complicated, each application has its own hardware requirements, so Michelle has to buy and then manage a server fleet that is unique to each application. Moreover, each application has its own unique deployment process and tooling. The database team gets new versions and updates in the mail via compact disk, so its process involves a database administrator (DBA) copying files from the CD to a central server and then using a set of custom shell scripts to push the files to the database servers, where another set of shell scripts handles installation and updates. Michelle handles the installation and updates of the company's financial system herself. This process involves downloading the software from the internet, at least saving her the hassle of dealing with CDs. But the financial software comes with its own set of tools for installing and managing updates. Several other teams are building the company's software product, and the applications these teams build have a completely different set of tools and procedures.

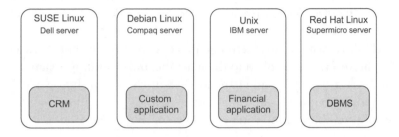

Figure 1.1   This diagram represents Michelle's world in 2002. The outer box represents physical machines and the operating systems running on them. The inner box represents the applications running on the machines and demonstrates how applications used to be more directly tied to both operating systems and machines.

If you weren't working in the industry during this time and didn't experience anything like Michelle's world, consider yourself lucky. Not only was that world chaotic and difficult to manage, it was also extremely wasteful. Virtualization came along next in the early to mid-2000s. These tools allowed sysadmins like Michelle to carve up their physical fleets so that each physical machine hosted several smaller yet independent virtual machines (VMs). Instead of each application running on its own dedicated physical machine, it now ran on a VM. And multiple VMs could be packed onto a single physical one. While virtualization made life for folks like Michelle better, it wasn't a silver bullet.

This was the way of things until the mid-2010s when two new technologies appeared on the horizon. The first was Docker, which introduced *containers* to the wider world. The concept of containers was not new. It had been around since 1979 (see Ell Marquez's "The History of Container Technology" at http://mng.bz/oro2). Before Docker, containers were mostly confined to large companies, like Sun Microsystems and Google, and hosting providers looking for ways to efficiently and securely provide virtualized environments for their customers. The second new technology to appear at this time was Kubernetes, a container *orchestrator* focused on automating the deployment and management of containers.

1.3   *What is a container, and how is it different from a virtual machine?*

As mentioned earlier, the first step in moving from Michelle's early world of physical machines and operating systems was the introduction of *virtual machines*. Virtual machines, or VMs, abstracted a computer's physical components (CPU, memory, disk, network, CD-Rom, etc.) so administrators could run multiple operating systems on a single physical machine. Each operating system running on the physical machine was distinct. Each had its own kernel, its own networking stack, and its own resources (e.g., CPU, memory, disk).

The VM world was a vast improvement in terms of cost and efficiency. The cost and efficiency gains, however, only applied to the machine and operating system layers. At the application layer, not much had changed. As you can see in figure 1.2, applications were still tightly coupled to an operating system. If you wanted to run two or more instances of your application, you needed two or more VMs.

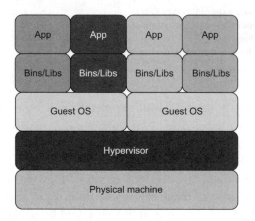

Figure 1.2   Applications running on VMs

Unlike VMs, a container does not have a kernel. It does not have its own networking stack. It does not control resources like CPU, memory, and disk. In fact, the term *container* is just a concept; it is not a concrete technical reality like a VM.

The term *container* is really just shorthand for process and resource isolation in the Linux kernel. So when we talk about containers, what we really are talking about are *namespaces* and *control groups* (*cgroups*), both of which are features of the Linux kernel. *Namespaces* are a mechanism to isolate processes and their resources from each other. *Cgroups* provide limits and accounting for a collection of processes.

But let's not get too bogged down with these lower-level details. You don't need to know about namespaces and cgroups to work through the rest of this book. If you are interested, however, I encourage you to watch Liz Rice's talk "Containers from Scratch" (https://www.youtube.com/watch?v=8fi7uSYlOdc).

With the introduction of containers, an application can be decoupled from the operating system layer, as seen in figure 1.3. With containers, if I have an app that starts up a server process that listens on port 80, I can now run multiple instances of that app on a single physical host. Or let's say that I have six different applications, each with their own server processes listening on port 80. Again, with containers, I can run those six applications on the same host without having to give each one a different port at the application layer.

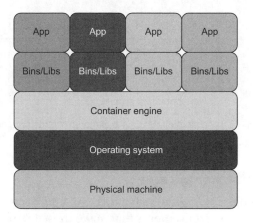

Figure 1.3   Applications running in containers

The real benefit of containers is that they give the application the impression that it is the sole application running on the operating system and thus has access to all of the operating system's resources.

1.4   What is an orchestrator?

The most recent step in the evolution of Michelle's world is using an *orchestrator* to deploy and manage her applications. An orchestrator is a system that provides automation for deploying, scaling, and otherwise managing containers. In many ways, an orchestrator is similar to a CPU scheduler. The difference is that the target objects of an orchestration system are containers instead of OS-level processes. (While containers are typically the primary focus of an orchestrator, some systems also provide for the orchestration of other types of workloads. HashiCorp's Nomad, for example, supports Java, command, and the QEMU VM runner workload types in addition to Docker.)

With containers and an orchestrator, Michelle's world changes drastically. In the past, the physical hardware and operating systems she deployed and managed were mostly dictated by requirements from application vendors. Her company's financial system, for example, had to run on AIX (a proprietary Unix OS owned by IBM), which meant the physical servers had to be RISC-based (https://riscv.org/) IBM machines. Why? Because the vendor that developed and sold the financial system certified that the system could run on AIX. If Michelle tried to run the financial system on, say, Debian Linux, the vendor would not provide support because it was not a certified OS. And this was just one of the many applications that Michelle operated for her company.

Now Michelle can deploy a standardized fleet of machines that all run the same OS. She no longer has to deal with multiple hardware vendors who deal in specialized servers. She no longer has to deal with administrative tools that are unique to each operating system. And, most importantly, she no longer needs the hodgepodge of deployment tools provided by application vendors. Instead, she can use the same tooling to deploy, scale, and manage all of her company's applications (table 1.1).

Table 1.1   Michelle's old and new worlds

Michelle's old world	Michelle's new world
Multiple hardware vendors	Single hardware vendor (or cloud provider)
Multiple operating systems	Single operating system
Runtime requirements dictated by application vendors	Application vendors build to standards (containers and orchestration)

1.5   *The components of an orchestration system*

So an orchestrator automates deploying, scaling, and managing containers. Next, let's identify the generic components and their requirements that make those features possible. They are as follows:

- The task
- The job
- The scheduler
- The manager
- The worker
- The cluster
- The command-line interface (CLI)

Some of these components can be seen in figure 1.4.

1.5.1   *The task*

The *task* is the smallest unit of work in an orchestration system and typically runs in a container. You can think of it like a process that runs on a single machine. A single task could run an instance of a reverse proxy like NGINX, or it could run an instance of an application like a RESTful API server; it could be a simple program that runs in an endless loop and does something silly, like ping a website and write the result to a database.

A task should specify the following:

1 The amount of memory, CPU, and disk it needs to run effectively
2 What the orchestrator should do in case of failures, typically called a *restart policy*
3 The name of the container image used to run the task

Task definitions may specify additional details, but these are the core requirements.

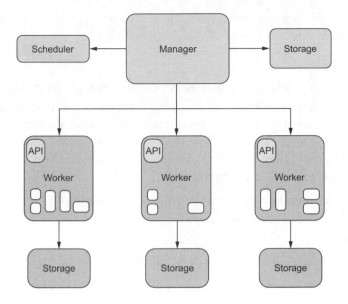

Figure 1.4 The basic components of an orchestration system. Regardless of what terms different orchestrators use, each has a scheduler, a manager, and a worker, and they all operate on tasks.

1.5.2 The job

The *job* is an aggregation of tasks. It has one or more tasks that typically form a larger logical grouping of tasks to perform a set of functions. For example, a job could be comprised of a RESTful API server and a reverse proxy.

> **Kubernetes and the concept of a job**
>
> If you're only familiar with Kubernetes, this definition of *job* may be confusing at first. In Kubernetesland, a job is a specific type of workload that has historically been referred to as a *batch job*—that is, a job that starts and then runs to completion. Kubernetes has multiple resource types that are Kubernetes-specific implementations of the *job* concept:
>
> - Deployment
> - ReplicaSet
> - StatefulSet
> - DaemonSet
> - Job
>
> In the context of this book, we'll use *job* in its more generic definition.

A job should specify details at a high level and will apply to all tasks it defines:

1. Each task that makes up the job
2. Which data centers the job should run in
3. How many instances of each task should run
4. The type of the job (should it run continuously or run to completion and stop?)

We won't be dealing with jobs in our implementation for the sake of simplicity. Instead, we'll work exclusively at the level of individual tasks.

1.5.3   *The scheduler*

The *scheduler* decides what machine can best host the tasks defined in the job. The decision-making process can be as simple as selecting a node from a set of machines in a round-robin fashion or as complex as the Enhanced Parallel Virtual Machine (E-PVM) scheduler (used as part of Google's Borg scheduler), which calculates a score based on a number of variables and then selects a node with the best score.

The scheduler should perform these functions:

1 Determine a set of candidate machines on which a task could run
2 Score the candidate machines from best to worst
3 Pick the machine with the best score

We'll implement both the round-robin and E-PVM schedulers later in the book.

1.5.4   *The manager*

The *manager* is the brain of an orchestrator and the main entry point for users. To run jobs in the orchestration system, users submit their jobs to the manager. The manager, using the scheduler, then finds a machine where the job's tasks can run. The manager also periodically collects metrics from each of its workers, which are used in the scheduling process.

The manager should do the following:

1 Accept requests from users to start and stop tasks.
2 Schedule tasks onto worker machines.
3 Keep track of tasks, their states, and the machine on which they run.

1.5.5   *The worker*

The *worker* provides the muscles of an orchestrator. It is responsible for running the tasks assigned to it by the manager. If a task fails for any reason, it must attempt to restart the task. The worker also makes metrics about its tasks and overall machine health available for the manager to poll.

The worker is responsible for the following:

1 Running tasks as Docker containers
2 Accepting tasks to run from a manager
3 Providing relevant statistics to the manager for the purpose of scheduling tasks
4 Keeping track of its tasks and their states

1.5.6   *The cluster*

The *cluster* is the logical grouping of all the previous components. An orchestration cluster could be run from a single physical or virtual machine. More commonly, however, a cluster is built from multiple machines, from as few as five to as many as thousands or more.

The cluster is the level at which topics like *high availability* (HA) and *scalability* come into play. When you start using an orchestrator to run production jobs, these topics become critical. For our purposes, we won't be discussing HA or scalability in any detail as they relate to the orchestrator we're going to build. Keep in mind, however, that the design and implementation choices we make will impact the ability to deploy our orchestrator in a way that would meet the HA and scalability needs of a production environment.

1.5.7 Command-line interface

Finally, our CLI, the main user interface, should allow a user to

1 Start and stop tasks
2 Get the status of tasks
3 See the state of machines (i.e., the workers)
4 Start the manager
5 Start the worker

All orchestration systems share these same basic components. Google's Borg, seen in figure 1.5, calls the manager the *BorgMaster* and the worker a *Borglet* but otherwise uses the same terms as previously defined.

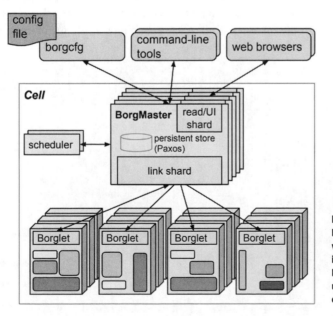

Figure 1.5 Google's Borg. At the bottom are a number of Borglets, or workers, which run individual tasks in containers. In the middle is the BorgMaster, or the manager, which uses the scheduler to place tasks on workers.

Apache Mesos, seen in figure 1.6, was presented at the Usenix HotCloud workshop in 2009 and was used by Twitter starting in 2010. Mesos calls the manager simply the *master*

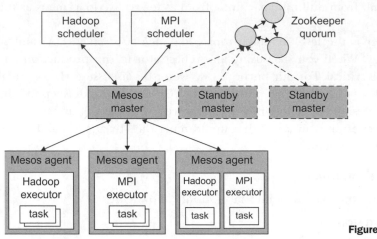

Figure 1.6   Apache Mesos

and the worker an *agent*. It differs slightly, however, from the Borg model in how it schedules tasks. It has a concept of a *framework*, which has two components: a *scheduler* that registers with the master to be offered resources, and an executor process that is launched on agent nodes to run the framework's tasks (http://mesos.apache.org/documentation/latest/architecture/).

Kubernetes, which was created at Google and influenced by Borg, calls the manager the *control plane* and the worker a *kubelet*. It rolls up the concepts of job and task into *Kubernetes objects*. Finally, Kubernetes maintains the usage of the terms *scheduler* and *cluster*. These components can be seen in the Kubernetes architecture diagram in figure 1.7.

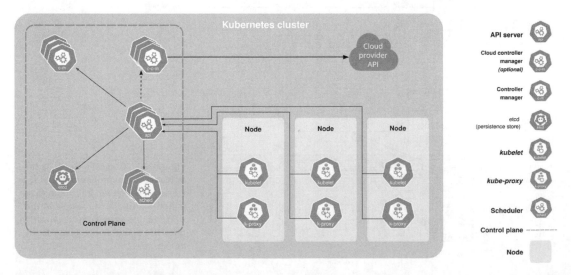

Figure 1.7   The Kubernetes architecture. The *control plane*, seen on the left, is equivalent to the manager function or to Borg's BorgMaster.

HashiCorp's Nomad, released a year after Kubernetes, uses more basic terms. The manager is the *server*, and the worker is the *client*. While not shown in figure 1.8, Nomad uses the terms *scheduler, job, task*, and *cluster* as we've defined here.

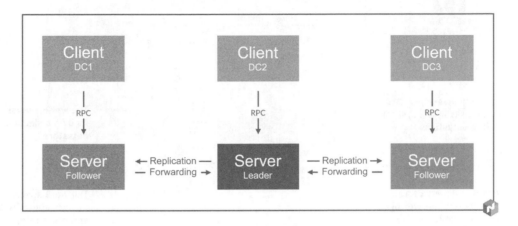

Figure 1.8   Nomad's architecture. While it appears more sparse, it still functions similarly to the other orchestrators.

1.6   Meet Cube

We're going to call our implementation *Cube*. If you're up on your *Star Trek: Next Generation* references, you'll recall that the Borg traveled in a cube-shaped spaceship.

Cube will have a much simpler design than Google's Borg, Kubernetes, or Nomad. And it won't be anywhere nearly as resilient as the Borg's ship. It will, however, contain all the same components as those systems.

The mental model in figure 1.9 expands on the architecture outlined in figure 1.4. In addition to the higher-level components, it dives a little deeper into the three main components: the manager, the worker, and the scheduler.

Starting with the scheduler in the lower left of the diagram, we see it contains three boxes: *feasibility, scoring,* and *picking*. These boxes represent the scheduler's generic phases, and they are arranged in the order in which the scheduler moves through the process of scheduling tasks onto workers:

- *Feasibility*—This phase assesses whether it's even possible to schedule a task onto a worker. There will be cases where a task cannot be scheduled onto any worker; there will also be cases where a task can be scheduled but only onto a subset of workers. We can think of this phase as similar to choosing which car to buy. My budget is $10,000, but depending on which car lot I go to, all the cars on the lot could cost more than $10,000, or only a subset of cars may fit into my price range.

Users interact with the system via the manager's API (typically a CLI or web UI).

The manager sends tasks to the worker and pulls metrics from it via the worker's API.

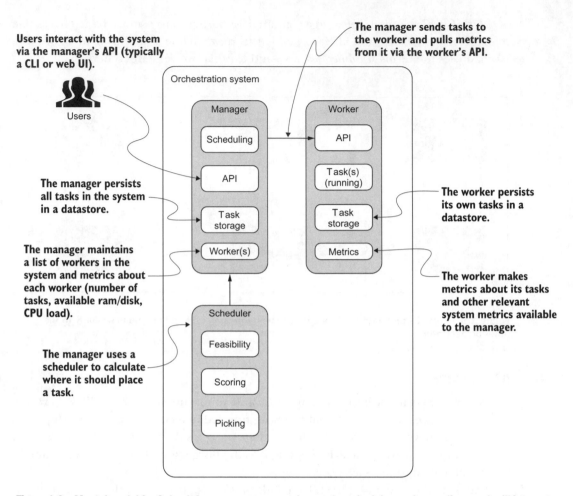

The manager persists all tasks in the system in a datastore.

The manager maintains a list of workers in the system and metrics about each worker (number of tasks, available ram/disk, CPU load).

The manager uses a scheduler to calculate where it should place a task.

The worker persists its own tasks in a datastore.

The worker makes metrics about its tasks and other relevant system metrics available to the manager.

Figure 1.9   Mental model for Cube. It has a manager, a worker, and a scheduler, and users (i.e., you) will interact with it via a command line.

- *Scoring*—This phase takes the workers identified by the feasibility phase and gives each one a score. This stage is the most important and can be accomplished in any number of ways. For example, to continue our car purchase analogy, I might give a score for each of three cars that fit within my budget based on variables like fuel efficiency, color, and safety rating.
- *Picking*—This phase is the simplest. From the list of scores, the scheduler picks the best one. This will be either the highest or lowest score.

Moving up the diagram, we come to the manager. The first box inside the manager component shows that the manager uses the scheduler we described previously. Next, there is the *API* box. The API is the primary mechanism for interacting with Cube. Users submit jobs and request jobs be stopped via the API. A user can also query the

API to get information about job and worker status. Next, there is the *Task Storage* box. The manager must keep track of all the jobs in the system to make good scheduling decisions, as well as to provide answers to user queries about job and worker statuses. Finally, the manager also keeps track of worker metrics, such as the number of jobs a worker is currently running, how much memory it has available, how much load the CPU is under, and how much disk space is free. This data, like the data in the job storage layer, is used for scheduling.

The final component in our diagram is the worker. Like the manager, it too has an API, although it serves a different purpose. The primary user of this API is the manager. The API provides the means for the manager to send tasks to the worker, to tell the worker to stop tasks, and to retrieve metrics about the worker's state. Next, the worker has a *task runtime*, which in our case will be Docker. Like the manager, the worker also keeps track of the work it is responsible for, which is done in the *Task Storage* layer. Finally, the worker provides metrics about its own state, which it makes available via its API.

1.7 What tools will we use?

To focus on our main goal, we're going to limit the number of tools and libraries we use. Here's the list of tools and libraries we're going to use:

- Go
- chi
- Docker SDK
- BoltDB
- goprocinfo
- Linux

As the title of this book says, we're going to write our code in the Go programming language. Both Kubernetes and Nomad are written in Go, so it is obviously a reasonable choice for large-scale systems. Go is also relatively lightweight, making it easy to learn quickly. If you haven't used Go before but have written non-trivial software in languages such as C/C++, Java, Rust, Python, or Ruby, then you should be fine. If you want more in-depth material about the Go language, either *The Go Programming Language* (www.gopl.io/) or *Get Programming with Go* (www.manning.com/books/get-programming-with-go) are good resources. That said, all the code presented will compile and run, so simply following along should also work.

There is no particular requirement for an IDE to write the code. Any text editor will do. Use whatever you're most comfortable with and makes you happy.

We'll focus our system on supporting Docker containers. This is a design choice. We could broaden our scope so our orchestrator could run a variety of jobs: containers, standalone executables, or Java JARs. Remember, however, our goal is not to build something that will rival existing orchestrators. This is a learning exercise. Narrowing our scope to focus solely on Docker containers will help us reach our learning goals more easily. That said, we will be using Docker's Go SDK (https://pkg.go.dev/github .com/docker/docker/client).

Our manager and worker are going to need a datastore. For this purpose, we're going to use BoltDB (https://github.com/boltdb/bolt), an embedded key/value store. There are two main benefits to using Bolt. First, by being embedded within our code, we don't have to run a database server. This feature means neither our manager nor our workers will need to talk across a network to read or write its data. Second, using a key/value store provides fast, simple access to our data.

The manager and worker will each provide an API to expose their functionality. The manager's API will be primarily user-facing, allowing users of the system to start and stop jobs, review job status, and get an overview of the nodes in the cluster. The worker's API is internal-facing and will provide the mechanism by which the manager sends jobs to workers and retrieves metrics from them. In many other languages, we might use a web framework to implement such an API. For example, if we were using Java, we might use Spring. Or if we were using Python, we might choose Django. While there are such frameworks available for Go, they aren't always necessary. In our case, we don't need a full web framework like Spring or Django. Instead, we're going to use a lightweight router called chi (https://github.com/go-chi/chi). We'll write handlers in plain Go and assign those handlers to routes.

To simplify the collection of worker metrics, we're going to use the `goprocinfo` library (https://github.com/c9s/goprocinfo). This library will abstract away some details related to getting metrics from the proc filesystem.

Finally, while you can write the code in this book on any operating system, it will need to be compiled and run on Linux. Any recent distribution should be sufficient.

For everything else, we'll rely on Go and its standard tools that are installed by default with every version of Go. Since we'll be using Go modules, you should use Go v1.14 or later. I've developed the code in this book using versions 1.20, 1.19, and 1.16.

1.8   *A word about hardware*

You won't need a bunch of hardware to complete this book. You can do everything on a single machine, whether that's a laptop, a desktop, or even a Raspberry Pi. The only requirements are that the machine is running Linux and it has enough memory and disk to hold the source code and compile it.

If you are going to do everything on a single machine, there are a couple more things to consider. You can run a single instance of the worker. This means when you submit a job to the manager, it will assign that job to the single worker. For that matter, any job will be assigned to that worker. For a better experience, and one that better exercises the scheduler and showcases the work you're going to do, you can run multiple instances of the worker. One way to do this is to simply open multiple terminals and run an instance of the worker in each. Alternatively, you can use something like tmux (https://github.com/tmux/tmux), seen in figure 1.10, which

```
tjb@pi-1:~ $ ./cube worker
Starting worker.
2021/06/13 20:18:35 Create new worker: Worker task queue - 0
2021/06/13 20:18:35 No tasks to process currently.
2021/06/13 20:18:35 Sleeping for 10 seconds.
2021/06/13 20:18:35 Updating task count
2021/06/13 20:18:35 Collecting stats
2021/06/13 20:18:45 No tasks to process currently.
2021/06/13 20:18:45 Sleeping for 10 seconds.
2021/06/13 20:18:50 Updating task count
2021/06/13 20:18:50 Collecting stats
2021/06/13 20:18:55 No tasks to process currently.
2021/06/13 20:18:55 Sleeping for 10 seconds.
2021/06/13 20:19:05 Updating task count
2021/06/13 20:19:05 No tasks to process currently.
2021/06/13 20:19:05 Sleeping for 10 seconds.
2021/06/13 20:19:05 Collecting stats
2021/06/13 20:19:15 No tasks to process currently.
2021/06/13 20:19:15 Sleeping for 10 seconds.
2021/06/13 20:19:20 Updating task count
2021/06/13 20:19:20 Collecting stats
2021/06/13 20:19:25 No tasks to process currently.
2021/06/13 20:19:25 Sleeping for 10 seconds.
```

```
tjb@pi-2:~ $ ./cube worker
Starting worker.
2021/06/13 20:18:35 Create new worker: Worker task queue - 0
2021/06/13 20:18:35 Collecting stats
2021/06/13 20:18:35 No tasks to process currently.
2021/06/13 20:18:35 Sleeping for 10 seconds.
2021/06/13 20:18:35 Updating task count
2021/06/13 20:18:45 No tasks to process currently.
2021/06/13 20:18:45 Sleeping for 10 seconds.
2021/06/13 20:18:50 Updating task count
2021/06/13 20:18:50 Collecting stats
2021/06/13 20:18:55 No tasks to process currently.
2021/06/13 20:18:55 Sleeping for 10 seconds.
2021/06/13 20:19:05 No tasks to process currently.
2021/06/13 20:19:05 Sleeping for 10 seconds.
2021/06/13 20:19:05 Updating task count
2021/06/13 20:19:05 Collecting stats
2021/06/13 20:19:15 No tasks to process currently.
2021/06/13 20:19:15 Sleeping for 10 seconds.
2021/06/13 20:19:20 Updating task count
2021/06/13 20:19:20 Collecting stats
2021/06/13 20:19:25 No tasks to process currently.
2021/06/13 20:19:25 Sleeping for 10 seconds.
```

```
tjb@pi-3:~ $ ./cube worker
Starting worker.
2021/06/13 20:18:35 Create new worker: Worker task queue - 0
2021/06/13 20:18:35 Updating task count
2021/06/13 20:18:35 No tasks to process currently.
2021/06/13 20:18:35 Sleeping for 10 seconds.
2021/06/13 20:18:35 Collecting stats
2021/06/13 20:18:45 No tasks to process currently.
2021/06/13 20:18:45 Sleeping for 10 seconds.
2021/06/13 20:18:50 Updating task count
2021/06/13 20:18:50 Collecting stats
2021/06/13 20:18:55 No tasks to process currently.
2021/06/13 20:18:55 Sleeping for 10 seconds.
2021/06/13 20:19:05 Updating task count
2021/06/13 20:19:05 No tasks to process currently.
2021/06/13 20:19:05 Sleeping for 10 seconds.
2021/06/13 20:19:05 Collecting stats
2021/06/13 20:19:15 No tasks to process currently.
2021/06/13 20:19:15 Sleeping for 10 seconds.
2021/06/13 20:19:20 Updating task count
2021/06/13 20:19:20 Collecting stats
2021/06/13 20:19:25 No tasks to process currently.
2021/06/13 20:19:25 Sleeping for 10 seconds.
]
```

```
[cube]  0:ssh*                                                              "tjb@borg:~" 15:19 13-Jun-21
```

Figure 1.10   A tmux session showing three Raspberry Pis running the Cube worker

achieves a similar outcome but allows you to detach from the terminal and leave everything running.

If you have extra hardware lying around (e.g., an old laptop or desktop or a couple of Raspberry Pis), you can use those as your worker nodes. Again, the only requirement is that they are running Linux. For example, in developing the code in preparation for writing this book, I used eight Raspberry Pis as workers. I used my laptop as the manager.

1.9   *What we won't be implementing or discussing*

So, to reiterate, our purpose here is not to build something that can be used to replace a production-grade system like Kubernetes. Engineering is about weighing tradeoffs against your requirements. This is a learning exercise to gain a better understanding of how orchestrators, in general, work. To that end, we won't be dealing with or discussing any of the following that might accompany discussions of production-grade systems:

- Distributed computing
- Service discovery
- High availability
- Load balancing
- Security

1.9.1   *Distributed computing*

Distributed computing is an architectural style where a system's components run on different computers, communicate across a network, and have to coordinate actions and states. The main benefits of this style are scalability and resiliency to failure. An orchestrator is a distributed system. It allows engineers to scale systems beyond the resources of a single computer, thus enabling those systems to handle larger and larger workloads. An orchestrator also provides resiliency to failure by making it relatively easy for engineers to run multiple instances of their services and for those instances to be managed in an automated way.

That said, we won't be going into the theory of distributed computing. If you're interested in that topic specifically, there are many resources that cover the subject in detail.

Resources on distributed computing include

- *Designing Data-Intensive Applications* (http://mng.bz/6nqZ)
- *Designing Distributed Systems* (http://mng.bz/5oqZ)

1.9.2   *Service discovery*

Service discovery provides a mechanism for users, either human or other machines, to discover service locations. Like all orchestration systems, Cube will allow us to run one or more instances of a task. When we ask Cube to run a task for us, we cannot know in advance where Cube will place the task (i.e., on which worker the task will run). If we have a cluster with three worker nodes, a task can potentially be scheduled onto any one of those three nodes.

To help find tasks once they are scheduled and running, we can use a service discovery system (e.g., Consul; www.consul.io) to answer queries about how to reach a service. While service discovery is indispensable in larger orchestration systems, it won't be necessary for our purposes.

Resources on service discovery include

- *Service Discovery in a Microservices Architecture* (http://mng.bz/0lpz/)
- *Service Discovery in Nomad* (http://mng.bz/W1yX)
- *Service Discovery in Kubernetes* (http://mng.bz/84Pg)

1.9.3   High availability

The term *availability* refers to the amount of time a system is available for usage by its intended user base. Often you'll hear the term *hgh availability* (HA) used, which refers to strategies to maximize the time a system is available for its users. Several examples of HA strategies are

- Elimination of single points of failure via redundancy
- Automated detection of and recovery from failures
- Isolation of failures to prevent total system outages

An orchestration system, by design, is a tool that enables engineers to implement these strategies. By running more than one instance of, say, a mission-critical web API, I can ensure the API won't become completely unavailable for my users if a single instance of it goes down for some reason. By running more than one instance of my web API on an orchestrator, I ensure that if one of the instances does fail for some reason, the orchestrator will detect it and attempt to recover from the failure. If any one instance of my web API fails, that failure will not affect the other instances (with some exceptions; see the following discussion).

At the same time, it is common to use these strategies to deploy the orchestration system itself. Production orchestration systems typically use multiple worker nodes. For example, worker nodes in a Borg cluster number in the tens of thousands. By running multiple worker nodes, the system permits users like me to run multiple instances of my mission-critical web API across a number of different machines. If one of those machines running my web API experiences a catastrophic failure (maybe a mouse took up residence in the machine's rack and accidentally unseated the machine's power cord), my application can still serve its users.

For our purposes in this book, we will implement our orchestrator so multiple instances of the worker can be easily run in a manner similar to Google's Borg. For the manager, however, we will only run a single instance. So while our workers can be run in an HA way, our manager cannot. Why?

The manager and worker components of our orchestration system—of any orchestration system—have different scopes. The worker's scope is narrow, concerned only with the tasks that it is responsible for running. If worker 2 fails for some reason, worker 1 doesn't care. Not only does it not care, but it doesn't even know worker 2 exists.

The manager's scope, however, encompasses the entire orchestration cluster. It maintains state for the cluster: how many worker nodes there are, the state of each worker (CPU, memory, and disk capacity, as well as how much of that capacity is already being used), and the state of each task submitted by users. To run multiple instances of the manager, there are many more questions to ask:

- Among the manager instances, will there be a *leader* that will handle all of the management responsibilities, or can any manager instance handle those responsibilities?
- How are state updates replicated to each instance of the manager?
- If state data gets out of sync, how do the managers decide which data to use?

These questions ultimately lead to the topic of *consensus*, which is a fundamental problem in distributed systems. While this topic is interesting, it isn't critical to our learning about and understanding how an orchestration system works. If our manager goes down, it won't affect our workers. They will continue to run the tasks already assigned to them. It does mean our cluster won't be able to accept new tasks, but for our purposes, we're going to decide that this is acceptable for the exercise at hand.

Resources on HA include

- "An Introduction to High Availability Computing: Concepts and Theory" (http://mng.bz/mj5y)
- *Learn Amazon Web Services in a Month of Lunches* (http://mng.bz/7vqV)

Resources on consensus include

- "Consensus: Reaching Agreement" (http://mng.bz/qjvN)
- *Paxos Made Simple* (http://mng.bz/K9Qn)
- *The Raft Consensus Algorithm* (https://raft.github.io/)

1.9.4   *Load balancing*

Load balancing is a strategy for building highly available, reliable, and responsive applications. Common load balancers (LBs) include NGINX, HAProxy, and AWS's assortment of load balancers (classic elastic LBs, network LBs, and the newer application LBs). While they are used in conjunction with orchestrators, they can become complex quickly because they are typically employed in multiple ways.

For example, it's common to have a public-facing LB that serves as an entry point to a system. This LB might know about each node in an orchestration system, and it will pick one of the nodes to which it forwards the request. The node receiving this request is itself running an LB that is integrated with a service discovery system and can thus forward the request to a node in the cluster running a task that can handle the request.

Load balancing as a topic is also complex. It can be as simple as using a round-robin algorithm, in which the LB maintains a list of nodes in the cluster and a pointer to the last node selected. When a request comes in, the LB selects the next node in the list. Or it can be as complex as choosing a node that is best able to meet some criteria, such as the resources available or the lowest number of connections. While load balancing is an important tool in building highly available production systems, it is not a fundamental component of an orchestration system.

Resources on load balancing include

- "Quick Introduction to Load Balancing and Load Balancers" (http://mng.bz/9QW8)
- "Types of Load Balancing Algorithms" (http://mng.bz/wjaB)

1.9.5 *Security*

Security is like an onion. It has many layers, many more than we can reasonably cover in this book. If we were going to run our orchestrator in production, we would need to answer questions like

- How do we secure the manager so only authenticated users can submit tasks or perform other management operations?
- Should we use authorization to segment users and the operations they can perform?
- How do we secure the workers so they only accept requests from a manager?
- Should network traffic between the manager and worker be encrypted?
- How should the system log events to audit who did what and when?

Resources on security include

- *API Security in Action* (https://www.manning.com/books/api-security-in-action)
- *Security by Design* (https://www.manning.com/books/secure-by-design)
- *Web Application Security* (http://mng.bz/Jdqz)

In the next chapter, we're going to start coding by translating our mental model into skeleton code.

Summary

- Orchestrators abstract machines and operating systems away from developers, thus leaving them to focus on their application.
- An orchestrator is a system comprised of a manager, worker, and scheduler. The primary objects of an orchestration system are tasks and jobs.
- Orchestrators are operated as a cluster of machines, with machines filling the roles of manager and worker.
- In orchestration systems, applications typically run in containers.
- Orchestrators allow for a level of standardization and automation that was difficult to achieve previously.

From mental model to skeleton code

2

This chapter covers

- Creating skeletons for task, worker, manager, and scheduler components
- Identifying the states of a task
- Using an interface to support different types of schedulers
- Writing a test program to verify that the code will compile and run

Once I have a mental model for a project, I like to translate that model into skeleton code. I do this quite frequently in my day job. It's similar to how carpenters frame a house: they define the exterior walls and interior rooms with two-by-fours and add trusses to give the roof a shape. This frame isn't the finished product, but it marks the boundaries of the structure, allowing others to come along and add details later in the construction.

In the same way, *skeleton code* provides the general shape and contours of the system I want to build. The final product may not conform exactly to this skeleton code. Bits and pieces may change, new pieces may be added or removed, and that's okay. This typically allows me to start thinking about the implementation in a concrete way without getting too deep into the weeds just yet.

If we look again at our mental model (figure 2.1), where should we start? You can see immediately that the three most obvious components are the *manager, worker,* and *scheduler.* The foundation of each of these components, however, is the *task,* so let's start with it.

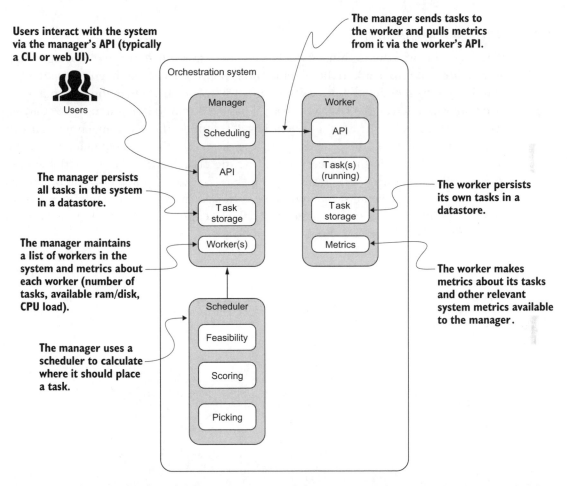

Figure 2.1 The Cube mental model shows the manager, worker, and scheduler as the major components of the system.

For the rest of the chapter, we'll be creating new files in our project directory. Take the time now to create the following directories and files:

```
.
├── main.go
├── manager
│   └── manager.go
├── node
```

```
|       └── node.go
├── scheduler
|       └── scheduler.go
├── task
|       └── task.go
└── worker
        └── worker.go
```

2.1   *The task skeleton*

The first thing we want to think about is the states a task will go through during its life. First, a user submits a task to the system. At this point, the task has been enqueued but is waiting to be scheduled. Let's call this initial state `Pending`. Once the system has figured out where to run the task, we can say it has been moved into a state of `Scheduled`. The `Scheduled` state means the system has determined there is a machine that can run the task, but it is in the process of sending the task to the selected machine, or the selected machine is in the process of starting the task. Next, if the selected machine successfully starts the task, it moves into the `Running` state. Upon a task completing its work successfully or being stopped by a user, the task moves into a state of `Completed`. If at any point the task crashes or stops working as expected, the task then moves into a state of `Failed`. Figure 2.2 shows this process.

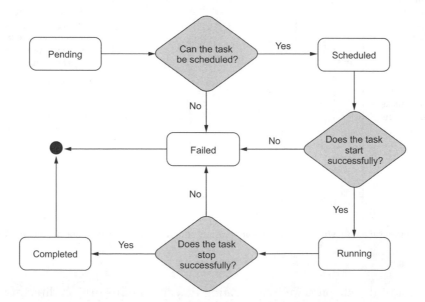

Figure 2.2   The states a task will go through during its life cycle

Now that we have identified the states of a task, let's create the `State` type.

Listing 2.1   The `State` type

```
package task

type State int

const (
    Pending State = iota
    Scheduled
    Running
    Completed
    Failed
)
```

Next, we should identify other attributes of a task that would be useful for our system. Obviously, an `ID` would allow us to uniquely identify individual tasks, and we'll use universally unique identifiers (UUID) for these. A human-readable `Name` would be good too because it means we can talk about `Tim's awesome task` instead of task `74560f1a-b141-40ec-885a-64e4b36b9f9c`. With these, we can sketch the beginning of our `Task` struct.

What is a UUID?

UUID stands for *universally unique identifier*. A UUID is 128 bits long and, in practice, unique. While it's not impossible to generate two identical UUIDs, the probability is extremely low. For more details about UUIDs, see RFC 4122 (https://tools.ietf.org/html/rfc4122).

Listing 2.2   The initial `Task` struct

```
import (
    "github.com/google/uuid"
)

type Task struct {
    ID      uuid.UUID
    Name    string
    State   State
}
```

Note that the `State` field is of type `State`, which we defined previously.

We have already said we're going to limit our orchestrator to dealing with Docker containers. As a result, we'll want to know what Docker image a task should use, and for that, let's use an attribute named `Image`. Given that our tasks will be Docker containers, there are several attributes that would be useful for a task to track. `Memory` and `Disk` will help the system identify the number of resources a task needs. `ExposedPorts` and `PortBindings` are used by Docker to ensure the machine allocates the proper network ports for the task and that it is available on the network. We'll also want a `RestartPolicy` attribute, which will tell the system what to do in the event a task stops or fails unexpectedly. With these attributes, we can update our `Task` struct.

Listing 2.3   Updating our `Task` struct with Docker-specific fields

```
import (
    "github.com/google/uuid"
    "github.com/docker/go-connections/nat"
)

type Task struct {
    ID              uuid.UUID
    Name            string
    State           State
    Image           string
    Memory          int
    Disk            int
    ExposedPorts    nat.PortSet
    PortBindings    map[string]string
    RestartPolicy   string
}
```

Finally, to know when a task starts and stops, we can add `StartTime` and `FinishTime` fields to our struct. While these aren't strictly necessary, they are helpful to display in a command-line interface (CLI). With these two attributes, we can flesh out the remainder of our `Task` struct.

Listing 2.4   Adding `StartTime` and `FinishTime` fields to the `Task` struct

```
import(
    ...
    "time"
)

type Task struct {
    ID              uuid.UUID
    ContainerID     string
    Name            string
    State           State
    Image           string
    CPU             float64
    Memory          int64
    Disk            int64
    ExposedPorts    nat.PortSet
    PortBindings    map[string]string
    RestartPolicy   string
    StartTime       time.Time
    FinishTime      time.Time
}
```

We have our `Task` struct defined, which represents a task that a user wants to run on our cluster. As I previously mentioned, a `Task` can be in one of several states: `Pending`,

Scheduled, Running, Failed, or Completed. The Task struct works fine when a user first requests a task to be run, but how does a user tell the system to stop a task? For this purpose, let's introduce the TaskEvent struct.

To identify a TaskEvent, it will need an ID, and like our Task, this will be done using a UUID. The event will need a State, which will indicate the state the task should transition to (e.g., from Running to Completed). Next, the event will have a Timestamp to record the time the event was requested. Finally, the event will contain a Task struct. Users won't directly interact with the TaskEvent struct. It will be an internal object that our system uses to trigger tasks from one state to another.

Listing 2.5   The TaskEvent struct

```
type TaskEvent struct {
    ID        uuid.UUID
    State     State
    Timestamp time.Time
    Task      Task
}
```

With our Task and TaskEvent structs defined, let's move on to sketching the next component, the Worker.

2.2 *The worker skeleton*

If we think of the *task* as the foundation of this orchestration system, then we can think of the *worker* as the next layer that sits atop the foundation. Let's remind ourselves what the worker's requirements are:

1 Run tasks as Docker containers
2 Accept tasks to run from a manager
3 Provide relevant statistics to the manager for the purpose of scheduling tasks
4 Keep track of its tasks and their state

Using the same process we used for defining the Task struct, let's create the Worker struct. Given the first and fourth requirements, we know that our worker will need to run and keep track of tasks. To do that, the worker will use a field named Db, which will be a map of UUIDs to tasks. To meet the second requirement, accepting tasks from a manager, the worker will want a Queue field. Using a queue will ensure that tasks are handled in first-in, first-out (FIFO) order. We won't be implementing our own queue, however; instead, we'll use the Queue from golang-collections. We'll also add a TaskCount field as a convenient way of keeping track of the number of tasks a worker has at any given time.

In your project directory, create a subdirectory called worker, and then change to that directory. Now, open a file named worker.go and type in the code in the following listing.

Listing 2.6   The beginnings of the `Worker` struct

```go
package worker

import (
    "fmt"
    "github.com/google/uuid"
    "github.com/golang-collections/collections/queue"

    "cube/task"
)

type Worker struct {
    Name        string
    Queue       queue.Queue
    Db          map[uuid.UUID]*task.Task
    TaskCount   int
}
```

Note that by using a `map` for the `Db` field, we get the benefit of a datastore without having to worry about the complexities of an external database server or embedded database library.

So we've identified the fields of our `Worker` struct. Now let's add some methods that will do the actual work. First, we'll give the struct a `RunTask` method. As its name suggests, it will handle running a task on the machine where the worker is running. Since a task can be in one of several states, the `RunTask` method will be responsible for identifying the task's current state and then either starting or stopping a task based on the state. Next, let's add a `StartTask` and a `StopTask` method, which will do exactly as their names suggest—start and stop tasks. Finally, let's give our worker a `CollectStats` method, which can be used to periodically collect statistics about the worker.

Listing 2.7   The skeleton of the `Worker` component

```go
func (w *Worker) CollectStats() {
    fmt.Println("I will collect stats")
}

func (w *Worker) RunTask() {
    fmt.Println("I will start or stop a task")
}

func (w *Worker) StartTask() {
    fmt.Println("I will start a task")
}

func (w *Worker) StopTask() {
    fmt.Println("I will stop a task")
}
```

Notice that each method simply prints out a line stating what it will do. Later in the book, we will revisit these methods to implement the real behavior represented by these statements.

2.3 The manager skeleton

Along with the `Worker`, the `Manager` is the other major component of our orchestration system. It will handle the bulk of the work.

As a reminder, here are the requirements for the manager we defined in chapter 1:

1 Accept requests from users to start and stop tasks
2 Schedule tasks onto worker machines
3 Keep track of tasks, their states, and the machine on which they run

In the `manager.go` file, let's create the struct named `Manager`. The `Manager` will have a queue, represented by the `pending` field, in which tasks will be placed upon first being submitted. The queue will allow the `Manager` to handle tasks on a FIFO basis. Next, the `Manager` will have two in-memory databases: one to store tasks and another to store task events. The databases are maps of strings to `Task` and `TaskEvent`, respectively.

Our `Manager` will need to keep track of the workers in the cluster. For this, let's use a field named, surprisingly, `workers`, which will be a slice of strings. Finally, let's add a couple of convenience fields that will make our lives easier down the road. It's easy to imagine that we'll want to know the jobs that are assigned to each worker. We'll use a field called `WorkerTaskMap`, which will be a map of strings to task UUIDs. Similarly, it'd be nice to have an easy way to find the worker running a task given a task name. Here we'll use a field called `TaskWorkerMap`, which is a map of task UUIDs to strings, where the string is the name of the worker.

Listing 2.8 The beginnings of our `Manager` skeleton

```
package manager

import(
    "cube/task"
    "fmt"

    "github.com/golang-collections/collections/queue"
    "github.com/google/uuid"
)

type Manager struct {
    Pending       queue.Queue
    TaskDb        map[string][]*task.Task
    EventDb       map[string][]*task.TaskEvent
    Workers       []string
    WorkerTaskMap map[string][]uuid.UUID
    TaskWorkerMap map[uuid.UUID]string
}
```

From our requirements, you can see that the manager needs to schedule tasks onto workers. So let's create a method on our `Manager` struct called `selectWorker` to perform that task. This method will be responsible for looking at the requirements specified in a `Task` and evaluating the resources available in the pool of workers to see which worker is best suited to run the task. Our requirements also say the `Manager` must keep track of tasks, their states, and the machine on which they run. To meet this requirement, create a method called `UpdateTasks`. Ultimately, this method will end up triggering a call to a worker's `CollectStats` method, but more about that later in the book.

Is our `Manager` skeleton missing anything? Ah, yes. So far, it can select a worker for a task and update existing tasks. There is another requirement that is implied in the requirements: the `Manager` obviously needs to send tasks to workers. Let's add this to our requirements and create a method on our `Manager` struct.

Listing 2.9   Adding methods to the `Manager`

```
func (m *Manager) SelectWorker() {
    fmt.Println("I will select an appropriate worker")
}

func (m *Manager) UpdateTasks() {
    fmt.Println("I will update tasks")
}

func (m *Manager) SendWork() {
    fmt.Println("I will send work to workers")
}
```

Like the `Worker`'s methods, the `Manager`'s methods only print out what they will do. The work of implementing these methods' actual behavior will come later.

2.4   *The scheduler skeleton*

The last of the four major components of our mental model is the scheduler. Its requirements are as follows:

1 Determine a set of candidate workers on which a task could run
2 Score the candidate workers from best to worst
3 Pick the worker with the best score

This skeleton, which we'll create in the `scheduler.go` file, will be different from our previous ones. Instead of defining structs and the methods of those structs, we're going to create an *interface*.

> **Interfaces in Go**
>
> Interfaces are the mechanism by which Go supports polymorphism. They are contracts that specify a set of behaviors, and any type that implements the behaviors can then be used anywhere that the interface type is specified.
>
> For more details about interfaces, see the Interfaces and Other Types section of the *Effective Go* blog post at http://mng.bz/j1n9.

Why an interface? As with everything in software engineering, tradeoffs are the norm. During my initial experiments with writing an orchestrator, I wanted a simple scheduler because I wanted to focus on other core features like running a task. For this purpose, my initial scheduler used a round-robin algorithm that kept a list of workers and identified which worker got the most recent task. Then, when the next task came in, the scheduler simply picked the next worker in its list.

   While the round-robin scheduler worked for this particular situation, it obviously has flaws. What happens if the next worker to be assigned a task doesn't have the available resources? Maybe the current tasks are using up all the memory and disk. Furthermore, I might want more flexibility in how tasks are assigned to workers. Maybe I'd want the scheduler to fill up one worker with tasks instead of spreading the tasks across multiple workers, where each worker could potentially only be running a single task. Conversely, maybe I'd want to spread out the tasks across the pool of resources to minimize the likelihood of resource starvation.

   Thus, we'll use an interface to specify the methods a type must implement to be considered a `Scheduler`. As you can see in the next listing, these methods are `SelectCandidateNodes`, `Score`, and `Pick`. Each of these methods map nicely onto the requirements for our scheduler.

Listing 2.10 The skeleton of the `Scheduler` component

```
package scheduler

type Scheduler interface {
    SelectCandidateNodes()
    Score()
    Pick()
}
```

2.5 *Other skeletons*

At this point, we've created skeletons for the four primary objects we see in our mental model: `Task`, `Worker`, `Manager`, and `Scheduler`. There is, however, another object that is hinted at in this model, the `Node`.

   Up to now, we've talked about the `Worker`. The `Worker` is the component that deals with our logical workload (i.e., tasks). The `Worker` has a physical aspect to it, however, in that it runs on a physical machine itself, and it also causes tasks to run on a physical machine. Moreover, it needs to know about the underlying machine to gather stats about the machine that the manager will use for scheduling decisions. We'll call this physical aspect of the `Worker` a `Node`.

In the context of Cube, a *node* is an object that represents any machine in our cluster. For example, the manager is one type of node in Cube. The worker, of which there can be more than one, is another type of node. The manager will make extensive use of node objects to represent workers.

For now, we're only going to define the fields that make up a `Node` struct, as seen in listing 2.11. First, a node will have a `Name`, for example, something as simple as "node-1." Next, a node will have an `Ip` address, which the manager will want to know in order to send tasks to it. A physical machine also has a certain amount of `Memory` and `Disk` space that tasks can use. These attributes represent maximum amounts. At any point in time, the tasks on a machine will be using some amount of memory and disk, which we can call `MemoryAllocated` and `DiskAllocated`. Finally, a `Node` will have zero or more tasks, which we can track using a `TaskCount` field.

> **Listing 2.11 The `Node` struct, representing a physical machine**

```
package node

type Node struct {
    Name            string
    Ip              string
    Cores           int
    Memory          int
    MemoryAllocated int
    Disk            int
    DiskAllocated   int
    Role            string
    TaskCount       int
}
```

2.6 *Taking our skeletons for a spin*

Now that we've created these skeletons, let's see whether we can use them in a simple test program. We want to ensure that the code we just wrote will compile and run. To do this, we're going to create instances of each of the skeletons, print the skeletons, and, finally, call each skeleton's methods.

The following list summarizes in more detail what our test program will do:

- Create a `Task` object
- Create a `TaskEvent` object
- Print the `Task` and `TaskEvent` objects
- Create a `Worker` object
- Print the `Worker` object
- Call the worker's methods
- Create a `Manager` object

- Call the manager's methods
- Create a `Node` object
- Print the `Node` object

Before we write this program, however, let's take care of a small administrative task that's necessary to get our code to compile. Remember, we said we're going to use the `Queue` implementation from the `golang-collections` package, and we're also using the `UUID` package from Google. We've also used the `nat` package from Docker. While we have imported them into our code, we haven't yet installed them locally. So let's do that now.

Listing 2.12 Using the `go get` command to install the third-party packages

```
$ go get github.com/golang-collections/collections/queue
$ go get github.com/google/uuid
$ go get github.com/docker/go-connections/nat
```

Now we are ready to test our skeletons, which we'll do in the following two listings.

Listing 2.13 Testing the skeletons with a minimal program: Part 1

```
package main

import (
    "cube/node"
    "cube/task"
    "fmt"
    "time"

    "github.com/golang-collections/collections/queue"
    "github.com/google/uuid"

    "cube/manager"
    "cube/worker"
)

func main() {
    t := task.Task{
        ID:     uuid.New(),
        Name:   "Task-1",
        State:  task.Pending,
        Image:  "Image-1",
        Memory: 1024,
        Disk:   1,
    }
```

Listing 2.14 Testing the skeletons with a minimal program: Part 2

```
te := task.TaskEvent{
        ID:     uuid.New(),
        State:  task.Pending,
```

```
        Timestamp: time.Now(),
        Task:      t,
    }

    fmt.Printf("task: %v\n", t)
    fmt.Printf("task event: %v\n", te)

    w := worker.Worker{
        Name: "worker-1",
        Queue: *queue.New(),
        Db:    make(map[uuid.UUID]*task.Task),
    }
    fmt.Printf("worker: %v\n", w)
    w.CollectStats()
    w.RunTask()
    w.StartTask()
    w.StopTask()

    m := manager.Manager{
        Pending: *queue.New(),
        TaskDb:  make(map[string][]task.Task),
        EventDb: make(map[string][]task.TaskEvent),
        Workers: []string{w.Name},
    }

    fmt.Printf("manager: %v\n", m)
    m.SelectWorker()
    m.UpdateTasks()
    m.SendWork()

    n := node.Node{
        Name:   "Node-1",
        Ip:     "192.168.1.1",
        Cores:  4,
        Memory: 1024,
        Disk:   25,
        Role:   "worker",
    }

    fmt.Printf("node: %v\n", n)
}
```

Now is the moment of truth! Time to compile and run our program. Do this using the go run main.go command, and you should see output like that in the following listing.

Listing 2.15   Testing the skeletons by running our minimal program

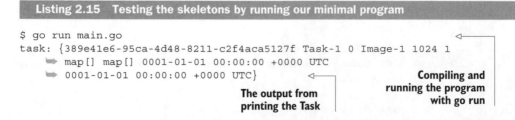

```
$ go run main.go
task: {389e41e6-95ca-4d48-8211-c2f4aca5127f Task-1 0 Image-1 1024 1
    map[] map[] 0001-01-01 00:00:00 +0000 UTC
    0001-01-01 00:00:00 +0000 UTC}
```

The output from printing the Task

Compiling and running the program with go run

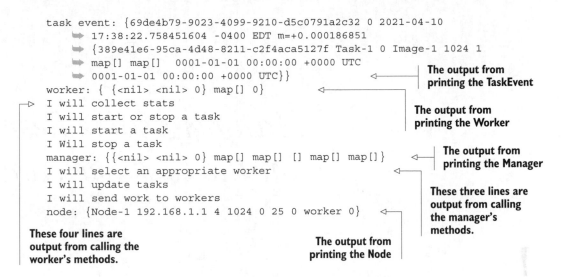

```
task event: {69de4b79-9023-4099-9210-d5c0791a2c32 0 2021-04-10
    ⇒ 17:38:22.758451604 -0400 EDT m=+0.000186851
    ⇒ {389e41e6-95ca-4d48-8211-c2f4aca5127f Task-1 0 Image-1 1024 1
    ⇒ map[] map[]  0001-01-01 00:00:00 +0000 UTC
    ⇒ 0001-01-01 00:00:00 +0000 UTC}}                          ◁──  The output from
worker: { {<nil> <nil> 0} map[] 0}              ◁──                  printing the TaskEvent
I will collect stats                                                The output from
I will start or stop a task                                         printing the Worker
I will start a task
I Will stop a task
manager: {{<nil> <nil> 0} map[] map[] [] map[] map[]}   ◁──  The output from
I will select an appropriate worker           ◁──                 printing the Manager
I will update tasks
I will send work to workers                                  These three lines are
node: {Node-1 192.168.1.1 4 1024 0 25 0 worker 0}   ◁──      output from calling
                                                             the manager's
                                                             methods.
```

These four lines are output from calling the worker's methods.

The output from printing the Node

Congrats! You've just written the skeleton of an orchestration system that compiles and runs. Take a moment to celebrate. In the following chapters, we'll use these skeletons as a starting point for more detailed discussions of each component before diving into the technical implementations.

Summary

- The code for the Cube orchestrator is organized into separate subdirectories inside our project: Manager, Node, Scheduler, Task, and Worker.
- Writing skeletons can help translate a mental model from an abstract concept into working code. Thus, we created skeletons for the Task, Worker, Manager, and Scheduler components of our orchestration system. This step also helped us identify additional concepts we didn't initially think of. The TaskEvent and Node components were not represented in our model but will be useful later in the book.
- We exercised our skeletons by writing a main program. While this program did not perform any operations, it did print messages to the terminal, allowing us to get a general idea of how things work.
- A task can be in one of five states: Pending, Scheduled, Running, Completed, or Failed. The worker and manager will use these states to perform actions on tasks, such as stopping and starting them.
- Go implements polymorphism by using interfaces. An interface is a type that specifies a set of behaviors, and any other type that implements those behaviors will be considered of the same type as the interface. Using an interface will allow us to implement multiple schedulers, each with slightly different behavior.

Hanging some flesh on the task skeleton

3

This chapter covers

- Reviewing how to start and stop Docker containers via the command line
- Introducing the Docker API calls for starting and stopping containers
- Implementing the `Task` concept to start and stop a container

Think about cooking your favorite meal. Let's say you like making homemade pizza. To end up pulling a delicious, hot pizza out of your oven, you have to perform a number of tasks. If you like onions, green peppers, or any other veggies on your pizza, you have to cut them up. You must knead the dough and spread it on a baking sheet. Next, you spread tomato sauce across the dough and sprinkle cheese over it. Finally, on top of the cheese, you layer your veggies and other ingredients.

A task in an orchestration system is similar to one of the individual steps in making a pizza. Like most companies these days, yours most likely has a website. That company's website runs on a web server, perhaps the ubiquitous Apache web server. That's a task. The website may use a database, like MySQL or PostgreSQL, to store dynamic content. That's a task.

In our pizza-making analogy, the pizza wasn't made in a vacuum. It was created in a specific context, which is a kitchen. The kitchen provides the necessary resources to make the pizza: a refrigerator where the cheese is stored, cabinets where the pizza sauce is kept, an oven in which to cook the pizza, and a knife to cut the pizza into slices.

Similarly, a task operates in a specific context. In our case, that context will be a Docker container. Like the kitchen, the container will provide the resources necessary for the task to run: it will provide CPU cycles, memory, and networking according to the needs of the task.

As a reminder, the task is the foundation of an orchestration system. Figure 1.1 shows a modified version of our mental model from chapter 1.

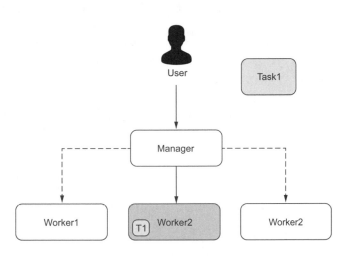

Figure 3.1 The main purpose of an orchestration system is to accept tasks from users and run them on the system's worker nodes. Here, we see a user submitting a task to the `Manager` node, which then selects `Worker2` to run the task. The dotted lines to `Worker1` and `Worker3` represent that these nodes were considered but ultimately not selected to run the task.

In the rest of this chapter, we'll flesh out the `Task` skeleton we wrote in the previous chapter. But first, let's quickly review some Docker basics.

3.1 Docker: Starting, stopping, and inspecting containers from the command line

If you are a developer, you have probably used Docker containers to run your application and its backend database on your laptop while working on your code. If you are a DevOps engineer, you may have deployed Docker containers to your company's production environment. Containers allow the developer to package their code, along with all its dependencies, and then ship the container to production. If a DevOps team is responsible for deployments to production, then they only have to worry about deploying the container. They don't have to worry about whether the machine where the container will run has the correct version of the PostgreSQL library that the application uses to connect to its database.

TIP If you need a more detailed review of Docker containers and how to control them, check out chapter 2 of *Docker in Action* (http://mng.bz/PRq8).

To run a Docker container, we can use the `docker run` command, an example of which can be seen in the next listing. Here, the `docker run` command is starting up a PostgreSQL database in a container, which might be used as a backend datastore while developing a new application.

Listing 3.1   Running the Postgres database server as a Docker container

```
$ docker run -it \
    -p 5432:5432 \
    --name cube-book \
    -e POSTGRES_USER=cube \
    -e POSTGRES_PASSWORD=secret \
    postgres
```

This command runs the container in the foreground, meaning we can see its log output (`-it`), gives the container the name of `postgres`, and sets the `POSTGRES_USER` and `POSTGRES_PASSWORD` environment variables.

Once a container is running, it performs the same functions it would if you were running it as a regular process on your laptop or desktop. In the case of the Postgres database from listing 3.1, I can now log into the database server using the `psql` command-line client and create a table like that in the following listing.

Listing 3.2   Logging in to the Postgres server and creating a table

```
$ psql -h localhost -p 5432 -U cube
Password for user cube:
psql (9.6.22, server 13.2 (Debian 13.2-1.pgdg100+1))
WARNING: psql major version 9.6, server major version 13.
        Some psql features might not work.
Type "help" for help.

cube=# \d
No relations found.
cube=# CREATE TABLE book (
isbn char(13) PRIMARY KEY,
title varchar(240) NOT NULL,
author varchar(140)
);
CREATE TABLE
cube=# \d
        List of relations
 Schema | Name | Type  | Owner
--------+------+-------+-------
 public | book | table | cube
(1 row)
```

Because we specified `-p 5432:5432` in the `docker run` command in the previous listing, we can tell the `psql` client to connect to that port on the local machine.

Once a container is up and running, we can get information about it using the `docker inspect` command. The output from this command is extensive, so I will only list the `State` info.

Listing 3.3   Using the `docker inspect` command

```
$ docker inspect cube-book
[
    {
        "Id": "a820c7abb54b723b5efc0946900baf58e093d8fdd238d4ec7cb5647",
        "Created": "2021-05-15T20:00:41.228528102Z",
        "Path": "docker-entrypoint.sh",
        "Args": [
            "postgres"
        ],
        "State": {
            "Status": "running",
            "Running": true,
            "Paused": false,
            "Restarting": false,
            "OOMKilled": false,
            "Dead": false,
            "Pid": 27599,
            "ExitCode": 0,
            "Error": "",
            "StartedAt": "2021-05-15T20:00:42.4656334Z",
            "FinishedAt": "0001-01-01T00:00:00Z"
        },
        ....
]
```

Finally, we can stop a Docker container using the `docker stop cube-book` command. There isn't any output from the command, but if we run the `docker inspect cube-book` command now, we'll see that the state has changed from `running` to `exited`.

Listing 3.4   Running `docker inspect cube-book` after `docker stop cube-book`

```
$ docker inspect cube-book
[
    {
        "Id": "a820c7abb54b723b5efc0946900baf58e093d8fdd238d4ec7cb5647",
        "Created": "2021-05-15T20:00:41.228528102Z",
        "Path": "docker-entrypoint.sh",
        "Args": [
            "postgres"
        ],
        "State": {
            "Status": "exited",
            "Running": false,
            "Paused": false,
            "Restarting": false,
            "OOMKilled": false,
```

```
            "Dead": false,
            "Pid": 0,
            "ExitCode": 0,
            "Error": "",
            "StartedAt": "2021-05-15T20:00:42.4656334Z",
            "FinishedAt": "2021-05-15T20:18:31.698919838Z"
        },
        ....
    ]
```

3.2 Docker: Starting, stopping, and inspecting containers from the API

In our orchestration system, the worker will be responsible for starting, stopping, and providing information about the tasks it's running. To perform these functions, the worker will use Docker's API. The API is accessible via the HTTP protocol using a client like `curl` or the HTTP library of a programming language. The following listing shows an example of using `curl` to get the same information we got from the `docker inspect` command previously.

Listing 3.5 Querying the Docker API with the `curl` HTTP client

```
curl --unix-socket \
    /var/run/docker.sock http://docker/containers/6970e8469684/json| jq .
{
  "Id": "6970e8469684d439c73577c4caee7261bf887a67433420e7dcd637cc53b8ffa7",
  "Created": "2021-05-15T20:58:36.283909602Z",
  "Path": "docker-entrypoint.sh",
  "Args": [
    "postgres"
  ],
  "State": {
    "Status": "running",
    "Running": true,
    "Paused": false,
    "Restarting": false,
    "OOMKilled": false,
    "Dead": false,
    "Pid": 270523,
    "ExitCode": 0,
    "Error": "",
    "StartedAt": "2021-05-15T20:58:36.541148947Z",
    "FinishedAt": "0001-01-01T00:00:00Z"
  },
  ....
}
```

Notice we're passing the `--unix-socket` flag to the `curl` command. By default, Docker listens on a `unix` socket, but it can be configured to listen on a `tcp` socket. The URL, `http://docker/containers/6970e8469684/json`, contains the ID of the container to inspect, which I got from the `docker ps` command on my machine. Finally, the output from `curl` is piped to the `jq` command, which prints the output in a more readable format than `curl`'s.

We could use Go's HTTP library in our orchestration system, but that would force us to deal with many low-level details like HTTP methods, status codes, and serializing requests and deserializing responses. Instead, we're going to use Docker's SDK, which handles all the low-level HTTP details for us and allows us to focus on our primary task: creating, running, and stopping containers. The SDK provides the following six methods that will meet our needs:

- `NewClientWithOpts`—A helper method that instantiates an instance of the client and returns it to the caller
- `ImagePull`—Pulls the image down to the local machine where it will be run
- `ContainerCreate`—Creates a new container with a given configuration
- `ContainerStart`—Sends a request to Docker Engine to start the newly created container
- `ContainerStop`—Sends a request to Docker Engine to stop a running container
- `ContainerRemove`—Removes the container from the host

NOTE Docker's Golang SDK has extensive documentation (https://pkg.go .dev/github.com/docker/docker) that's worth reading. In particular, the docs about the Go client (https://pkg.go.dev/github.com/docker/docker/ client) are relevant to our work throughout the rest of this book.

The `docker` command-line examples we reviewed in the previous section use the Go SDK under the hood. Later in this chapter, we'll implement a `Run()` method that uses the `ImagePull`, `ContainerCreate`, and `Container-Start` methods to create and start a container. Figure 3.2 provides a graphic representation of our custom code and the `docker` command using the SDK.

By using the Go SDK for controlling the Docker containers in our orchestration system, we don't have to reinvent the wheel. We can simply reuse the same code used by the `docker` command every day.

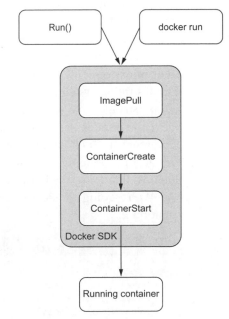

Figure 3.2 Regardless of the starting point, all paths to creating and running a container go through the Docker SDK.

3.3 Task configuration

To run our tasks as containers, they need a configuration. What is a configuration? Think back to our pizza analogy from the beginning of the chapter. One of the tasks in making our pizza was cutting the onions (if you don't like onions, insert your veggie of choice). To perform that task, we would use a knife and a cutting board, and we would cut the onions in a particular way. Perhaps we cut them into thin, even slices or dice them into small cubes. This is all part of the "configuration" of the task of cutting onions. (Okay, I'm probably stretching the pizza analogy a bit far, but I think you get the point.)

For a task in our orchestration system, we'll describe its configuration using the `Config` struct in listing 3.6. This struct encapsulates all the necessary bits of information about a task's configuration. The comments should make the intent of each field obvious, but there are a couple of fields worth highlighting.

The `Name` field will be used to identify a task in our orchestration system, and it will perform double duty as the name of the running container. Throughout the rest of the book, we'll use this field to name our containers like `test-container-1`.

The `Image` field, as you probably guessed, holds the name of the image the container will run. Remember, an image can be thought of as a package: it contains the collection of files and instructions necessary to run a program. This field can be set to a value as simple as `postgres`, or it can be set to a more specific value that includes a version, like `postgres:13`.

The `Memory` and `Disk` fields will serve two purposes. The scheduler will use them to find a node in the cluster capable of running a task. They will also be used to tell the Docker daemon the number of resources a task requires.

The `Env` field allows a user to specify environment variables that will get passed into the container. In our command to run a Postgres container, we set two environment variables: `-e POSTGRES_USER=cube` to specify the database user and `-e POSTGRES_PASSWORD=secret` to specify that user's password.

Finally, the `RestartPolicy` field tells the Docker daemon what to do if a container dies unexpectedly. This field is one of the mechanisms that provides resilience in our orchestration system. As you can see from the comment, the acceptable values are an empty string, `always`, `unless-stopped`, or `on-failure`. Setting this field to `always` will, as its name implies, restart a container if it stops. Setting it to `unless-stopped` will restart a container unless it has been stopped (e.g., by `docker stop`). Setting it to `on-failure` will restart the container if it exits due to an error (i.e., a nonzero exit code). There are a few details that are spelled out in the documentation (http://mng.bz/1JdQ).

We're going to add the `Config` struct in the next listing to the `task.go` file from chapter 2.

> **Listing 3.6 The `Config` struct that will hold the configuration for orchestration tasks**

```
type Config struct {
    Name          string
    AttachStdin   bool
    AttachStdout  bool
    AttachStderr  bool
    ExposedPorts  nat.PortSet
    Cmd           []string
    Image         string
```

```
Cpu           float64
Memory        int64
Disk          int64
Env           []string
RestartPolicy string
}
```

3.4   *Starting and stopping tasks*

Now that we've talked about a task's configuration, let's move on to starting and stopping a task. Remember, the worker in our orchestration system will be responsible for running tasks for us. That responsibility will mostly involve starting and stopping tasks.

Let's start by adding the code for the `Docker` struct you see in listing 3.7 to the `task.go` file. This struct will encapsulate everything we need to run our task as a Docker container. The `Client` field will hold a Docker client object that we'll use to interact with the Docker API. The `Config` field will hold the task's configuration. And once a task is running, it will also contain the `ContainerId`. This ID will allow us to interact with the running task.

Listing 3.7   The `Docker` struct

```
type Docker struct {
    Client *client.Client
    Config  Config
}
```

For the sake of convenience, let's create a struct called `DockerResult`. We can use this struct as the return value in methods that start and stop containers, providing a wrapper around common information that is useful for callers. The struct contains an `Error` field to hold any error messages. It has an `Action` field that can be used to identify the action being taken, for example, start or stop. It has a `ContainerId` field to identify the container to which the result pertains. And, finally, there is a `Result` field that can hold arbitrary text that provides more information about the result of the operation.

Listing 3.8   The `DockerResult` struct

```
type DockerResult struct {
    Error       error
    Action      string
    ContainerId string
    Result      string
}
```

Now we're ready for the exciting part: actually writing the code to create and run a task as a container. To do this, let's start by adding a method to the `Docker` struct we created earlier. Let's call that method `Run`.

The first part of our `Run` method will pull the Docker image our task will use from a container registry such as Docker Hub. A container registry is simply a repository of images and allows for the easy distribution of the images it hosts. To pull the image, the `Run` method first creates a context, which is a type that holds values that can be passed across boundaries such as APIs and processes. It's common to use a context to pass along deadlines or cancellation signals in requests to an API. In our case, we'll use an empty context returned from the `Background` function.

Next, `Run` calls the `ImagePull` method on the Docker client object, passing the context object, the image name, and any options necessary to pull the image. The `ImagePull` method returns two values: an object that fulfills the `io.ReadCloser` interface and an error object. It stores these values in the `reader` and `err` variables.

The next step in the method checks the error value returned from `ImagePull`. If the value is not `nil`, the method prints the error message and returns as a `DockerResult`.

Finally, the method copies the value of the `reader` variable to `os.Stdout` via the `io.Copy` function. `io.Copy` is a function from the `io` package in Golang's standard library, and it simply copies data to a destination (`os.Stdout`) from a source (`reader`). Because we'll be working from the command line whenever we're running the components of our orchestration system, it's useful to write the `reader` variable to `Stdout` as a way to communicate what happened in the `ImagePull` method.

Listing 3.9 The start of our `Run()` method

```go
func (d *Docker) Run() DockerResult {
    ctx := context.Background()
    reader, err := d.Client.ImagePull(
        ctx, d.Config.Image, types.ImagePullOptions{})
    if err != nil {
        log.Printf("Error pulling image %s: %v\n", d.Config.Image, err)
        return DockerResult{Error: err}
    }
    io.Copy(os.Stdout, reader)
}
```

Similar to running a container from the command line, the method begins by pulling the container's image.

Once the `Run` method has pulled the image and checked for errors (and found none, we hope), the next bit of business on the agenda is to prepare the configuration to be sent to Docker. Before we do that, however, let's take a look at the signature of the `ContainerCreate` method from the Docker client. This is the method we'll use to create the container. As you can see in listing 3.10, `ContainerCreate` takes several arguments. Similar to the `ImagePull` method used earlier, it takes a `context.Context` as its first argument. The next argument is the actual container configuration, which is a pointer to a `container.Config` type. We'll copy the values from our own `Config` type into this one. The third argument is a pointer to a `container.HostConfig` type. This type will hold the configuration a task requires of the host on which the container will run, for example, a Linux machine. The fourth argument is also a pointer and points to a `network.NetworkingConfig` type. This type can be used to specify networking details, such as the network ID container, any links to other containers that are needed, and IP addresses. For our purposes, we won't use the network configuration, instead allowing Docker to handle those details for us. The fifth argument is another pointer, and it points to a `specs.Platform` type. This type can be used to specify details about the platform on which the image runs. It allows you to specify things like the CPU architecture and the operating system. We won't be making use of this argument either. The sixth and final argument to `ContainerCreate` is the container name, passed as a string.

Listing 3.10 The Docker client's `ContainerCreate` method

```
func (cli *Client) ContainerCreate(
    ctx context.Context,
    config *container.Config,
    hostConfig *container.HostConfig,
    networkingConfig *network.NetworkingConfig,
    platform *specs.Platform,
    containerName string) (container.ContainerCreateCreatedBody, error)
```

Now we know what information we need to pass along in the `ContainerCreate` method, so let's gather it from our `Config` type and massage it into the appropriate types that `ContainerCreate` will accept. What we'll end up with is what you see in listing 3.11.

First, we'll create a variable called `rp`. This variable will hold a `container.Restart-Policy` type, and it will contain the `RestartPolicy` we defined earlier in our `Config` struct in listing 3.6.

Following the `rp` variable, let's declare a variable called `r`. This variable will hold the resources required by the container in a `container.Resources` type. The most common resources we'll use for our orchestration system will be memory.

Next, let's create a variable called `cc` to hold our container configuration. This variable will be of the type `container.Config`, and into it, we'll copy two values from our `Config` type. The first is the `Image` our container will use. The second is any environment variables, which go into the `Env` field.

Finally, we take the `rp` and `r` variables we defined and add them to a third variable called `hc`. This variable is a `container.HostConfig` type. In addition to specifying the `RestartPolicy` and `Resources` in the `hc` variable, we'll also set the `PublishAllPorts` field to `true`. What does this field do? Remember our example `docker run` command in listing 3.2, where we start up a PostgreSQL container? In that command, we used `-p 5432:5432` to tell Docker that we wanted to map port 5432 on the host running our container to port 5432 inside the container. Well, that's not the best way to expose a container's ports on a host. There is an easier way. Instead, we can set `PublishAllPorts` to `true`, and Docker will expose those ports automatically by randomly choosing available ports on the host.

The following listing creates four variables to hold configuration information, which gets passed to the `ContainerCreate` method.

Listing 3.11　The next phase of running a container

```
func (d *Docker) Run() DockerResult {

    // previous code not listed

    rp := container.RestartPolicy{
        Name: d.Config.RestartPolicy,
    }

    r := container.Resources{
        Memory: d.Config.Memory,
        NanoCPUs: int64(d.Config.Cpu * math.Pow(10, 9)),
    }

    cc := container.Config{
        Image: d.Config.Image,
        Tty: false,
        Env: d.Config.Env,
        ExposedPorts: d.Config.ExposedPorts,
    }

    hc := container.HostConfig{
        RestartPolicy: rp,
        Resources:     r,
        PublishAllPorts: true,
    }
```

We've done all the necessary prep work, and now we can create the container and start it. We've already touched on the `ContainerCreate` method in listing 3.10, so all that's left to do is to call it like in listing 3.12. One thing to notice, however, is that we pass `nil` values as the fourth and fifth arguments, which, as you'll recall from listing 3.10, are the `networking` and `platform` arguments. We won't be making use of these features in our orchestration system, so we can ignore them for now.

As with the `ImagePull` method earlier, `ContainerCreate` returns two values: a response, which is a pointer to a `container.ContainerCreateCreatedBody` type, and an error type. The `ContainerCreateCreatedBody` type gets stored in the `resp` variable, and we put the error in the `err` variable. Next, we check the `err` variable for any errors and, if we find any, print them and return them in a `DockerResult` type.

Great! We've got all our ingredients together, and we've formed them into a container. All that's left to do is start it. To perform this final step, we call the `Container-Start` method.

Besides a context argument, `ContainerStart` takes the `ID` of an existing container, which we get from the `resp` variable returned from `ContainerCreate`, and any options necessary to start the container. In our case, we don't need any options, so we simply pass an empty `types.ContainerStartOptions`. `ContainerStart` only returns one type, an error, so we check it in the same way we have with the other method calls we've made. If there is an error, we print it and then return it in a `DockerResult`.

Listing 3.12 The penultimate phase

```
func (d *Docker) Run() DockerResult {

    // previous code not listed

    resp, err := d.Client.ContainerCreate(ctx, &cc, &hc, nil, nil,
  ➥ d.Config.Name)
    if err != nil {
        log.Printf("Error creating container using image %s: %v\n",
  ➥ d.Config.Image, err)
        return DockerResult{Error: err}
    }

    err = d.Client.ContainerStart(ctx, resp.ID,
     types.ContainerStartOptions{})
    if err != nil {
        log.Printf("Error starting container %s: %v\n", resp.ID, err)
        return DockerResult{Error: err}
    }
```

At this point, if all was successful, we have a container running the task. All that's left to do now is to take care of some bookkeeping, which you can see in listing 3.13. We start by adding the container ID to the configuration object (which will ultimately be stored, but let's not get ahead of ourselves!). Similar to printing the results of the `ImagePull` operation to `stdout`, we do the same with the result of starting the container. This is accomplished by calling the `ContainerLogs` method and then writing the return value to `stdout` using the `stdcopy.StdCopy(os.Stdout, os.Stderr, out)` call.

Listing 3.13 The final phase of creating and running a container

```
func (d *Docker) Run() DockerResult {

    // previous code not listed

    d.Config.Runtime.ContainerID = resp.ID

    out, err := cli.ContainerLogs(
        ctx,
        resp.ID,
        types.ContainerLogsOptions{ShowStdout: true, ShowStderr: true}
    )
    if err != nil {
        log.Printf("Error getting logs for container %s: %v\n", resp.ID, err)
        return DockerResult{Error: err}
    }

    stdcopy.StdCopy(os.Stdout, os.Stderr, out)
```

```
    return DockerResult{ContainerId: resp.ID, Action: "start",
➥   Result: "success"}
}
```

As a reminder, the `Run` method we've written in listings 3.9, 3.11, 3.12, and 3.13 perform the same operations as the `docker run` command. When you type `docker run` on the command line, under the hood, the `docker` binary is using the same SDK methods we're using in our code to create and run the container.

Now that we can create a container and start it, let's write the code to stop a container. Compared to our `Run` method, the `Stop` method will be much simpler, as you can see in listing 3.14. Because there isn't the necessary prep work to do for stopping a container, the process simply involves calling the `ContainerStop` method with the `ContainerID` and then calling the `ContainerRemove` method with the `ContainerID` and the requisite options. Again, in both operations, the code checks the value of the `err` returned from the method. As with the `Run` method, our `Stop` method performs the same operations carried out by the `docker stop` and `docker rm` commands.

Listing 3.14 Stopping a container

```
func (d *Docker) Stop(id string) DockerResult {
    log.Printf("Attempting to stop container %v", id)
    ctx := context.Background()
    err := d.Client.ContainerStop(ctx, id, nil)
    if err != nil {
        log.Printf("Error stopping container %s: %v\n", id, err)
        return DockerResult{Error: err}
    }

    err = d.Client.ContainerRemove(ctx, id, types.ContainerRemoveOptions{
        RemoveVolumes: true,
        RemoveLinks:   false,
        Force:         false,
    })
    if err != nil {
        log.Printf("Error removing container %s: %v\n", id, err)
        return DockerResult{Error: err}
    }

    return DockerResult{Action: "stop", Result: "success", Error: nil}
}
```

Now, let's update our `main.go` program that we created in chapter 2 to create and stop a container.

First, add the `createContainer` function in listing 3.15 to the bottom of the `main.go` file. Inside it, we'll set up the configuration for the task and store it in a variable called `c`, and then we'll create a new Docker client and store it in `dc`. Next, let's create the `d` object, which is of type `task.Docker`. From this object, we call the `Run()` method to create the container.

Listing 3.15   The `createContainer` function

```go
func createContainer() (*task.Docker, *task.DockerResult) {
    c := task.Config{
        Name:   "test-container-1",
        Image: "postgres:13",
        Env: []string{
            "POSTGRES_USER=cube",
            "POSTGRES_PASSWORD=secret",
        },
    }

    dc, _ := client.NewClientWithOpts(client.FromEnv)
    d := task.Docker{
        Client: dc,
        Config: c,
    }

    result := d.Run()
    if result.Error != nil {
        fmt.Printf("%v\n", result.Error)
        return nil, nil
    }

    fmt.Printf(
        "Container %s is running with config %v\n", result.ContainerId, c)
    return &d, &result
}
```

Second, add the `stopContainer` function below `createContainer`. This function accepts a single argument, `d`, which is the same `d` object created in `createContainer` in listing 3.15. All that's left to do is call `d.Stop()`.

Listing 3.16   The `stopContainer` function

```go
func stopContainer(d *task.Docker, id string) *task.DockerResult {
    result := d.Docker.Stop(id)
    if result.Error != nil {
        fmt.Printf("%v\n", result.Error)
        return nil
    }

    fmt.Printf(
        "Container %s has been stopped and removed\n", result.ContainerId)
    return &result
}
```

Finally, we call the `createContainer` and `stopContainer` functions we created from our `main()` function in `main.go`. To do that, add the code from listing 3.17 to the bottom of your main function.

As you can see, the code is fairly simple. It starts by printing a useful message that it's going to create a container; it then calls the createContainer() function and stores the results in two variables, dockerTask and createResult. Then it checks for errors by comparing the value of createResult.Error to nil. If it finds an error, it prints it and exits by calling os.Exit(1). To stop the container, the main function simply calls stopContainer and passes it the dockerTask object returned by the earlier call to createContainer.

Listing 3.17 Calling the createContainer and stopContainer functions

```
func main() {

    // previous code not shown

    fmt.Printf("create a test container\n")
    dockerTask, createResult := createContainer()
    if createResult.Error != nil {
        fmt.Printf("%v", createResult.Error)
        os.Exit(1)
    }

    time.Sleep(time.Second * 5)
    fmt.Printf("stopping container %s\n", createResult.ContainerId)
    _ = stop_container(dockerTask, createResult.ContainerId)
}
```

Time for another moment of truth. Let's run the code!

Listing 3.18 Running the code to create and stop a container

```
$ go run main.go
 task: {2c66f7c4-2484-4cf8-a22b-81c3dd24294d Task-1 0 Image-1 1024 1
    map[] map[]   0001-01-01 00:00:00 +0000 UTC
    0001-01-01 00:00:00 +0000 UTC}
task event: {f7045213-732e-49f9-9ca0-ef781e58d30c 0 2021-05-16
    16:00:41.890181309 -0400 EDT m=+0.001923263
    {2c66f7c4-2484-4cf8-a22b-81c3dd24294d Task-1 0 Image-1 1024 1
    map[] map[]   0001-01-01 00:00:00 +0000 UTC 0001-01-01
    00:00:00 +0000 UTC}}
worker: { {<nil> <nil> 0} map[] 0}
I will collect stats
I will start or stop a task
I will start a task
I Will stop a task
manager: {{<nil> <nil> 0} map[] map[] [] map[] map[]}
I will select an appropriate worker
I will update tasks
I will send work to workers
node: {Node-1 192.168.1.1 4 1024 0 25 0 worker 0}
create a test container
"status":"Pulling from library/postgres","id":"13"}
{"status":"Digest: sha256:117c3ea384ce21421541515ed"}
```

Running our testing program with the go run command

Everything up to this point is from chapter 2.

This is the start of our new code to create a container.

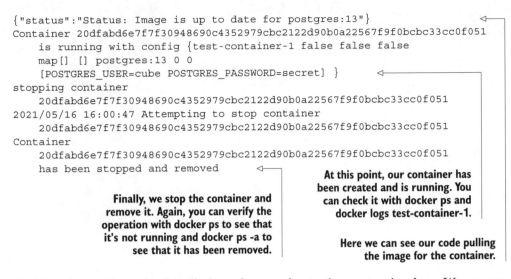

```
{"status":"Status: Image is up to date for postgres:13"}
Container 20dfabd6e7f7f30948690c4352979cbc2122d90b0a22567f9f0bcbc33cc0f051
    is running with config {test-container-1 false false false
    map[] [] postgres:13 0 0
    [POSTGRES_USER=cube POSTGRES_PASSWORD=secret] }
stopping container
    20dfabd6e7f7f30948690c4352979cbc2122d90b0a22567f9f0bcbc33cc0f051
2021/05/16 16:00:47 Attempting to stop container
    20dfabd6e7f7f30948690c4352979cbc2122d90b0a22567f9f0bcbc33cc0f051
Container
    20dfabd6e7f7f30948690c4352979cbc2122d90b0a22567f9f0bcbc33cc0f051
    has been stopped and removed
```

Finally, we stop the container and remove it. Again, you can verify the operation with docker ps to see that it's not running and docker ps -a to see that it has been removed.

At this point, our container has been created and is running. You can check it with docker ps and docker logs test-container-1.

Here we can see our code pulling the image for the container.

At this point, we have the foundation of our orchestration system in place. We can create, run, stop, and remove containers, which provide the technical implementation of our `Task` concept. The other components in our system—namely, the `Worker` and `Manager`—will use this `Task` implementation to perform their necessary roles.

Summary

- The task concept, and its technical implementation, is the fundamental unit of our orchestration system. All the other components—worker, manager, and scheduler—exist for the purpose of starting, stopping, and inspecting tasks.
- The Docker API provides the ability to manipulate containers programmatically. The three most important methods are `ContainerCreate`, `ContainerStart`, and `ContainerStop`. These methods allow a developer to perform the same operations from their code that they can do from the command line (i.e., `docker run`, `docker start`, and `docker stop`).
- A container has a configuration. The configuration can be broken down into the following categories: identification (i.e., how to identify containers), resource allocation, networking, and error handling.
- A task is the smallest unit of work performed by our orchestration system and can be thought of as similar to running a program on your laptop or desktop.
- We use Docker in this book because it abstracts away many of the concerns of the underlying operating system. We could implement our orchestration system to run tasks as regular operating system processes. Doing so, however, means our system would need to be intimately familiar with the details of how processes run across OSs (e.g., Linux, Mac, Windows).
- An orchestration system consists of multiple machines, called a cluster.

Part 2

Worker

The second part of this book focuses on the Cube worker component. As its name suggests, the worker is responsible for performing the work in an orchestration system. The subject of that work is the *task*. If you've used Docker, then you're familiar with starting containers using the Docker command-line interface. In this model, *you* are the worker. In Cube, we replace you with a program that conceptually performs operations similar to you starting and stopping a Docker container.

In chapter 4, we will flesh out the implementation of the `Worker` object. The implementation focuses on starting and stopping a task.

In chapter 5, we will build an API for the `Worker`. The `Manager` object, which will be the subject of part 3, will be the user of this API.

In chapter 6, we will create a framework that allows the worker to expose metrics on its API. These metrics will be used by the `Manager` and the `Scheduler` components in later chapters.

Workers 4
of the Cube, unite!

This chapter covers

- Reviewing the purpose of the worker component in an orchestration system
- Reviewing the `Task` and `Docker` structs
- Defining and implementing an algorithm for processing incoming tasks
- Building a simple state machine to transition tasks between states
- Implementing the worker's methods for starting and stopping tasks

Think about running a web server that serves static pages. In many cases, running a single instance of our web server on a single physical or virtual machine is good enough. As the site grows in popularity, however, this setup poses several problems:

- *Resource availability*—Given the other processes running on the machine, is there enough memory, CPU, and disk space to meet the needs of our web server?
- *Resilience*—If the machine running the web server goes down, our site goes down with it.

Running multiple instances of our web server helps us solve these problems.

In this chapter, we will focus on fleshing out the `Worker` skeleton sketched out in chapter 2. It will use the `Task` implementation we covered in chapter 3. At the end of the chapter, we'll use our implementation of the worker to run multiple instances of a simple web server like that in our previously described scenario.

4.1   The Cube worker

With an orchestration system, the worker component allows us to easily scale applications such as our web server in the previous scenario. Figure 4.1 shows how we could run three instances of our website, represented by the boxes `W1`, `W2`, and `W3`, with each instance running on a separate worker. In this diagram, it's important to realize that the term `Worker` is doing double duty: it represents a physical or virtual machine and the worker component of the orchestration system that runs on that machine.

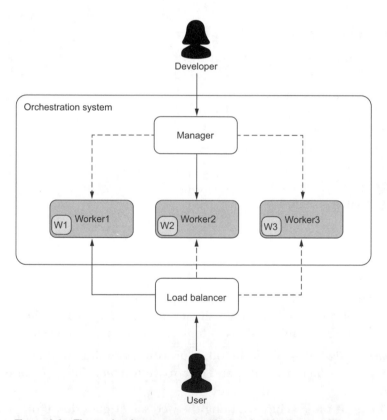

Figure 4.1   The worker boxes serve double duty in this diagram. They represent a physical or virtual machine on which the `Worker` component of the orchestration system runs.

Now we're less likely to experience resource availability issues. Because we're running three instances of our site on three different workers, user requests can be spread across the three instances instead of going to a single instance running on a single machine.

Similarly, our site is now more resilient to failures. For example, if `Worker1` in figure 4.2 crashes, it will take the `W3` instance of our site with it. While this might make us sad and create some work for us to bring `Worker1` back online, the users of our site shouldn't notice the difference. They'll be able to continue making requests to our site and getting back the expected static content.

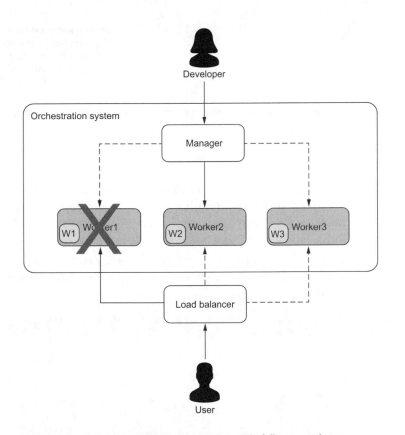

Figure 4.2 In the scenario where a worker node fails, our web server running on the other nodes can still respond to requests.

The worker is composed of smaller pieces that perform specific roles. Those pieces, seen in figure 4.3, are an API, a runtime, a task queue, a task database (DB), and metrics. In this chapter, we're going to focus only on three of these components: the runtime, the task queue, and the task DB. We'll work with the other two components in the following chapters.

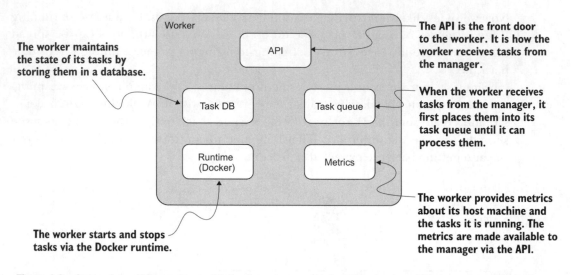

The worker maintains the state of its tasks by storing them in a database.

The API is the front door to the worker. It is how the worker receives tasks from the manager.

When the worker receives tasks from the manager, it first places them into its task queue until it can process them.

The worker starts and stops tasks via the Docker runtime.

The worker provides metrics about its host machine and the tasks it is running. The metrics are made available to the manager via the API.

Figure 4.3   Our worker will be made up of these five components, but this chapter will focus only on the runtime, task queue, and task DB.

4.2   Tasks and Docker

In chapter 1, we said a *task* is the smallest unit of work in an orchestration system. Then, in chapter 3, we implemented that definition in the Task struct, which we can see again in listing 4.1. This struct is the primary focus of the worker. It receives a task from the manager and then runs it. We'll use this struct throughout this chapter.

As the smallest unit of work, a task performs its work by being run as a Docker container. So there is a one-to-one correlation between a task and a container. The worker uses this struct to start and stop tasks.

Listing 4.1   Task struct defined in chapter 2

```
type Task struct {
    ID              uuid.UUID
    ContainerID     string
    Name            string
    State           State
    Image           string
    Memory          int64
    Disk            int64
    ExposedPorts    nat.PortSet
    PortBindings    map[string]string
    RestartPolicy   string
    StartTime       time.Time
    FinishTime      time.Time
}
```

In chapter 3, we also defined the Docker struct seen in the following listing. The worker will use this struct to start and stop the tasks as Docker containers.

Listing 4.2 `Docker` struct defined in chapter 3

```
type Docker struct {
    Client    *client.Client
    Config    Config
}
```

The two objects will be the core of the process that will allow our worker to start and stop tasks.

4.3 *The role of the queue*

Take a peek at listing 4.3 to remind yourself what the `Worker` struct looks like. The struct is in the same state in which we left it in chapter 2.

The worker will use the `Queue` field in the `Worker` struct as a temporary holding area for incoming tasks that need to be processed. When the manager sends a task to the worker, the task lands in the queue, which the worker will process on a first in, first out basis.

Listing 4.3 Worker skeleton from chapter 2

```
package worker


import (
    "fmt"

    "github.com/google/uuid"
    "github.com/golang-collections/collections/queue"
)


type Worker struct {
    Name      string
    Queue     queue.Queue
    Db        map[uuid.UUID]*task.Task
    TaskCount int
}
```

It's important to note that the `Queue` field is itself a struct, which defines several methods we can use to push items onto the queue (`Enqueue`), pop items off of the queue (`Dequeue`), and get the length of the queue (`Len`). The `Queue` field is an example of *composition* in Go. Thus, we can use other structs to compose new, higher-level objects.

Also notice that `Queue` is being imported from the `github.com/golang-collections/collections/queue` package. So we're reusing a `Queue` implementation that someone else has written for us. If you haven't done so already, you'll need to specify this package as a dependency (see the appendix).

4.4   *The role of the DB*

The worker will use the Db field to store the state about its tasks. This field is a map, where keys are of type uuid.UUID from the github.com/google/uuid package and values are of type task from our task package. There is one thing to note about using a map for the Db field. We're starting with a map here out of convenience. This will allow us to write working code quickly. But this comes with a tradeoff: anytime we restart the worker, we will lose data. This tradeoff is acceptable for the purpose of getting started, but later we'll replace this map with a persistent data store that won't lose data when we restart the worker.

4.5   *Counting tasks*

Finally, the TaskCount field provides a simple count of the tasks the worker has been assigned. We won't make use of this field until the next chapter.

4.6   *Implementing the worker's methods*

Now that we've reviewed the fields in our Worker struct, let's move on and talk about the methods that we stubbed out in chapter 2. The RunTask, StartTask, and StopTask methods seen in the next listing don't do much right now other than print out a statement, but by the end of the chapter, we will have fully implemented each of them.

> **Listing 4.4   The stubbed-out versions of RunTask, StartTask, and StopTask**

```
func (w *Worker) RunTask() {
    fmt.Println("I will start or stop a task")
}

func (w *Worker) StartTask() {
    fmt.Println("I will start a task")
}

func (w *Worker) StopTask() {
    fmt.Println("I will stop a task")
}
```

We're going to implement these methods in reverse order from what you see in listing 4.4. The reason for implementing them in this order is that the RunTask method will use the other two methods to start and stop tasks.

4.6.1   *Implementing the StopTask method*

There is nothing complicated about the StopTask method. It has a single purpose: to stop running tasks, remembering that a task corresponds to a running container. The implementation, seen in listing 4.5, can be summarized as the following set of steps:

1 Create an instance of the Docker struct that allows us to talk to the Docker daemon using the Docker SDK.
2 Call the Stop() method on the Docker struct.

   3 Check whether there were any errors in stopping the task.

   4 Update the `FinishTime` field on the task `t`.

   5 Save the updated task `t` to the worker's `Db` field.

   6 Print an informative message and return the result of the operation.

> **Listing 4.5   Our implementation of the `StopTask` method**

```
func (w *Worker) StopTask(t task.Task) task.DockerResult {
    config := task.NewConfig(&t)
    d := task.NewDocker(config)

    result := d.Stop(t.ContainerID)
    if result.Error != nil {
        log.Printf("Error stopping container %v: %v\n", t.ContainerID,
            result.Error)
    }
    t.FinishTime = time.Now().UTC()
    t.State = task.Completed
    w.Db[t.ID] = &t
    log.Printf("Stopped and removed container %v for task %v\n",
        t.ContainerID, t.ID)

    return result
}
```

Notice that the `StopTask` method returns a `task.DockerResult` type. The definition of that type can be seen in listing 4.6. If you remember, Go supports multiple return types. We could have enumerated each field in the `DockerResult` struct as a return type to the `StopTask` method. While there is nothing technically wrong with that approach, using the `DockerResult` approach allows us to wrap all the bits related to the outcome of an operation into a single struct. When we want to know anything about the result of an operation, we simply consult the `DockerResult` struct.

> **Listing 4.6   A reminder of what the `DockerResult` type looks like**

```
type DockerResult struct {
    Error       error
    Action      string
    ContainerId string
    Result      string
}
```

4.6.2   Implementing the StartTask method

Next, let's implement the `StartTask` method. Similar to the `StopTask` method, `StartTask` is fairly simple, but the process to start a task has a few more steps. The enumerated steps are as follows:

   1 Update the `StartTime` field on the task `t`.

   2 Create an instance of the `Docker` struct to talk to the Docker daemon.

   3 Call the `Run()` method on the `Docker` struct.

   4 Check whether there were any errors in starting the task.

   5 Add the running container's ID to the tasks `t.Runtime.ContainerId` field.

   6 Save the updated task `t` to the worker's `Db` field.

   7 Return the result of the operation.

The implementation of these steps can be seen in the following listing.

Listing 4.7 Our implementation of the `StartTask` method

```go
func (w *Worker) StartTask(t task.Task) task.DockerResult {
    t.StartTime = time.Now().UTC()
    config := task.NewConfig(&t)
    d := task.NewDocker(config)
    result := d.Run()
    if result.Error != nil {
        log.Printf("Err running task %v: %v\n", t.ID, result.Error)
        t.State = task.Failed
        w.Db[t.ID] = &t
        return result
    }

    t.ContainerID = result.ContainerId
    t.State = task.Running
    w.Db[t.ID] = &t

    return result
}
```

By recording the `StartTime` in the `StartTask` method, combined with recording `FinishTime` in the `StopTask` method, we'll later be able to use these timestamps in other output. For example, later in the book, we'll write a command-line interface that allows us to interact with our orchestrator, and the `StartTime` and `FinishTime` values can be output as part of a task's status.

Before we move on from these two methods, I want to point out that neither of them interact directly with the Docker SDK. Instead, they simply call the `Run` and `Stop` methods on the `Docker` object we created. It is the `Docker` object that handles the direct interaction with the Docker client. By encapsulating the interaction with Docker in the `Docker` object, our worker does not need to know anything about the underlying implementation details.

The `StartTask` and `StopTask` methods are the foundation of our worker. But looking at the skeleton we created in chapter 2, we see there is another foundational method missing. How do we add a task to the worker? Remember, we said the worker would use its `Queue` field as a temporary storage for incoming tasks, and when it was ready, it would pop a task of the queue and perform the necessary operation.

Let's fix this problem by adding the `AddTask` method seen in the next listing. This method performs a single task: it adds the task `t` to the `Queue`.

```
Listing 4.8   The worker's AddTask method
```

```
func (w *Worker) AddTask(t task.Task) {
    w.Queue.Enqueue(t)
}
```

4.6.3   An interlude on task state

All that's left to do now is to implement the RunTask method. Before we do that, how-ever, let's pause for a moment and recall the purpose of the RunTask method. In chapter 2, we said the RunTask method will be responsible for identifying the task's current state and then either starting or stopping a task based on the state. But why do we even need RunTask?

There are two possible scenarios for handling tasks:

- A task is being submitted for the first time, so the worker will not know about it.
- A task is being submitted for the *n_th* time, where the task submitted represents the *desired* state to which the *current* task should transition.

When processing the tasks it receives from the manager, the worker will need to deter-mine which of these scenarios it is dealing with. We're going to use a naive heuristic to help the worker solve this problem.

Remember that our worker has the Queue and Db fields. For our naive implementa-tion, the worker will use the Queue field to represent the desired state of a task. When the worker pops a task off the queue, it will interpret it as "put task *t* in the state *s*." The worker will interpret tasks it already has in its Db field as existing tasks—that is, tasks it has already seen at least once. If a task is in the Queue but not the Db, then this is the first time the worker is seeing the task, and we default to starting it.

In addition to identifying which of the two scenarios it is dealing with, the worker will also need to verify if the transition from the current state to the desired state is a valid one.

Let's review the states we defined in chapter 2. The next listing shows that we have states Pending, Scheduled, Running, Completed, and Failed.

```
Listing 4.9   The State type, which defines the valid states for a task
```

```
const (
    Pending State = iota
    Scheduled
    Running
    Completed
    Failed
)
```

But what do these states represent? We explained these states in chapter 2, but let's do a quick refresher:

- *Pending*—This is the initial state, the starting point, for every task.

- *Scheduled*—A task moves to this state once the manager has scheduled it onto a worker.
- *Running*—A task moves to this state when a worker successfully starts the task (i.e., starts the container).
- *Completed*—A task moves to this state when it completes its work in a normal way (i.e., it does not fail).
- *Failed*—If a task fails, it moves to this state.

To reinforce what these states represent, we can also recall the state diagram from chapter 2, seen here in figure 4.4.

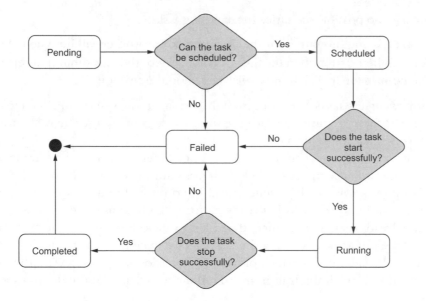

Figure 4.4   The states a task will go through during its life cycle

So we've defined what the states mean as they relate to a task, but we still haven't defined *how* a task transitions from one state to the next. Nor have we talked about what transitions are valid. For example, if a worker is already running a task, which means it's in the Running state, can it transition to the Scheduled state? If a task has failed, should it be able to transition from the Failed state to the Scheduled state?

So before getting back to the RunTask method, it looks like we need to figure out this issue of how to handle state transitions. To do this, we can model our states and transitions using the state table seen in table 4.1.

This table has three columns that represent the CurrentState of a task, an Event that triggers a state transition, and the NextState to which the task should transition. Each row in the table represents a specific *valid* transition. Notice that there is not a transition from Running to Scheduled, or from Failed to Scheduled.

Table 4.1 State transition table showing the valid transitions from one state to another

CurrentState	Event	NextState
Pending	ScheduleEvent	Scheduled
Pending	ScheduleEvent	Failed
Scheduled	StartTask	Running
Scheduled	StartTask	Failed
Running	StopTask	Completed

Now that we have a better understanding of the states and transitions between them, we can translate our understanding into code. Orchestrators like Borg, Kubernetes, and Nomad use a state machine to deal with the issue of state transitions. However, to keep the number of concepts and technologies we have to deal with to a minimum, we're going to hard-code our state transitions into the `stateTransitionMap` type you see in listing 4.10. This map encodes the transitions we identified in table 4.1.

The `stateTransitionMap` creates a map between a `State` and a slice of states, `[]State`. Thus, the keys in this map are the current state, and the values are the valid transition states. For example, the `Pending` state can only transition to the `Scheduled` state. The `Scheduled` state, however, can transition to `Running`, `Completed`, or `Failed`.

Listing 4.10 The `stateTransitionMap` map

```
var stateTransitionMap = map[State][]State{
    Pending:   []State{Scheduled},
    Scheduled: []State{Scheduled, Running, Failed},
    Running:   []State{Running, Completed, Failed},
    Completed: []State{},
    Failed:    []State{},
}
```

In addition to `stateTransitionMap`, we're going to implement the `Contains` and `ValidStateTransition` helper functions, seen in listing 4.11. These functions will perform the actual logic to verify that a task can transition from one state to the next.

Let's start with the `Contains` function. It takes two arguments: `states`, a slice of type `State`, and `state` of type `State`. If it finds `state` in the slice of `states`, it returns `true`; otherwise, it returns `false`.

The `ValidStateTransition` function is a wrapper around the `Contains` function. It provides a convenient way for callers of the function to ask, "Hey, can a task transition from this state to that state?" All the heavy lifting is done by the `Contains` function.

You should add the code in the following listing to the `state.go` file in the `task` directory of your project.

Listing 4.11   Helper methods

```go
func Contains(states []State, state State) bool {
    for _, s := range states {
        if s == state {
            return true
        }
    }
    return false
}

func ValidStateTransition(src State, dst State) bool {
    return Contains(stateTransitionMap[src], dst)
}
```

4.6.4 *Implementing the RunTask method*

Now we can finally talk more specifically about the RunTask method. It took us a while to get here, but we needed to iron out those other details before it even made sense to discuss this method. And because we did that leg work, implementing the RunTask method will go a bit more smoothly.

As we said earlier in the chapter, the RunTask method will identify the task's current state and then either start or stop it based on that state. We can use a fairly naive algorithm to determine whether the worker should start or stop a task. It looks like this:

1 Pull a task off the queue.
2 Convert it from an interface to a task.Task type.
3 Retrieve the task from the worker's Db.
4 Check whether the state transition is valid.
5 If the task from the queue is in the state Scheduled, call StartTask.
6 If the task from the queue is in the state Completed, call StopTask.
7 Else, there is an invalid transition, so return an error.

All that's left to do now is to implement these steps in our code, which can be seen in the following listing.

Listing 4.12   Our implementation of the RunTask method

```go
func (w *Worker) RunTask() task.DockerResult {
    t := w.Queue.Dequeue()                          // Calls the Dequeue()
    if t == nil {                                    // method
        log.Println("No tasks in the queue")
        return task.DockerResult{Error: nil}
    }

    taskQueued := t.(task.Task)                      // Converts the task
                                                     // to the proper type

    taskPersisted := w.Db[taskQueued.ID]             // Attempts to retrieve
    if taskPersisted == nil {                         // the same task from
                                                     // the Db
```

```
        taskPersisted = &taskQueued
        w.Db[taskQueued.ID] = &taskQueued
}

var result task.DockerResult
if task.ValidStateTransition(
    ➥ taskPersisted.State, taskQueued.State) {
    switch taskQueued.State {
    case task.Scheduled:
        result = w.StartTask(taskQueued)
    case task.Completed:
        result = w.StopTask(taskQueued)
    default:
        result.Error = errors.New("We should not get here")
    }
} else {
    err := fmt.Errorf("Invalid transition from %v to %v",
        ➥ taskPersisted.State, taskQueued.State)
    result.Error = err
}
return result
}
```

If there is a valid state transition and a task from the queue has a state of Scheduled, calls the StartTask method

If the task from the queue has a state of Completed, calls the StopTask method

If there is no valid transition, sets the Error field of the result variable

Returns the result

We start by calling the `Dequeue()` method to pop a task off the worker's queue. Notice that we're checking whether we received a task from the queue. If we didn't, which means the queue was empty, then we log a message and return a result with a nil `Error` field. Next, we have to convert the task we popped off the queue to the proper type, which is `task.Task`. This step is necessary because the `Queue`'s `Dequeue` method returns an interface type. Now we have a task from the queue, so we need to attempt to get the same task from the `Db`. If we don't find the task in the `Db`, it means this is the first time we're seeing the task, and we add it. Then we get to use the `Valid-StateTransition` function we created earlier in the chapter. Notice that we're passing the state from the `Db`, `taskPersisted.State`, and the state from the `Queue`, `task-Queued.State`. If there is a valid state transition and a task from the queue has a state of `Scheduled`, then we call the `StartTask` method. Or if there is a valid state transition but the task from the queue has a state of `Completed`, we call the `StopTask` method. If there isn't a valid transition—in other words, transitioning from `task-Persisted.State` to `taskQueued.State` is not valid—then we set the `Error` field of the `result` variable.

4.7 Putting it all together

Whew, we've made it. We covered a lot of territory in implementing the methods for our worker. If you remember chapter 3, we ended by writing a program that used the work we did earlier in the chapter. We're going to continue that practice in this chapter.

Before we do, however, remember that in chapter 3, we built out the `Task` and `Docker` structs, and that work allowed us to start and stop containers. The work we did in this chapter sits on top of the work from the last chapter. So once again, we're going to write a program that will start and stop tasks. The worker operates on the level of the `Task`, and the `Docker` struct operates on the lower level of the container.

Now let's write a program to pull everything together into a functioning worker. You can either comment out the code from the `main.go` file you used in the last chapter or create a new `main.go` file to use for this chapter.

The program is simple. We create a worker `w`, which has the `Queue` and `Db` fields as we talked about at the beginning of the chapter. Next, we create a task `t`. This task starts with a state of `Scheduled`, and it uses a Docker image named `strm/helloworld-http`. More about this image in a bit. After creating a worker and a task, we call the worker's `AddTask` method and pass it task `t`. Then it calls the worker's `RunTask` method. This method will pull the task `t` off the queue and do the right thing. It captures the return value from the `RunTask` method and stores it in the variable `result`. (Bonus points if you remember what type is returned from `RunTask`.)

At this point, we have a running container. After sleeping for 30 seconds (feel free to change the sleep time to whatever you want), we start the process of stopping the task. We change the task's state to `Completed`, call `AddTask` again and pass it the same task, and finally call `RunTask` again. This time, when `RunTask` pulls the task off the queue, the task will have a container ID and a different state. As a result, the task gets stopped. The following listing shows our program to create a worker, add a task, start it, and finally stop it.

Listing 4.13   Pulling everything together into a functioning worker

```go
// previous code not shown

func main() {
    db := make(map[uuid.UUID]*task.Task)
    w := worker.Worker{
        Queue: *queue.New(),
        Db:    db,
    }

    t := task.Task{
        ID:    uuid.New(),
        Name:  "test-container-1",
        State: task.Scheduled,
        Image: "strm/helloworld-http",
    }

    // first time the worker will see the task
    fmt.Println("starting task")
    w.AddTask(t)
    result := w.RunTask()
    if result.Error != nil {
        panic(result.Error)
    }

    t.ContainerID = result.ContainerId
```

```
fmt.Printf("task %s is running in container %s\n", t.ID, t.ContainerID)
fmt.Println("Sleepy time")
time.Sleep(time.Second * 30)

fmt.Printf("stopping task %s\n", t.ID)
t.State = task.Completed
w.AddTask(t)
result = w.RunTask()
if result.Error != nil {
    panic(result.Error)
}
}
```

Let's pause for a moment and talk about the image used in the previous code listing. At the beginning of the chapter, we talked about the scenario of scaling a static website using an orchestrator, specifically the worker component. This image, strm/helloworld-http provides a concrete example of a static website: it runs a web server that serves a single file. To verify this behavior, when you run the program, type the docker ps command in a separate terminal. You should see output similar to listing 4.14. In that output, you can find the port the web server is running on by looking at the PORTS column. Then open your browser and type localhost:<port>. In the case of the output in the following listing, I would type localhost:49161 in my browser. The output has been truncated to make it more readable.

Listing 4.14   Truncated output from the `docker  ps` command

```
$ docker ps
CONTAINER ID    IMAGE                   PORTS                   NAMES
4723a4201829    strm/helloworld-http    0.0.0.0:49161->80/tcp   test-container-1
```

When I browse to the server on my machine, I see "Hello from 90566e236f88". Go ahead and run the program. You should see output similar to the following listing.

Listing 4.15   Running your main program

```
$ go run main.go
starting task
{"status":"Pulling from strm/helloworld-http","id":"latest"}
{"status":"Digest:
    ➥ sha256:bd44b0ca80c26b5eba984bf498a9c3bab0eb1c59d30d8df
    ➥ cb2c073937ee4e45"}
{"status":"Status: Image is up to date for strm/helloworld-http:latest"}
task bfe7d381-e56b-4c4d-acaf-cbf47353a30a is running in
    ➥ container e13af1f4b9cbac6f871d1d343ea8f7958dae5f1897954bf6
    ➥ b4a2c58ad7520dcb
Sleepy time
stopping task bfe7d381-e56b-4c4d-acaf-cbf47353a30a
2021/08/08 21:13:09 Attempting to stop container
    ➥ e13af1f4b9cbac6f871d1d343ea8f7958dae5f1897954bf6b4a2c58ad7520dcb
2021/08/08 21:13:19 Stopped and removed container
    ➥ e13af1f4b9cbac6f871d1d343ea8f7958dae5f1897954bf6b4a2c58ad7520dcb
    ➥ for task bfe7d381-e56b-4c4d-acaf-cbf47353a30a
```

Congratulations! You now have a functional worker. Before moving on to the next chapter, play around with what you've built. In particular, modify the `main` function from listing 4.13 to create multiple workers, and then add tasks to each them.

Summary

- Tasks are executed as containers, meaning there is a one-to-one relationship between a task and a container.
- The worker performs two basic actions on tasks, either starting or stopping them. These actions result in tasks transitioning from one state to the next valid state.
- The worker shows how the Go language supports object composition. The worker itself is a composition of other objects; in particular, the worker's `Queue` field is a struct defined in the `github.com/golang-collections/collections/queue` package
- The worker, as we've designed and implemented it, is simple. We've used clear and concise processes that are easy to implement in code.
- The worker does not interact directly with the Docker SDK. Instead, it uses our `Docker` struct, which is a wrapper around the SDK. By encapsulating the interaction with the SDK in the `Docker` struct, we can keep the `StartTask` and `StopTask` methods small and readable.

An API for the worker

This chapter covers

- Understanding the purpose of the worker API
- Implementing methods to handle API requests
- Creating a server to listen for API requests
- Starting, stopping, and listing tasks via the API

In chapter 4, we implemented the core features of the worker: pulling tasks off its queue and then starting or stopping them. Those core features alone, however, do not make the worker complete. We need a way to expose those core features so a manager, which will be the exclusive user, running on a different machine can make use of them. To do this, we're going to wrap the worker's core functionality in an application programming interface, or API.

The API will be simple, as you can see in figure 5.1, providing the means for a manager to perform these basic operations:

- Send a task to the worker (which results in the worker starting the task as a container)
- Get a list of the worker's tasks
- Stop a running task

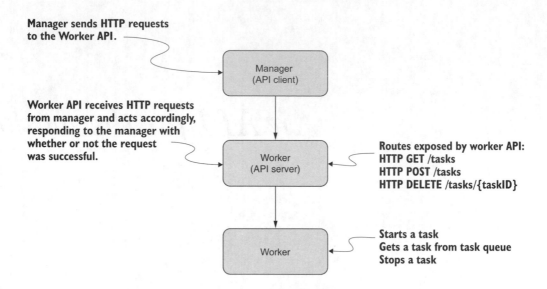

Manager sends HTTP requests to the Worker API.

Manager
(API client)

Worker API receives HTTP requests from manager and acts accordingly, responding to the manager with whether or not the request was successful.

Worker
(API server)

Routes exposed by worker API:
HTTP GET /tasks
HTTP POST /tasks
HTTP DELETE /tasks/{taskID}

Worker

Starts a task
Gets a task from task queue
Stops a task

Figure 5.1   The API for our orchestrator provides a simple interface to the worker.

5.1   Overview of the worker API

We've enumerated the operations that the worker's API will support: sending a task to a worker to be started, getting a list of tasks, and stopping a task. But how will we implement those operations? We're going to implement those operations using a web API. This choice means that the worker's API can be exposed across a network and that it will use the HTTP protocol. Like most web APIs, the worker's API will use three primary components:

- *Handlers*—Functions that are capable of responding to requests
- *Routes*—Patterns that can be used to match the URL of incoming requests
- *Router*—An object that uses routes to match incoming requests with the appropriate handler

We could implement our API using nothing but the http package from the Go standard library. That can be tedious, however, because the http package is missing one critical piece: the ability to define *parameterized routes*. What is a parameterized route? It's a route that defines a URL where one or more parts of the URL path are unknown and may change from one request to the next. This is particularly useful for things like identifiers. For example, if a route like /tasks called with an HTTP GET request returns a list of all tasks, then a route like /tasks/5 returns a single item, the task whose identifier is the integer 5. Since each task should have a unique identifier, however, we need to provide a pattern when defining this kind of route in a web API. The way to do this is to use a parameter for the part of the URL path that can be different with each request. In the case of tasks, we can use a route defined as /tasks/{taskID}.

Because the `http` package from the standard library doesn't provide a robust and easy way to define parameterized routes, we're going to use a lightweight, third-party router called chi (https://github.com/go-chi/chi). Conceptually, our API will look like what you see in figure 5.2. Requests will be sent to an HTTP server, which you can see in the box. This server provides a function called `ListenAndServe`, which is the lowest layer in our stack and will handle the low-level details of listening for incoming requests. The next three layers—routes, router, and handlers—are all provided by chi.

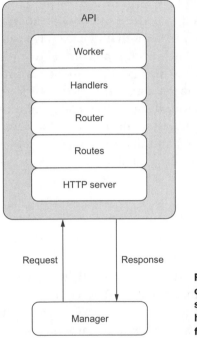

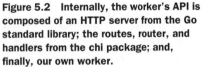

Figure 5.2 Internally, the worker's API is composed of an HTTP server from the Go standard library; the routes, router, and handlers from the chi package; and, finally, our own worker.

For our worker API, we'll use the routes defined in table 5.1. Because we're exposing our worker's functionality via a web API, the routes will involve standard HTTP methods like GET, POST, and DELETE. The first route in the table, `/tasks`, will use the HTTP GET method and will return a list of tasks. The second route is the same as the first, but it uses the POST method, which will start a task. The third route, `/tasks/{taskID}`, will stop the running task identified by the parameter `{taskID}`.

Table 5.1 Routes used by our worker API

Method	Route	Description
GET	/tasks	Gets a list of all tasks
POST	/tasks	Creates a task
DELETE	/tasks/{taskID}	Stops the task identified by `taskID`

If you work with REST (representational state transfer) APIs at your day job, this should look familiar. If you're not familiar with REST or you are new to the world of APIs, don't worry. It's not necessary to be a REST expert to grok what we're building in this chapter. At a very hand-wavy level, REST is an architectural style that builds on the client-server model of application development. If you want to learn more about REST, you can start with a gentle introduction like the blog post "API 101: What Is a REST API?" (https://blog.postman.com/rest-api-definition/).

5.2 *Data format, requests, and responses*

Before we get into writing any code, we need to address one more important item. From your experience browsing the internet, you know that when you type an address into your browser, you get back data. Type in https://espn.com, and you get data about sports. Type in https://nytimes.com, and you get data about current events. Type in https://www.funnycatpix.com, and you get data that is pictures of cats.

Like these websites, the worker API deals with data, both sending and receiving it. However, its data is not about news or cats but tasks. Furthermore, the data that the worker API deals with will take a specific form, and that form is JSON, which stands for *JavaScript Object Notation*. You're probably already familiar with JSON, as it's the lingua franca of many modern APIs. This decision has two consequences:

- Any data sent to the API (e.g., for our POST /tasks route in table 5.1) must be encoded as JSON data in the body of the request.
- Any data returned from the API (e.g., for our GET /tasks route) must be encoded as JSON data in the body of the response.

For our worker, we only have one route, the POST /tasks route, that will accept a body. But what data does our worker expect to be in the body of that request?

If you remember from the last chapter, the worker has a StartTask method that takes a task.Task type as an argument. That type holds all the necessary data we need to start the task as a Docker container. But what the worker API will receive (from the manager) is a task.TaskEvent type, which contains a task.Task. So the job of the API is to extract that task from the request and add it to the worker's queue. Thus, a request to our POST /tasks route will look like that in the following listing. The task.TaskEvent here was used in chapter 4.

Listing 5.1 The worker API receiving a `task.TaskEvent` from the manager

```
{
    "ID": "6be4cb6b-61d1-40cb-bc7b-9cacefefa60c",
    "State": 2,
    "Task": {
        "State": 1,
        "ID": "21b23589-5d2d-4731-b5c9-a97e9832d021",
        "Name": "test-chapter-5",
        "Image": "strm/helloworld-http"
    }
}
```

The response to our POST /tasks request will have a status code of 201 and includes a JSON-encoded representation of the task in the response body. Why a 201 and not a 200 response code? We could use a 200 response status. According to the HTTP spec described in RFC 7231, "The 200 (OK) status code indicates that the request has succeeded. The payload sent in a 200 response depends on the request method" (https://datatracker.ietf.org/doc/html/rfc7231#section-6.3.1). Thus, the 200 response code is the generic case telling the requester, "Yes, I received your request, and it was successful." The 201 response code, however, handles the more specific case. For a POST request, it tells the requester, "Yes, I received your request, and I created a new resource." In our case, that new resource is the task sent in the request body.

Like the POST /tasks route, the GET /tasks route returns a body in its response. This route ultimately calls the GetTasks method on our worker, which returns a slice of pointers to task.Task types, effectively a list of tasks. Our API in this situation will take that slice returned from GetTasks, encode it as JSON, and then return it. The following listing shows an example of what such a response might look like. In this example, there are two tasks.

> **Listing 5.2 The worker API returning a list of tasks for the GET /tasks route**

```
[
  {
    "ID": "21b23589-5d2d-4731-b5c9-a97e9832d021",
    "ContainerID": "4f67af51b173564ffd50a3c7f",
    "Name": "test-chapter-5",
    "State": 2,
    "Image": "strm/helloworld-http",
    "Memory": 0,
    "Disk": 0,
    "ExposedPorts": null,
    "PortBindings": null,
    "RestartPolicy": "",
    "StartTime": "0001-01-01T00:00:00Z",
    "FinishTime": "0001-01-01T00:00:00Z"
  },
  {
    "ID": "266592cd-960d-4091-981c-8c25c44b1018",
    "ContainerID": "180d207fa788d5261e6ccf927",
    "Name": "test-chapter-5-1",
    "State": 2,
    "Image": "strm/helloworld-http",
    "Memory": 0,
    "Disk": 0,
    "ExposedPorts": null,
    "PortBindings": null,
    "RestartPolicy": "",
    "StartTime": "0001-01-01T00:00:00Z",
    "FinishTime": "0001-01-01T00:00:00Z"
  }
]
```

In addition to the list of tasks, the response will also have a status code of 200.

Finally, let's talk about the DELETE /tasks/{taskID} route. Like the GET /tasks route, this one will not take a body in the request. Remember, we said earlier that the {taskID} part of the route is a parameter and allows the route to be called with arbitrary IDs. So this route allows us to stop a task for the given taskID. This route will only return a status code of 204; it will not include a body in the response. So with this new information, let's update table 5.1.

Table 5.2 Updated table 5.1 showing for each request whether the route accepts a request body, whether it returns a response body, and what status code is returned for a successful request

Method	Route	Description	Request body	Response body	Status code
GET	/tasks	Gets a list of all tasks	None	List of tasks	200
POST	/tasks	Creates a task	JSON-encoded task.TaskEvent	None	201
DELETE	/tasks/{taskID}	Stops the task identified by taskID	None	None	204

5.3 *The API struct*

At this point, we've set the stage for writing the code for the worker API. We've identified the main components of our API, defined the data format used by that API, and enumerated the routes the API will support.

We're going to start by representing our API in code as the struct seen in listing 5.3. You should create a file named api.go in the worker/ directory of your code where you can place this struct.

This struct serves several purposes. First, it contains the Address and Port fields, which define the local IP address of the machine where the API runs and the port on which the API will listen for requests. These fields will be used to start the API server, which we will implement later in the chapter. Second, it contains the Worker field, which will be a reference to an instance of a Worker object. Remember, we said the API will wrap the worker to expose the worker's core functionality to the manager. This field is the means by which that functionality is exposed. Third, the struct contains the Router field, which is a pointer to an instance of chi.Mux. This field brings in all the functionality provided by the chi router.

Listing 5.3 The API struct that will power our worker

```
type Api struct {
    Address string
    Port    int
    Worker  *Worker
    Router  *chi.Mux
}
```

> **Definition**
> The term *mux* stands for *multiplexer* and can be used synonymously with *request router*.

5.4 Handling requests

With the API struct defined, we've given the API a general shape, or form, at a high level. This shape will contain the API's three components: handlers, routes, and a router. Let's dive deeper into the API and implement the handlers that will be able to respond to the routes we defined in table 5.1.

As we've already said, a *handler* is a function capable of responding to a request. For our API to handle incoming requests, we need to define handler methods on the API struct. We're going to use the following three methods, which I'll list here with their method signatures:

- `StartTaskHandler(w http.ResponseWriter, r *http.Request)`
- `GetTasksHandler(w http.ResponseWriter, r *http.Request)`
- `StopTaskHandler(w http.ResponseWriter, r *http.Request)`

There is nothing terribly complicated about these handler methods. Each method takes the same arguments, an `http.ReponseWriter` type and a pointer to an `http.Request` type. Both of these types are defined in the `http` package in Go's standard library. The `http.ResponseWriter`'s w will contain data related to responses. The `http.Request`'s r will hold data related to requests.

To implement these handlers, create a file named `handlers.go` in the `worker` directory of your project and then open that file in a text editor. We'll start by adding the `StartTaskHandler` method seen in listing 5.4. At a high level, this method reads the body of a request from `r.Body`, converts the incoming data it finds in that body from JSON to an instance of our `task.TaskEvent` type, and then adds that `task.TaskEvent` to the worker's queue. It wraps up by printing a log message and then adding a response code to the `http.ResponseWriter`. It takes incoming requests to start a task, reads the body of the request, converts it from JSON to a `task.TaskEvent`, and then puts that on the worker's queue.

Listing 5.4 The worker's `StartTaskHandler` method

```
func (a *Api) StartTaskHandler(w http.ResponseWriter, r *http.Request) {
    d := json.NewDecoder(r.Body)
    d.DisallowUnknownFields()
```

Creates an instance of json.Decoder by calling the NewDecoder function, passing in the request body r.Body

Calls the DisallowUnknownFields() method, which will cause the Decode() method to return an error if there are fields in the body that are not defined in the destination struct—in our case, task.TaskEvent

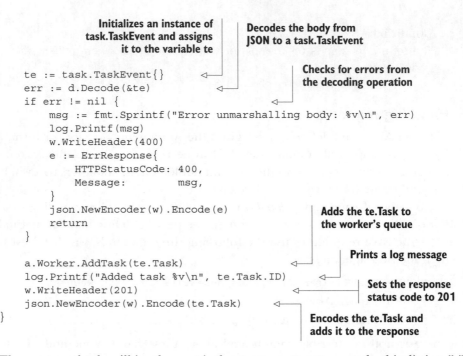

Initializes an instance of task.TaskEvent and assigns it to the variable te

Decodes the body from JSON to a task.TaskEvent

Checks for errors from the decoding operation

```
te := task.TaskEvent{}
err := d.Decode(&te)
if err != nil {
    msg := fmt.Sprintf("Error unmarshalling body: %v\n", err)
    log.Printf(msg)
    w.WriteHeader(400)
    e := ErrResponse{
        HTTPStatusCode: 400,
        Message:        msg,
    }
    json.NewEncoder(w).Encode(e)
    return
}

a.Worker.AddTask(te.Task)
log.Printf("Added task %v\n", te.Task.ID)
w.WriteHeader(201)
json.NewEncoder(w).Encode(te.Task)
}
```

Adds the te.Task to the worker's queue

Prints a log message

Sets the response status code to 201

Encodes the te.Task and adds it to the response

The next method we'll implement is the `GetTasksHandler` method in listing 5.5. This method looks simple, but there is a lot going on inside it. It starts off by setting the `Content-Type` header to let the client know we're sending it JSON data. Then, similar to `StartTaskHandler`, it adds a response code. And then we come to the final line in the method. It may look a little complicated, but it's really just a compact way to express the following operations:

- Gets an instance of a `json.Encoder` type by calling the `json.NewEncoder()` method
- Gets all the worker's tasks by calling the worker's `GetTasks` method
- Transforms the list of tasks into JSON by calling the `Encode` method on the `json.Encoder` object

Listing 5.5 The worker's `GetTasksHandler`

```
func (a *Api) GetTasksHandler(w http.ResponseWriter, r *http.Request) {
    w.Header().Set("Content-Type", "application/json")
    w.WriteHeader(200)
    json.NewEncoder(w).Encode(a.Worker.GetTasks())
}
```

The final handler to implement is the `StopTaskHandler`. If we glance back at table 5.2, we can see that stopping a task is accomplished by sending a request with a path of `/tasks/{taskID}`. An example of what this path will look like when a real request is made is `/tasks/6be4cb6b-61d1-40cb-bc7b-9cacefefa60c`. This is all that's needed to stop a task because the worker already knows about the task: it has it stored in its Db field.

The first thing the StopTaskHandler must do is read the taskID from the request path. As you can see in listing 5.6, we're doing that by using a helper function named URLParam from the chi package. We're not going to worry about how the helper method is getting the taskID for us; all we care about is that it simplifies our life a bit and gives us the data we need to get on with the job of stopping a task.

Now that we have the taskID, we have to convert it from a string, which is the type that chi.URLParam returns to us, into a uuid.UUID type. This conversion is done by calling the uuid.Parse() method and passing it the string version of the taskID. Why do we have to perform this step? It's necessary because the worker's Db field is a map that has keys of type uuid.UUID. So if we were to try to look up a task using a string, the compiler would yell at us.

Okay, now we have a taskID and have converted it to the correct type. The next thing we want to do is check whether the worker knows about this task. If it doesn't, we should return a response with a 404 status code. If it does, we change the state to task.Completed and add it to the worker's queue. This is what the remaining of the method is doing. The worker's StopTaskHandler uses the taskID from the request path to add a task to the worker's queue that will stop the specified task.

Listing 5.6   The worker's StopTaskHandler

> Extracts the {taskID} from the
> request path and stores it in taskID

```go
func (a *Api) StopTaskHandler(w http.ResponseWriter, r *http.Request) {
    taskID := chi.URLParam(r, "taskID")
    if taskID == "" {
        log.Printf("No taskID passed in request.\n")
        w.WriteHeader(400)
    }
```

> Checks whether
> taskID is an empty
> string; if it is, returns
> a 400 status code

> Converts the taskID from a string
> to a uuid.UUID and stores it in tID

```go
    tID, _ := uuid.Parse(taskID)
    _, ok := a.Worker.Db[tID]
    if !ok {
        log.Printf("No task with ID %v found", tID)
        w.WriteHeader(404)
    }
```

> Queries the worker's
> datastore for the UUID.
> This idiom is called the
> "comma, ok" idiom, and
> will set the ok variable
> to true if the tID key is
> found in the datastore;
> otherwise, it will set ok to
> false. Also, we're using the
> blank identifier, which is a
> placeholder whose value
> we don't care about.

> Checks the value of ok; if it's false,
> returns a 404 status code because the
> worker doesn't know about the task

```go
    taskToStop := a.Worker.Db[tID]
    taskCopy := *taskToStop
```

> Retrieves a
> pointer to the
> task with an ID
> of tID and stores
> it in taskToStop

> Makes a copy of
> taskToStop and stores
> it in taskCopy

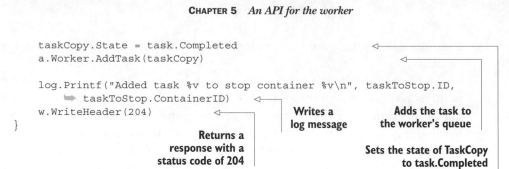

```
        taskCopy.State = task.Completed
        a.Worker.AddTask(taskCopy)

        log.Printf("Added task %v to stop container %v\n", taskToStop.ID,
            ➥ taskToStop.ContainerID)
        w.WriteHeader(204)
}
```

Returns a response with a status code of 204

Writes a log message

Adds the task to the worker's queue

Sets the state of TaskCopy to task.Completed

There is one little gotcha in our `StopTaskHandler` that's worth explaining in more detail. Notice that we're making a copy of the task in the worker's datastore. Why is this necessary?

As I mentioned in chapter 4, we're using the worker's datastore to represent the current state of tasks, while we're using the worker's queue to represent the desired state of tasks. As a result of this decision, the API cannot simply retrieve the task from the worker's datastore, set the state to `task.Completed`, and then put the task onto the worker's queue. The reason is that the values in the datastore are pointers to `task.Task` types. If we were to change the state on `taskToStop`, we would be changing the state field on the task in the datastore. We would then add the same task to the worker's queue, and when it popped the task off to work on it, it would complain about not being able to transition a task from the state `task.Completed` to `task.Completed`. Hence, we make a copy, change the state on the copy, and add it to the queue.

5.5   *Serving the API*

Up to this point, we've been setting the stage for serving the worker's API. We've created our `API` struct that contains the two components that will make this possible: the `Worker` and `Router` fields. Each of these is a pointer to another type. The `Worker` field is a pointer to our own `Worker` type that we created in chapter 3, and it will provide all the functionality to start and stop tasks and get a list of tasks the worker knows about. The `Router` field is a pointer to a `Mux` object provided by the chi package, and it will provide the functionality for defining routes and routing requests to the handlers we defined earlier.

To serve the worker's API, we need to make two additions to the code we've written so far. Both additions will be made to the `api.go` file.

The first addition is to add the `initRouter()` method to the `Api` struct, as you see in listing 5.7. This method, as its name suggests, initializes our router. It starts by creating an instance of a `Router` by calling `chi.NewRouter()`. Then it goes about setting up the routes we defined in table 5.2. We won't get into the internals of how the chi package creates these routes.

Listing 5.7   The `initRouter()` method

```
func (a *Api) initRouter() {
    a.Router = chi.NewRouter()
```

Creates a new router

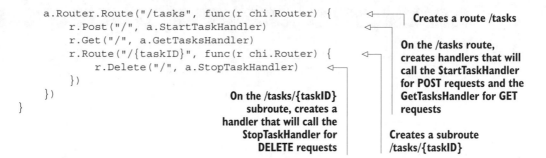

```
a.Router.Route("/tasks", func(r chi.Router) {          ◄──────      Creates a route /tasks
    r.Post("/", a.StartTaskHandler)                    ◄──────
    r.Get("/", a.GetTasksHandler)                                   On the /tasks route,
    r.Route("/{taskID}", func(r chi.Router) {          ◄──────      creates handlers that will
        r.Delete("/", a.StopTaskHandler)               ◄──────      call the StartTaskHandler
    })                                                              for POST requests and the
})                                                                  GetTasksHandler for GET
}                                                                   requests
```

On the /tasks/{taskID}
subroute, creates a
handler that will call the
StopTaskHandler for
DELETE requests

Creates a subroute
/tasks/{taskID}

The final addition is to add the `Start()` method to the `Api` struct, as you see in listing 5.8. This method calls the `initRouter` method defined in listing 5.4, and then it starts an HTTP server that will listen for requests. The `ListenAndServe` function is provided by the `http` package from Go's standard library. It takes an address (e.g. `127.0.0.1:5555`), which we're building with the `fmt.Sprintf` function, and a handler, which for our purposes is the router that gets created in the `initRouter()` method.

Listing 5.8 The `Start()` method: Initializes our router and starts listening for requests

```
func (a *Api) Start() {
    a.initRouter()
    http.ListenAndServe(fmt.Sprintf("%s:%d", a.Address, a.Port), a.Router)
}
```

5.6 *Putting it all together*

Like we've done in previous chapters, it's time to take the code we've written and actually run it. To do this, we're going to continue our use of `main.go`, in which we'll write our `main` function. You can either reuse the `main.go` file from the last chapter and just delete the contents of the main function or start with a fresh file.

In your `main.go` file, add the `main()` function from listing 5.9. This function uses all the work we've done up to this point. It creates an instance of our worker, `w`, which has a `Queue` and a `Db`. It creates an instance of our API, `api`, which uses the `host` and `port` values that it reads from the local environment. Finally, the `main()` function performs the two operations that bring everything to life.

The first of these operations is to call a function `runTasks` and pass it a pointer to the worker `w`. But it also does something else. It has this funny `go` term before calling the `runTasks` function. What is that about? If you've used threads in other languages, the `go runTasks(&w)` line is similar to using threads. In Go, threads are called *goroutines*, and they provide the ability to perform concurrent programming. We won't go into the details of goroutines here because there are other resources dedicated solely to this topic. For our purposes, all we need to know is that we're creating a goroutine, and inside it, we will run the `runTasks` function. After creating the goroutine, we can continue on in the main function and start our API by calling `api.Start()`.

Listing 5.9   Running our worker from `main.go`

```go
func main() {
    host := os.Getenv("CUBE_HOST")
    port, _ := strconv.Atoi(os.Getenv("CUBE_PORT"))

    fmt.Println("Starting Cube worker")

    w := worker.Worker{
        Queue: *queue.New(),
        Db:    make(map[uuid.UUID]*task.Task),
    }
    api := worker.Api{Address: host, Port: port, Worker: &w}

    go runTasks(&w)
    api.Start()
}
```

Now, let's talk about the `runTasks` function, which you can see in listing 5.10. This function runs in a separate goroutine from the main function, and it's fairly simple. It's a continuous loop that checks the worker's queue for tasks and calls the worker's `RunTask` method when it finds tasks that need to run. For our own convenience, we're sleeping for 10 seconds between each iteration of the loop. This slows things down for us so we can easily read any log messages.

Listing 5.10   The `runTasks` function

```go
func runTasks(w *worker.Worker) {
    for {
        if w.Queue.Len() != 0 {
            result := w.RunTask()
            if result.Error != nil {
                log.Printf("Error running task: %v\n", result.Error)
            }
        } else {
            log.Printf("No tasks to process currently.\n")
        }
        log.Println("Sleeping for 10 seconds.")
        time.Sleep(10 * time.Second)
    }

}
```

There is a reason that we've structured our main function like this. Recall the handler functions we wrote earlier in the chapter; they were performing a very narrow set of operations, namely:

- Reading requests sent to the server
- Getting a list of tasks from the worker (in the case of the `GetTasksHandler`)
- Putting a task on the worker's queue
- Sending a response to the requester

Notice that the API is not calling any worker methods that perform task operations (i.e., it is not starting or stopping tasks). Structuring our code in this way allows us to separate the concern of handling requests from the concern of performing the operations to start and stop tasks. Thus, we make it easier on ourselves to reason about our codebase. If we want to add a feature or fix a bug with the API, we know we need to work in the `api.go` file. If we want to do the same for request handling, we need to work in the `handlers.go` file. And for anything related to the operations of starting and stopping tasks, we need to work in the `worker.go` file.

Okay, time to make some magic. Running our code should result in a number of log messages being printed to the terminal like this:

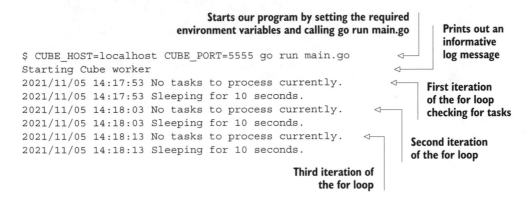

As you can see when we first start the worker API, it doesn't do much. It tells us it doesn't have any tasks to process, sleeps for 10 seconds, and then wakes up again and tells us the same thing. This isn't very exciting. Let's spice things up by interacting with the worker API. We'll start with getting a list of tasks using the `curl` command in a separate terminal:

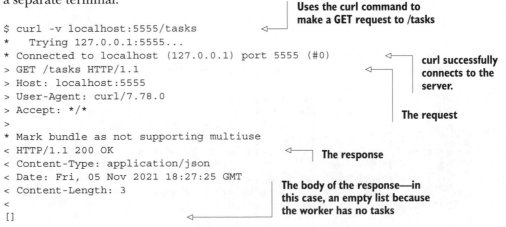

Great! We can query the API to get a list of tasks. As expected, though, the response is an empty list because the worker doesn't have any tasks yet. Let's remedy that by sending it a request to start a task:

--request allows us to specify the request is a POST.

--header allows us to specify that we're sending the server JSON data in the body.

--data allows us to specify the JSON data that should be sent in the request body, which, in this case, is a task.TaskEvent.

```
curl -v --request POST \
  --header 'Content-Type: application/json' \
  --data '{
    "ID": "266592cd-960d-4091-981c-8c25c44b1018",
    "State": 2,
    "Task": {
        "State": 1,
        "ID": "266592cd-960d-4091-981c-8c25c44b1018",
        "Name": "test-chapter-5-1",
        "Image": "strm/helloworld-http"
    }
}'
localhost:5555/tasks
```

When you run the `curl` command, you should see output like the following. Notice that the status code in the response is `HTTP/1.1 201 Created`, and there is no response body:

```
*   Trying 127.0.0.1:5555...
* Connected to localhost (127.0.0.1) port 5555 (#0)
> POST /tasks HTTP/1.1
> Host: localhost:5555
> User-Agent: curl/7.80.0
> Accept: */*
> Content-Type: application/json
> Content-Length: 243
>
* Mark bundle as not supporting multiuse
< HTTP/1.1 201 Created
< Date: Mon, 29 Nov 2021 22:24:51 GMT
<
* Connection #0 to host localhost left intact
```

At the same time that you run the `curl` command, you should see log messages in the terminal where the API is running. Those log messages should look like this:

```
2021/11/05 14:47:47 Added task 266592cd-960d-4091-981c-8c25c44b1018
Found task in queue: {266592cd-960d-4091-981c-8c25c44b1018
    ➥ test-chapter-5-1 1 strm/helloworld-http 0 0 map[] map[]
    ➥ 0001-01-01 00:00:00 +0000 UTC 0001-01-01 00:00:00 +0000 UTC}:
{"status":"Pulling from strm/helloworld-http","id":"latest"}
{"status":"Digest:
    ➥ sha256:bd44b0ca80c26b5eba984bf49"}
{"status":"Status: Image is up to date for strm/helloworld-http:latest"}
2021/11/05 14:47:53 Sleeping for 10 seconds.
```

Great! At this point, we've created a task by calling the worker API's `POST /tasks` route. Now, when we make a `GET` request to `/tasks`, instead of seeing an empty list, we should see output like this:

```
$ curl -v localhost:5555/tasks
*   Trying 127.0.0.1:5555...
* Connected to localhost (127.0.0.1) port 5555 (#0)
> GET /tasks HTTP/1.1
> Host: localhost:5555
> User-Agent: curl/7.78.0
> Accept: */*
>
* Mark bundle as not supporting multiuse
< HTTP/1.1 200 OK
< Content-Type: application/json
< Date: Fri, 05 Nov 2021 19:17:55 GMT
< Content-Length: 346
<
[
  {
    "ID":"266592cd-960d-4091-981c-8c25c44b1018",
    "ContainerID": "6df4e15a5c840b0ece1aede53",
    "Name":"test-chapter-5-1",
    "State":2,
    "Image":"strm/helloworld-http",
    "Memory":0,
    "Disk":0,
    "ExposedPorts":null,
    "PortBindings":null,
    "RestartPolicy":"",
    "StartTime":"0001-01-01T00:00:00Z",
    "FinishTime":"0001-01-01T00:00:00Z"
  }
]
```

Also, we should see a container running on our local machine, which we can verify using the docker ps:

```
$ docker ps --format "table {{.ID}}\t{{.Image}}\t{{.Status}}\t{{.Names}}"
CONTAINER ID   IMAGE                 STATUS          NAMES
6df4e15a5c84   strm/helloworld-http  Up 35 minutes   test-chapter-5-1
```

So far, we've queried the worker API to get a list of tasks by making a GET request to the /tasks route. Seeing the worker didn't have any, we created one by making a POST request to the /tasks route. Upon querying the API again by making a subsequent GET request /tasks, we got back a list containing our task.

Now let's exercise the last bit of the worker's API functionality and stop our task. We can do this by making a DELETE request to the /tasks/<taskID> route, using the ID field from our previous GET request:

```
$ curl -v --request DELETE
    ➥ "localhost:5555/tasks/266592cd-960d-4091-981c-8c25c44b1018"
*   Trying 127.0.0.1:5555...
* Connected to localhost (127.0.0.1) port 5555 (#0)
> DELETE /tasks/266592cd-960d-4091-981c-8c25c44b1018 HTTP/1.1
> Host: localhost:5555
```

```
> User-Agent: curl/7.78.0
> Accept: */*
>
* Mark bundle as not supporting multiuse
< HTTP/1.1 204 No Content
< Date: Fri, 05 Nov 2021 19:25:47 GMT
```

In addition to seeing that our request received an `HTTP/1.1 204 No Content` response, we should see log output from the worker API that looks like the following:

```
2021/11/05 15:25:47 Added task 266592cd-960d-4091-981c-8c25c44b1018 to stop
    ➥ container 6df4e15a5c840b0ece1aede53
Found task in queue:
    ➥ {266592cd-960d-4091-981c-8c25c44b1018
    ➥ 6df4e15a5c840b0ece1aede5378e344fb672c2516196117dd37c3ae055b402d2
    ➥ test-chapter-5-1 3 strm/helloworld-http 0 0 map[] map[]
    ➥ 0001-01-01 00:00:00 +0000 UTC 0001-01-01 00:00:00 +0000 UTC}:
2021/11/05 15:25:54 Attempting to stop container
    ➥ 6df4e15a5c840b0ece1aede53
2021/11/05 15:26:05 Stopped and removed container
    ➥ 6df4e15a5c840b0ece1aede5378e344fb672c2516196117dd37c3ae055b402d2
    ➥ for task 266592cd-960d-4091-981c-8c25c44b1018
2021/11/05 15:26:05 Sleeping for 10 seconds.
```

We can confirm it's been stopped by checking the output of `docker ps` again:

```
$ docker ps
CONTAINER ID    IMAGE     COMMAND    CREATED    STATUS    PORTS     NAMES
```

We can also confirm by querying the API and checking the state of our task. In the response to our `GET /tasks` request, we should see the `State` of the task is `3`:

```
$ curl -v localhost:5555/tasks
*    Trying 127.0.0.1:5555...
* Connected to localhost (127.0.0.1) port 5555 (#0)
> GET /tasks HTTP/1.1
> Host: localhost:5555
> User-Agent: curl/7.78.0
> Accept: */*
>
* Mark bundle as not supporting multiuse
< HTTP/1.1 200 OK
< Content-Type: application/json
< Date: Fri, 05 Nov 2021 19:31:36 GMT
< Content-Length: 356
<
[
  {
    "ID":"266592cd-960d-4091-981c-8c25c44b1018",
    "ContainerID":
      ➥ "20d50c12fb2243f96183b81c00942a123cd2a48e463cc971dafedcadedfbd2d8",
    "Name":"test-chapter-5-1",
    "State":3,
```

```
    "Image":"strm/helloworld-http",
    "Memory":0,
    "Disk":0,
    "ExposedPorts":null,
    "PortBindings":null,
    "RestartPolicy":"",
    "StartTime":"0001-01-01T00:00:00Z",
    "FinishTime":"2021-11-05T19:30:04.661208966Z"
  }
]
```

Summary

- The API wraps the worker's functionality and exposes it as an HTTP server, thus making it accessible over a network. This strategy of exposing the worker's functionality as a web API will allow the manager to start and stop tasks, as well as query the state of tasks across one or more workers.

- The API is made up of handlers, routes, and a router. *Handlers* are functions that accept a request and know how to process it and return a response. *Routes* are patterns that can be used to match the URL of incoming requests (e.g., /tasks). Finally, a *router* is the glue that makes it all work by using the routes to route requests to the handlers.

- The API uses the standard HTTP methods like GET, POST, and DELETE to define the operations that will occur for a given route. For example, calling GET /tasks will return a list of tasks from the worker.

- While the API wraps the worker's functionality, it does not interact with that functionality itself. Instead, it simply performs some administrative work and then places the task on the worker's queue.

6

Metrics

This chapter covers

- Explaining why the worker needs to collect metrics
- Defining the metrics
- Creating a process to collect metrics
- Implementing a handler on the existing API

Imagine you're the host at a busy restaurant on a Friday night. You have six servers waiting on customers sitting at tables spread across the room. Each customer at each of those tables has different requirements. One customer might be there to have drinks and appetizers with a group of friends they haven't seen in a while. Another customer might be there for a full dinner, complete with an appetizer and dessert. Yet another customer might have strict dietary requirements and only eat plant-based food.

Now a new customer walks in. It's a family of four: two adults and two teenage children. Where do you seat them? Do you place them at the table in the section being served by John, who already has three tables with four customers each? Do you place them at the table in Jill's section, which has six tables with a single customer each? Or do you place them in Willie's section, which has a single table with three customers?

This scenario is exactly what the manager in an orchestration system deals with. Instead of six servers waiting on tables, you have six machines. Instead of customers, you have tasks, and instead of being hungry and wanting food and drinks, the tasks want computing resources like CPU, memory, and disk. The manager's job in an orchestration system, like the host in the restaurant, is to place incoming tasks on the best worker machine that can meet the task's resource needs.

For the manager to do its job, however, it needs metrics that reflect how much work a worker is already doing. Those metrics are provided by the worker.

6.1 What metrics should we collect?

Before we dive deeper into metrics, it's good to refresh our memory about the worker and its components at a higher level. As you can see in figure 6.1, the two components that we'll be dealing with are the API and Metrics. In previous chapters, we covered the Task DB, Task Queue, and Runtime components. In the last chapter, we covered the API, which resulted in building an API server that wraps the worker's lower-level operations for starting and stopping tasks. Now we want to dig deeper into the Metrics component, which will expose metrics on the same API.

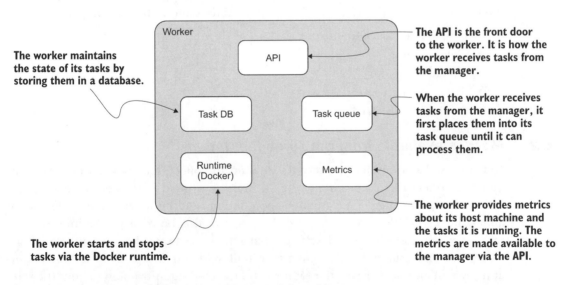

Figure 6.1   Remembering the big picture of the worker's components

For a worker to tell a manager how much work it's currently doing, what metrics will paint a reasonably accurate picture? Remember, we're not building a production-ready orchestrator. Systems like Borg, Kubernetes, and Nomad will have better metrics, both in quantity and quality, than will our system. That's okay. We're trying to understand how an orchestration system works at a fundamental level, not replace existing systems.

In thinking about these metrics, let's look back at listing 3.6, in which we defined the `Task` struct. Three fields in that struct are relevant to this discussion: `CPU`, `Memory`, and `Disk`. These fields represent how much CPU, memory, and disk space a task needs to perform its work. The values will be specified by humans like you and me when we submit our tasks to the system. If our task will be doing a lot of heavy computation, maybe it will need lots of CPU and memory. If our task uses a Docker image that is particularly large for some reason, we may want to specify an amount that provides a little overhead so there is room for the worker to download the image when it starts the task:

```
type Task struct {
    // prior fields not listed

    Cpu          float64
    Memory       int64
    Disk         int64

    // following fields not listed
}
```

If these are the resources that a user will specify when it submits a task to the system, then it makes sense that we should collect metrics about these resources from each of the workers. In particular, we're interested in metrics about the following:

- CPU usage (as a percentage)
- Total memory
- Available memory
- Total disk space
- Available disk space

6.2 *Metrics available from the /proc filesystem*

Now that we've identified the metrics we want to collect, let's talk about how we're going to collect them. On Linux systems, there is a pseudo-filesystem named /proc, which contains a range of information about the state of the system. A deep discussion about the /proc filesystem is beyond the scope of this book; if you're interested in more details, there are good sources that cover the topic. For our purposes, it's enough to understand that /proc is a special filesystem that is part of the Linux operating system and holds a wealth of information, including information about the state of the system's CPU, memory, and disk resources.

> **More info about /proc**
>
> If you're interested in more information about the /proc filesystem, there are many resources available on the web. Here are a couple to get started:
>
> - https://tldp.org/LDP/sag/html/proc-fs.html
> - http://mng.bz/27do

The nice thing about /proc is that it appears like any other filesystem, which means users can interact with it the same way they interact with other normal filesystems. Items in /proc appear as files, which means standard tools like ls and cat can be used on them.

The files in the /proc filesystem that we're going to work with are as follows:

- /proc/stat—Contains information about processes running on the system
- /proc/meminfo—Contains information about memory usage
- /proc/loadavg—Contains information about the system's load average

These files are the source of data that you see in many Linux commands like ps, stat, and top.

To get a sense of the data contained in these files, use the cat command to poke around in them. For example, running the command cat/proc/stat on my laptop (which is running Manjaro Linux), I see a bunch of data about each of my CPUs. According to the proc man page (see man 5 proc), each line contains 10 values, which represent the amount of time spent in various states. Those states are

- user—Time spent in user mode
- nice—Time spent in user mode with low priority (nice)
- system—Time spent in system mode
- idle—Time spent in the idle task
- iowait—Time waiting for I/O to complete
- irq—Time servicing interrupts
- softirq—Time servicing softirqs
- steal—Stolen time, which is the time spent in other operating systems when running in a virtualized environment
- guest—Time spent running a virtual CPU for guest operating systems under the control of the Linux kernel
- guest_nice—Time spent running a niced guest

Listing 6.1 Using cat to look at the /proc/stat file

```
$ cat /proc/stat
cpu   724661 181 374910 105390121 4468 59434 23083 0 0 0      ◁───  An aggregation of
cpu0  59580 33 29642 8786508 191 3560 2244 0 0 0          ◁──┐      the cpuN values
cpu1  60502 3 31300 8779359 150 9016 2729 0 0 0             │
cpu2  58574 7 32002 8785331 139 3688 3159 0 0 0             │      Values for an
cpu3  59564 9 30935 8787000 137 3259 2017 0 0 0             │      individual CPU
cpu4  59555 6 29208 8786670 369 3312 1950 0 0 0
cpu5  63148 16 37486 8755311 430 16914 2993 0 0 0
cpu6  60653 76 31349 8780196 483 4168 2040 0 0 0
cpu7  62622 2 33386 8781129 533 3402 1325 0 0 0
cpu8  60286 1 31729 8783928 542 3175 1219 0 0 0
cpu9  59229 2 29664 8787395 571 3038 1118 0 0 0
cpu10 59550 1 28925 8789436 468 2945 1100 0 0 0
cpu11 61392 18 29278 8787854 449 2952 1184 0 0 0
```

Running the command `cat/proc/meminfo` shows data about the memory being used by my system. This data is used by commands like `free`. For our purposes, we will focus on two values provided by `/proc/meminfo` (see `/proc/meminfo` in `man 5 proc` for more details):

- `MemTotal`—Total usable RAM (i.e., physical RAM minus a few reserved bits and the kernel binary code)
- `MemAvailable`—An estimate of how much memory is available for starting new applications without swapping

Listing 6.2   Using `cat` to look at the `/proc/meminfo` file

```
$ cat /proc/meminfo
MemTotal:       32488372 kB
MemFree:        21697264 kB
MemAvailable:   25975132 kB
Buffers:          512724 kB
Cached:          5829084 kB
SwapCached:            0 kB
Active:          1978056 kB
Inactive:        6165696 kB
Active(anon):      18368 kB
Inactive(anon):  3766080 kB
Active(file):    1959688 kB
Inactive(file):  2399616 kB
Unevictable:     1836208 kB
Mlocked:              32 kB
SwapTotal:             0 kB
SwapFree:              0 kB
Dirty:                 0 kB
[additional data truncated]
```

Running the command `cat/proc/loadavg` shows data about the system's load average (see listing 6.3). The first three fields in the output should look familiar, as they are the same as what you see when you run the `uptime` command. These numbers represent the number of jobs in the run queue (state R) or waiting for disk I/O averaged over 1, 5, and 15 minutes. The fourth field contains two values separated by a slash (i.e., this is not a fraction): the first value is the number of currently runnable kernel processes or threads, and the second value is the number of kernel processes and threads that currently exist on the system (see `/proc/loadavg` in `man 5 proc`).

Listing 6.3   Using `cat` to look at the `/proc/loadavg` file

```
$ cat /proc/loadavg
0.14 0.16 0.18 1/1787 176550
```

While we will use the `/proc` filesystem for CPU and memory metrics, we won't use it to gather disk metrics. We could use it, for there is the `/proc/diskstats` file. But we're going to collect disk metrics a different way, which we'll talk more about in a minute.

Since the metrics we're interested in are available from the /proc filesystem, we could write our own code to interact with /proc and pull out the data we need. We're not, however, going to take that route. Instead, we're going to use a third-party library called goprocinfo.

6.3 Collecting metrics with goprocinfo

The goprocinfo library (https://github.com/c9s/goprocinfo) provides a range of types that allow us to interact with the /proc filesystem. For our purposes, we will focus on four types that will greatly simplify our work. They are as follows:

- LoadAvg (http://mng.bz/Rm0R), which provides the ReadLoadAvg() method and makes available the data from /proc/loadavg
- CpuStat (http://mng.bz/ZRDN), which provides the ReadStat() method and makes available the data from /proc/stat
- MemInfo (http://mng.bz/A8me), which provides the ReadMemInfo() method and makes available the data from /proc/meminfo
- Disk (http://mng.bz/PRD8), which provides the ReadDisk() method and makes available disk-related data using the syscall package from Go's standard library

We won't use every piece of data contained in each of these types, as we will see shortly.

To make it easy to use these metrics, let's create a wrapper around them. We'll start by adding the Stats struct you see in listing 6.4 into the stats.go file under the worker. This wrapper type contains five fields that will provide us with everything we need. The MemStats field will hold all the memory-related data we need and will be a pointer to the MemInfo type from goprocinfo. The DiskStats field will hold all the necessary disk-related data and will be a pointer to goprocinfo's Disk type. The CpuStats field will contain all the CPU-related data and will be a pointer to goprocinfo's CPUStat type. Finally, the LoadStats field will hold the relevant load-related data and will be a pointer to goprocinfo's LoadAvg type.

> **Listing 6.4 The Stats type we'll use to hold all the worker's metrics**

```
type Stats struct {
    MemStats  *linux.MemInfo
    DiskStats *linux.Disk
    CpuStats  *linux.CPUStat
    LoadStats *linux.LoadAvg
}
```

Now that we have defined our Stats type, let's take a step back and think about the kinds of metrics that might be useful. Starting with memory, what might we be interested in? It'd be good to know how much total memory the worker has. Knowing how much memory is available for new programs would also probably be useful. It'd also be good to know how much memory is being used. Similarly, it'd be useful to know how much memory is being used as a percentage of total memory.

With these memory metrics identified, let's add some helper methods to the `Stats` type that will make it quick and easy to get this data. We'll start with a method named `MemTotalKb`, seen in the next listing. This method simply returns the value of the `Mem-Stats.MemTotal` field. We add the suffix `Kb` to the method name as a quick reminder of the units being used.

Listing 6.5   The `MemTotalKb()` helper method

```
func (s *Stats) MemTotalKb() uint64 {
    return s.MemStats.MemTotal
}
```

Next, let's add the `MemAvailableKb` method, as seen in the next listing. Like `MemTotalKb`, it simply returns the value from a field in the `MemStats` field—in this case, `MemAvailable`.

Listing 6.6   The `MemAvailableKb()` helper method

```
func (s *Stats) MemAvailableKb() uint64 {
    return s.MemStats.MemAvailable
}
```

The `MemTotalKb` and `MemAvailable` methods let us figure out the last two memory-related metrics we identified: how much memory is being used as an absolute value and as a percentage of total memory. These metrics are provided by the `MemUsedKb` and `MemUsedPercent` methods in the following listing.

Listing 6.7   The `MemUsedKb()` and `MemUsedPercent()` helper methods

```
func (s *Stats) MemUsedKb() uint64 {
    return s.MemStats.MemTotal - s.MemStats.MemAvailable
}

func (s *Stats) MemUsedPercent() uint64 {
    return s.MemStats.MemAvailable / s.MemStats.MemTotal
}
```

Now let's turn our attention to disk-related metrics. Similar to our memory metrics, it'd be good to know how much total disk is available on a worker machine, how much is free, and how much is being used. Unlike the memory-related methods, our disk-related methods won't need to perform any calculations. The data is provided to us directly from `goprocinfo`'s `Disk` type. So let's create the `DiskTotal`, `DiskFree`, and `DiskUsed` methods, as shown in the following listing.

Listing 6.8   Helper methods for disk-related metrics

```
func (s *Stats) DiskTotal() uint64 {
    return s.DiskStats.All
}
```

```
func (s *Stats) DiskFree() uint64 {
    return s.DiskStats.Free
}

func (s *Stats) DiskUsed() uint64 {
    return s.DiskStats.Used
}
```

Finally, let's talk about CPU-related metrics. The two most commonly used metrics are *load average* and *usage*. As we mentioned earlier, load average can be seen in the output of the `uptime` command, which comes from `/proc/loadavg`:

```
$ uptime
 14:38:18 up 6 days, 22:39,  2 users,  load average: 0.43, 0.32, 0.33

$ cat /proc/loadavg
0.43 0.32 0.33 1/2462 865995
```

For CPU usage, however, the story is slightly more complicated. When discussing CPU usage, we typically talk in terms of percentages. For example, on my laptop, the CPU usage is currently 2%. But what does that mean?

As we discussed previously, on a Linux operating system, a CPU spends its time in various states. Moreover, we can see how much time our CPU(s) are spending in each of the states (`user`, `nice`, `system`, `idle`, etc.) by looking at `/proc/stat`. Knowing how much time our CPUs are spending in these individual states is nice, but it doesn't translate into that single percentage we use when we say, "The CPU percentage is 2%."

Unfortunately, the `CPUStat` type provided by the `goprocinfo` library doesn't provide us with any useful helper methods to calculate the CPU usage; it simply provides us with the `CPUStat` type:

```
type CPUStat struct {
    Id        string `json:"id"`
    User      uint64 `json:"user"`
    Nice      uint64 `json:"nice"`
    System    uint64 `json:"system"`
    Idle      uint64 `json:"idle"`
    IOWait    uint64 `json:"iowait"`
    IRQ       uint64 `json:"irq"`
    SoftIRQ   uint64 `json:"softirq"`
    Steal     uint64 `json:"steal"`
    Guest     uint64 `json:"guest"`
    GuestNice uint64 `json:"guest_nice"`
}
```

So it is up to us to calculate this percentage ourselves. Luckily, we don't have to do too much work because this problem has been discussed in a StackOverflow post titled "Accurate Calculation of CPU Usage Given in Percentage in Linux" (http://mng.bz/ xj17). According to this post, the general algorithm for performing this calculation is

1 Sum the values for the idle states.

2 Sum the values for the non-idle states.

3 Sum the total of idle and non-idle states.

4 Subtract the idle from the total and divide the result by the total.

Thus, we can code this algorithm as in the following listing.

Listing 6.9   Using the `CpuUsage()` method to get CPU usage as a percentage

```go
func (s *Stats) CpuUsage() float64 {
    idle := s.CpuStats.Idle + s.CpuStats.IOWait
    nonIdle := s.CpuStats.User + s.CpuStats.Nice + s.CpuStats.System +
        s.CpuStats.IRQ + s.CpuStats.SoftIRQ + s.CpuStats.Steal
    total := idle + nonIdle

    if total == 0 {
        return 0.00
    }

    return (float64(total) - float64(idle)) / float64(total)
}
```

At this point, we have laid the foundation for gathering metrics that reflect the amount of work an individual worker is performing. All that is left now is to wrap up our work into a few functions that will return a fully populated `Stats` type that we can use in the worker's API.

The first of these functions is the `GetStats()` function seen in listing 6.10. This function sets the fields `MemStats`, `DiskStats`, `CpuStats`, and `LoadStats` in the `Stats` struct by calling the appropriate helper functions. Thus, it populates an instance of the `Stats` type and returns a pointer to the caller.

Listing 6.10   The `GetStats()` function

```go
func GetStats() *Stats {
    return &Stats{
        MemStats:  GetMemoryInfo(),
        DiskStats: GetDiskInfo(),
        CpuStats:  GetCpuStats(),
        LoadStats: GetLoadAvg(),
    }
}
```

Each of the helper functions used in the `GetStats` function takes a similar format. It starts by calling the relevant function from the `goprocinfo` library. It then checks whether any errors were returned from the function call. And finally, it returns the data in the relevant struct.

It's worth noting that if there is an error in calling the relevant `goprocinfo` function, we simply print an error message and return a pointer to the appropriate type (e.g., &linux.MemInfo{}), as in listing 6.11. The returned type will be populated with the appropriate zero value (i.e., the empty string "" for strings and 0 for numbers). Helper functions return metrics from the /proc filesystem, with the exception of the GetDiskInfo() function. Under the hood, it uses the syscall package from Go's standard library.

Listing 6.11   Helper functions used by GetStats()

```
func GetMemoryInfo() *linux.MemInfo {
    memstats, err := linux.ReadMemInfo("/proc/meminfo")
    if err != nil {
        log.Printf("Error reading from /proc/meminfo")
        return &linux.MemInfo{}
    }

    return memstats
}


// GetDiskInfo See https://godoc.org/github.com/c9s/goprocinfo/linux#Disk
func GetDiskInfo() *linux.Disk {
    diskstats, err := linux.ReadDisk("/")
    if err != nil {
        log.Printf("Error reading from /")
        return &linux.Disk{}
    }

    return diskstats
}


// GetCpuInfo See https://godoc.org/github.com/c9s/goprocinfo/linux#CPUStat
func GetCpuStats() *linux.CPUStat {
    stats, err := linux.ReadStat("/proc/stat")
    if err != nil {
        log.Printf("Error reading from /proc/stat")
        return &linux.CPUStat{}
    }

    return &stats.CPUStatAll
}


// GetLoadAvg See https://godoc.org/github.com/c9s/goprocinfo/linux#LoadAvg
func GetLoadAvg() *linux.LoadAvg {
    loadavg, err := linux.ReadLoadAvg("/proc/loadavg")
    if err != nil {
        log.Printf("Error reading from /proc/loadavg")
        return &linux.LoadAvg{}
    }

    return loadavg
}
```

6.4   *Exposing the metrics on the API*

Now that we've done all the hard work, there are only three things left to do to expose the worker's metrics on its API:

- Add a method to the worker to regularly collect metrics
- Add a handler method to the API
- Add a /stats route to the API

To regularly collect our metrics, let's add a method called CollectStats to our worker in the worker.go file. This method, seen in listing 6.12, uses an infinite loop, inside of which we call the GetStats() function we created earlier. Note that we also set the worker's TaskCount field. Finally, we sleep for 15 seconds. Why sleep for fifteen seconds? This is an arbitrary decision that is mainly intended to slow down how frequently our system is performing actions so that we humans can observe what is going on. In a real production system, where users might be submitting tens, hundreds, or even thousands of tasks per minute, we'd want to collect metrics in a more real-time fashion.

> **Listing 6.12   The worker's new CollectStats() method**

```go
func (w *Worker) CollectStats() {
    for {
        log.Println("Collecting stats")
        w.Stats = GetStats()
        w.Stats.TaskCount = w.TaskCount
        time.Sleep(15 * time.Second)
    }
}
```

Next, let's add the new handler method, called GetStatsHandler, to the API in the handlers.go file. Like the other handlers we created in chapter 5, this one takes two arguments: an http.ResponseWriter named w and a pointer to an http.Request named r. The body of the method is pretty simple. It sets the Content-Type header to application/json to let the caller know the response contains JSON-encoded content. It then sets the response code to 200. Finally, it encodes the worker's Stats field. Thus, GetStatsHandler is simply encoding and returning the metrics in the worker's Stats field, which gets refreshed every 15 seconds by the CollectStats method. The API's new GetStatsHandler() method will be used for requests to the new /stats route created in the following listing.

> **Listing 6.13   The API's new GetStatsHandler() method**

```go
func (a *Api) GetStatsHandler(w http.ResponseWriter, r *http.Request) {
    w.Header().Set("Content-Type", "application/json")
    w.WriteHeader(200)
    json.NewEncoder(w).Encode(a.Worker.Stats)
}
```

The last thing to do is to update the API's routes in the `api.go` file. Here, we will create a new route, `/stats`. That route will only support `GET` requests and will call the `GetStatsHandler` we created previously.

Listing 6.14 Adding the new `/stats` route to the `api.go` file

```
a.Router.Route("/stats", func(r chi.Router) {
    r.Get("/", a.GetStatsHandler)
})
```

Since we've added this new route to our API, let's update the route table from chapter 5 to provide a complete picture of what it now looks like in table 6.1.

Table 6.1 Our updated route table for the worker API

Method	Route	Description	Request body	Response body	Status code
GET	/tasks	Gets a list of all tasks	None	List of tasks	200
POST	/tasks	Creates a task	JSON-encoded `task.TaskEvent`	None	201
DELETE	/tasks/{taskID}	Stops the task identified by `taskID`	None	None	204
GET	/stats	Gets metrics about the worker	None	JSON-encoded `stats.Stats`	200

6.5 Putting it all together

Before we put this all together and take it for a test run, let's quickly review what we've done:

- We created a new file, `stats.go`.
- In `stats.go` we created a new `Stats` type to hold the worker's metrics.
- Also in `stats.go`, we created a `GetStats()` function that uses the `goprocinfo` library to collect metrics and populate the `Stats` type with data.
- We added the `CollectStats` method to the worker, which will call the `GetStats()` function in an infinite loop.
- We added the `GetStatsHandler` method to the worker's handlers in `handlers.go`.
- We added a new route, `/stats`, to the worker's API.

At a conceptual level, this work looks like that in figure 6.2.

Now, to see our work in action, we need to write a program, as we've done in past chapters, that will glue all of our work together. In this case, we can reuse the program we wrote in chapter 5. We only need to make one minor change.

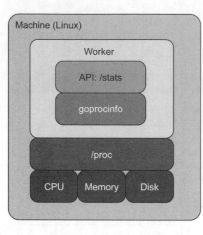

Figure 6.2   The worker runs on a Linux machine and serves an API that includes the /stats endpoint. The metrics served on the /stats endpoint are collected using the goprocinfo library, which interacts directly with the Linux /proc filesystem.

Open up the `main.go` program we used in chapter 5. In the `main()` function, after the call to `runTasks`, add a call to the worker's new `CollectStats` method. And, like the `runTasks` method, execute that call to `CollectStats` in a separate goroutine.

Listing 6.15   Updating the `main()` function from our `main.go` file

```go
func main() {
    host := os.Getenv("CUBE_HOST")
    port, _ := strconv.Atoi(os.Getenv("CUBE_PORT"))

    fmt.Println("Starting Cube worker")

    w := worker.Worker{
        Queue: *queue.New(),
        Db:    make(map[uuid.UUID]*task.Task),
    }
    api := worker.Api{Address: host, Port: port, Worker: &w}

    go runTasks(&w)
    go w.CollectStats()
    api.Start()
}
```

After updating the `main.go` file, start up the API the same way you did in chapter 5. You'll notice that the API's log output shows that it's collecting stats every 15 seconds:

```
$ CUBE_HOST=localhost CUBE_PORT=5555 go run main.go
Starting Cube worker
2021/12/28 14:03:35 No tasks to process currently.
2021/12/28 14:03:35 Sleeping for 10 seconds.
2021/12/28 14:03:35 Collecting stats
2021/12/28 14:03:45 No tasks to process currently.
2021/12/28 14:03:45 Sleeping for 10 seconds.
2021/12/28 14:03:50 Collecting stats
```

Now that the API is running, query the new /stats endpoint from a different terminal. You should see output about memory, disk, and CPU usage:

```
$ curl localhost:5555/stats|jq .
{
  "MemStats": {
    "mem_total": 32488372,
    "mem_free": 14399056,
    "mem_available": 23306576,
    [....]
  },
  "DiskStats": {
    "all": 1006660349952,
    "used": 39346565120,
    "free": 967313784832,
    "freeInodes": 61645909
  },
  "CpuStats": {
    "id": "cpu",
    "user": 4819423,
    "nice": 701,
    "system": 2140212,
    "idle": 502094668,
    "iowait": 14448,
    "irq": 561115,
    "softirq": 178454,
    "steal": 0,
    "guest": 0,
    "guest_nice": 0
  },
  "LoadStats": {
    "last1min": 0.78,
    "last5min": 0.55,
    "last15min": 0.43,
    "process_running": 2,
    "process_total": 2336,
    "last_pid": 581117
  },
  "TaskCount": 0
}
```

Summary

- The worker exposes metrics about the state of the machine where it is running. The metrics—about CPU, memory, and disk usage—will be used by the manager to make scheduling decisions.
- To make gathering metrics easier, we use a third-party library called goprocinfo. This library handles most of the low-level work necessary to get metrics from the /proc filesystem.
- The metrics are made available on the same API that we built in chapter 5. Thus, the manager will have a uniform way to interact with workers: making HTTP calls to /tasks to perform task operations and making calls to /stats to gather metrics about a worker's current state.

Part 3

Manager

The third part of this book focuses on the Cube manager component. Whereas the worker is responsible for running individual tasks on a single node within a pool of nodes, the manager is responsible for managing the entire system. The manager's responsibilities include

- Responding to requests from users
- Scheduling tasks on workers
- Periodically collecting information about the state of tasks and workers in the system
- Checking the health of running tasks and attempting to get them into a healthy state when something goes wrong

In chapter 7, we will flesh out the implementation details of the Manager object. This implementation will include a naive scheduler, which we will iterate on in a later chapter.

In chapter 8, we will build an API for the Manager object. This API will be the mechanism by which users will interact with Cube.

In chapter 9, we will explore some common failure scenarios and consider the options for dealing with them. Then we will implement a solution to handle task failures.

7

The manager
enters the room

This chapter covers

- Reviewing the purpose of the manager
- Designing a naive scheduling algorithm
- Implementing the manager's methods for scheduling and updating tasks

In chapters 4, 5, and 6, we implemented the Worker component of Cube, our orchestration system. We focused on the core functionality of the worker in chapter 4, which enabled the worker to start and stop tasks. In chapter 5, we added an API to the worker. This API wrapped the functionality we built in chapter 4 and made it available from standard HTTP clients (e.g., curl). And finally, in chapter 6, we added the ability for our worker to collect metrics about itself and expose those on the same API. With this work, we can run multiple workers, with each worker running multiple tasks.

Now, we'll move our attention to the Manager component of Cube. As we mentioned in chapter 1, the manager is the brain of an orchestrator. While we have multiple workers, we wouldn't want to ask the users of our orchestration system to submit their tasks directly to a worker. Why? This would place an unnecessary burden on users, forcing them to be aware of how many workers existed and how many tasks they were already running and to then pick one. Instead, we encapsulate all of that administrative work into the manager. The users submit their tasks to the manager, and it figures out which worker in the system can best handle the task.

Unlike workers, the Cube orchestrator will have a single manager. This is a practical design decision meant to simplify the number of problems we need to consider in our manager implementation.

By the end of this chapter, we will have implemented a manager that can submit tasks to workers, using a naive round-robin scheduling algorithm.

7.1   The Cube manager

The manager component allows us to isolate administrative concerns from execution concerns. This is a design principle known as *separation of concerns. Administrative* concerns in an orchestration system (figure 7.1) include things like the following:

- Handling requests from users
- Assigning tasks to workers who are best able to perform them (i.e., scheduling)
- Keeping track of task and worker state
- Restarting failed tasks

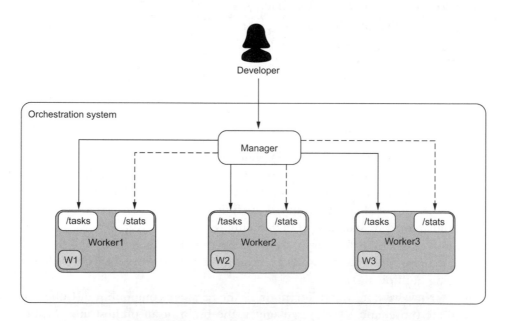

Figure 7.1   The manager is responsible for administrative tasks, similar to the function of a restaurant host seating customers. It will use the worker's `/tasks` and `/stats` API endpoints to perform its administrative duties.

Every orchestration system has a manager component. Google's Borg calls it the *Borg-Master*. HashiCorp's Nomad uses the unimaginative yet functional term *server*. Kubernetes doesn't have a singular name for this component, but instead specifically identifies the subcomponents (API server, controller manager, etcd, scheduler).

Control plane vs. data plane

Another way to think of the separation of concerns is the concept of *control plane versus data plane*. In the world of networking, you'll find these terms used frequently, and they refer to the plane of existence.

In a network, the control plane *controls* how data moves from point A to point B. This plane is responsible for things like creating routing tables, which are determined by different protocols, such as the Border Gateway Protocol (BGP) and the Open Shortest Path First (OSPF) protocol. This plane performs functions similar to the administrative concerns of our manager.

Unlike the control plane, the data plane does the actual work of moving the data around. This plane performs functions similar to the execution concerns of our worker.

7.1.1 The components that make up the manager

Like our worker, our manager will comprise several subcomponents, as seen in figure 7.2. The manager will have a Task DB, which, like the worker, will store tasks. In contrast to the worker's Task DB, however, the manager's will contain all tasks in the system.

The manager will also have an Event DB, which will store events (i.e., task.Task-Event). This subcomponent is mostly a convenient way for us to separate metadata from task-specific data. Metadata includes things like the timestamp when a user submitted a task to the system. We'll make use of it later in chapter 12 when we implement a CLI for the manager.

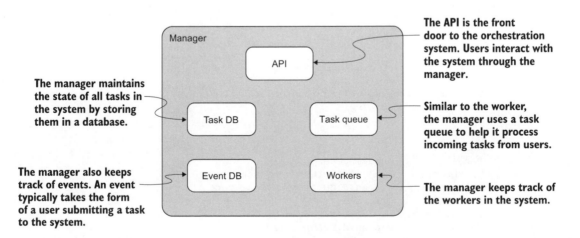

Figure 7.2   The manager's components are similar to the worker's, with the addition of an Event DB and a list of Workers.

Like the worker, for the initial implementation of the manager, we're going to use an in-memory map to store tasks and events. The manager's `Workers` subcomponent is a list of the workers it manages. Like the worker, it will also have a `Task Queue`. And finally, the manager will have an API, similar to the worker (figure 7.2). (As we did with the worker, we're going to address the manager's API in a separate chapter, so we'll defer further discussion of it until then.)

With this foundation laid, we can move on to implementation.

7.2 *The Manager struct*

Like the worker, we created a skeleton of the manager implementation in chapter 2. At the core of that manager skeleton is the `Manager` struct, which will contain fields that represent the subcomponents previously identified. You can see this struct in listing 7.1, which should be in the same state we left it in chapter 2.

Since it has been a while, let's remind ourselves of the requirements for our manager. In chapter 1, we identified these requirements:

1 Accepts requests from users to start and stop tasks
2 Schedules tasks onto worker machines
3 Keeps track of tasks, their states, and the machine on which they run

If you need more of a reminder about the `Manager` struct and its field, please look back at section 2.3.

Listing 7.1   The `Manager` struct

```go
package manager

import (
    "bytes"
    "cube/task"
    "cube/worker"
    "encoding/json"
    "fmt"
    "log"
    "net/http"

    "github.com/golang-collections/collections/queue"
    "github.com/google/uuid"
)

type Manager struct {
    Pending       queue.Queue
    TaskDb        map[uuid.UUID]*task.Task
    EventDb       map[uuid.UUID]*task.TaskEvent
    Workers       []string
    WorkerTaskMap map[string][]uuid.UUID
    TaskWorkerMap map[uuid.UUID]string
}
```

7.3 Implementing the manager's methods

Now that we've reminded ourselves of what the `Manager` struct looks like, let's move forward and remember what skeleton methods we had previously defined on the struct.

> **Listing 7.2 The stubbed-out versions of the manager's methods**

```
func (m *Manager) SelectWorker() {
    fmt.Println("I will select an appropriate worker")
}

func (m *Manager) UpdateTasks() {
    fmt.Println("I will update tasks")
}

func (m *Manager) SendWork() {
    fmt.Println("I will send work to workers")
}
```

We're going to implement these methods in the following order:

- `SelectWorker`
- `SendWork`
- `UpdateTasks`

7.3.1 Implementing the SelectWorker method

The `SelectWorker` method will serve as the scheduler in this early phase of implementing our manager. Its sole purpose will be to pick one of the workers from the manager's list of workers (i.e., the `Workers` field, which is a slice of strings). We're going to start with a naive round-robin scheduling algorithm that begins by simply selecting the first worker from the list of `Workers` and storing it in a variable. From this point forward, the algorithm looks like so:

1. Check whether we are at the end of the `Workers` list.
2. If we are not, select the next worker in the list.
3. Else, return to the beginning and select the first worker in the list.

To implement this algorithm, we need to make a minor change to the `Manager` struct. As you can see in the following listing, we've added the field `LastWorker`. We'll use this field to store an integer, which will be an index into the `Workers` slice, thus giving us a worker.

> **Listing 7.3 Adding the `LastWorker` field to the `Manager` struct**

```
type Manager struct {
    // previous fields omitted
    LastWorker    int
```

Let's move on now to the actual scheduling algorithm. As you can see in listing 7.4, it's only nine lines of code (not counting the method signature). We start the process by declaring the variable `newWorker`, which represents the lucky worker chosen to run a task. Then we use an `if/else` block to choose the worker. In this block, we first check whether the worker we chose during the last run is the last worker in our list of workers. If not, we set `newWorker` to the next worker in the list of workers, and we increment the value of `LastWorker` by 1. If the previous worker chosen is the last one in our list, we start over from the beginning, selecting the first worker in the list and setting `LastWorker` accordingly. Finally, we return the worker to the caller.

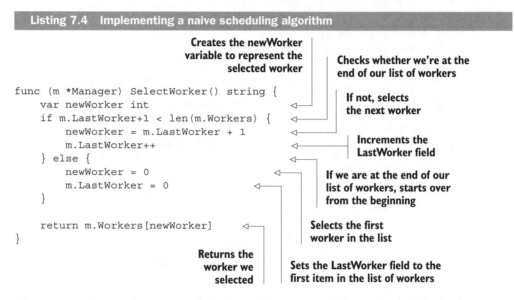

Listing 7.4 Implementing a naive scheduling algorithm

It's worth taking a moment to talk about the format of the strings stored in the manager's `Workers` field. The field itself is of type `[]string`, so technically, the value of the strings could be anything. In practice, however, these are going to take the form of `<hostname>:<port>`. If you recall from chapters 5 and 6, when we started the worker's API, we specified the `CUBE_HOST` and `CUBE_PORT` environment variables. The former we set to `localhost`, and the latter we set to `5555`. So the manager's `Workers` field contains a list of `<hostname>:<port>` values, which specify the address where the worker's API is running.

7.3.2 *Implementing the SendWork method*

The next method we need to implement is the manager's `SendWork` method. It is the workhorse of the manager and performs the following process:

1 Checks whether there are task events in the `Pending` queue
2 If there are, selects a worker to run a task
3 Pulls a task event off the pending queue
4 Sets the state of the task to `Scheduled`
5 Performs some administrative work that makes it easy for the manager to keep track of which workers tasks are running on

6 JSON-encodes the task event

7 Sends the task event to the selected worker

8 Checks the response from the worker

Let's implement steps 1 to 6 in the process with the code in listing 7.5. We use an `if/else` block that sets up our conditional flow: it checks the length of the manager's `Pending` queue, and if the length is greater than zero—meaning there are tasks to process—it moves on to the next steps.

Listing 7.5 The manager's `SendWork` method

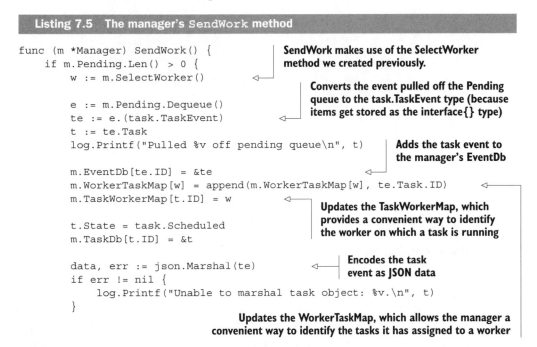

```go
func (m *Manager) SendWork() {
    if m.Pending.Len() > 0 {
        w := m.SelectWorker()

        e := m.Pending.Dequeue()
        te := e.(task.TaskEvent)
        t := te.Task
        log.Printf("Pulled %v off pending queue\n", t)

        m.EventDb[te.ID] = &te
        m.WorkerTaskMap[w] = append(m.WorkerTaskMap[w], te.Task.ID)
        m.TaskWorkerMap[t.ID] = w

        t.State = task.Scheduled
        m.TaskDb[t.ID] = &t

        data, err := json.Marshal(te)
        if err != nil {
            log.Printf("Unable to marshal task object: %v.\n", t)
        }
```

> SendWork makes use of the SelectWorker method we created previously.

> Converts the event pulled off the Pending queue to the task.TaskEvent type (because items get stored as the interface{} type)

> Adds the task event to the manager's EventDb

> Updates the TaskWorkerMap, which provides a convenient way to identify the worker on which a task is running

> Encodes the task event as JSON data

> Updates the WorkerTaskMap, which allows the manager a convenient way to identify the tasks it has assigned to a worker

Once the `SendWork` method has pulled a task off the `Pending` queue and encoded it as JSON, all that's left to do is send the task to the selected worker. These final two steps are implemented in listing 7.6. Sending the task to the worker involves building the URL using the worker's `host` and `port`, which we got when we called the manager's `SelectWorker` method previously. From there, we use the `Post` function from the `net/http` package in the standard library. Then we decode the response body and print it. Notice that we're also checking errors along the way.

Listing 7.6 The final two steps of the `SendWork` method

```go
url := fmt.Sprintf("http://%s/tasks", w)
        resp, err := http.Post(url, "application/json", bytes.NewBuffer(data))
        if err != nil {
            log.Printf("Error connecting to %v: %v\n", w, err)
            m.Pending.Enqueue(te)
            return
        }
```

```
        d := json.NewDecoder(resp.Body)
        if resp.StatusCode != http.StatusCreated {
            e := worker.ErrResponse{}
            err := d.Decode(&e)
            if err != nil {
                fmt.Printf("Error decoding response: %s\n", err.Error())
                return
            }
            log.Printf("Response error (%d): %s", e.HTTPStatusCode, e.Message)
            return
        }

        t = task.Task{}
        err = d.Decode(&t)
        if err != nil {
            fmt.Printf("Error decoding response: %s\n", err.Error())
            return
        }
        log.Printf("%#v\n", t)
    } else {
        log.Println("No work in the queue")
    }
}
```

As you can see from this code, the manager is interacting with the worker via the worker API we implemented in chapter 5.

7.3.3   *Implementing the UpdateTasks method*

At this point, our manager can select a worker to run a task and then send that task to the selected worker. It has also stored the task in its `TaskDB` and `EventsDB` databases. But the manager's view of the task is only from its own perspective. Sure, it sent the task to the worker, and if all went well, the worker responded with `http.Status-Created` (i.e., `201`). But even if we receive an `http.StatusCreated` response, that just tells us that the worker received the task and added it to its queue. This response gives us no indication that the task was started successfully and is currently running. What if the task failed when the worker attempted to start it? How might a task fail, you ask? Here are a few ways:

- The user specified a nonexistent Docker image so that when the worker attempts to start the task, Docker complains that it can't find the image.
- The worker's disk is full, so it doesn't have enough space to download the Docker image.
- There is a bug in the application running inside the Docker container that prevents it from starting correctly (maybe the creator of the container image left out an important environment variable that the application needs to start up properly).

These are just several ways a task might fail. While the manager doesn't necessarily need to know about every possible way a task might fail, what it does need to do is check in with the worker periodically to get status updates on the tasks it's running. Moreover, the manager needs to get status updates for every worker in the cluster. With this in mind, let's implement the manager's `UpdateTasks` method.

The general shape of updating tasks from each worker is straightforward. For each worker, we perform the following steps:

1 Query the worker to get a list of its tasks.
2 For each task, update its state in the manager's database so it matches the state from the worker.

The first step can be seen in listing 7.7. It should look familiar by this point. The manager starts by making a GET /tasks HTTP request to a worker using the `Get` method from the net/http package. It checks for any errors, such as connection problems (maybe the worker was down for some reason). If the manager was able to connect to the worker, it then checks the response code and ensures it received an `http.StatusOK` (i.e., `200`) response code. Finally, it decodes the JSON data in the body of the response, which should result in a list of the worker's tasks.

Listing 7.7   Step 1 of the process to update the manager's tasks

```
func (m *Manager) UpdateTasks() {
    for _, worker := range m.Workers {
        log.Printf("Checking worker %v for task updates", worker)
        url := fmt.Sprintf("http://%s/tasks", worker)
        resp, err := http.Get(url)
        if err != nil {
            log.Printf("Error connecting to %v: %v\n", worker, err)
        }

        if resp.StatusCode != http.StatusOK {
            log.Printf("Error sending request: %v\n", err)
        }

        d := json.NewDecoder(resp.Body)
        var tasks []*task.Task
        err = d.Decode(&tasks)
        if err != nil {
            log.Printf("Error unmarshalling tasks: %s\n", err.Error())
        }
    }
}
```

The second step, seen in listing 7.8, runs inside the main `for` loop from listing 7.7. There is nothing particularly sophisticated or clever about how we're updating the tasks. We start by checking whether the task's state in the manager is the same as that of the worker; if not, we set the state to the state reported by the worker. (In this way, the manager treats the workers as the authoritative source for the "state of the world"—that is, the current state of the tasks in the system.) Once we've updated the task's state, we then update its `StartTime` and `FinishTime`. And finally, we update the task's `ContainerID`.

Listing 7.8   Step 2 of the process to update the manager's tasks

```
for _, t := range tasks {
        log.Printf("Attempting to update task %v\n", t.ID)

        _, ok := m.TaskDb[t.ID]
        if !ok {
            log.Printf("Task with ID %s not found\n", t.ID)
            return
        }

        if m.TaskDb[t.ID].State != t.State {
            m.TaskDb[t.ID].State = t.State
        }

        m.TaskDb[t.ID].StartTime = t.StartTime
        m.TaskDb[t.ID].FinishTime = t.FinishTime
        m.TaskDb[t.ID].ContainerID = t.ContainerID
    }
}
```

With the implementation of the `UpdateTasks` method, we have now completed the core functionality of our manager. Let's quickly summarize what we've accomplished thus far before continuing:

- With the `SelectWorker` method, we've implemented a simple but naive scheduling algorithm to assign tasks to workers.
- With the `SendWork` method, we've implemented a process that uses the `Select-Worker` method and sends individual tasks to assigned workers via that worker's API.
- With the `UpdateTasks` method, we've implemented a process for the manager to update its view of the state of all the tasks in the system.

That's a large chunk of work that we've just completed. Take a moment to celebrate your achievement before moving on to the next section!

7.3.4   *Adding a task to the manager*

While we have implemented the core functionality of the manager, there are a couple more methods that we still need to implement. The first of these methods is the `AddTask` method, as seen in listing 7.9. This method should look familiar, as it's similar to the `AddTask` method we created for the worker. It also serves a similar purpose: it's how tasks are added to the manager's queue.

Listing 7.9   The manager's `AddTask` method

```
func (m *Manager) AddTask(te task.TaskEvent) {
    m.Pending.Enqueue(te)
}
```

7.3.5 Creating a manager

Finally, let's create the New function, as shown in listing 7.10. This is a helper function that takes in a list of workers, creates an instance of the manager, and returns a pointer to it. The bulk of the work performed by this function is initializing the necessary subcomponents used by the manager. It sets up the taskDB and eventDb databases. Next, it initializes the workerTaskMap and taskWorkerMap maps that help the manager more easily identify where tasks are running. While this function isn't technically called a *constructor*, as in some other object-oriented languages, it performs a similar function and will be used in the process of starting the manager.

Listing 7.10 Initializing a new manager with the New() function

```
func New(workers []string) *Manager {
    taskDb := make(map[uuid.UUID]*task.Task)
    eventDb := make(map[uuid.UUID]*task.TaskEvent)
    workerTaskMap := make(map[string][]uuid.UUID)
    taskWorkerMap := make(map[uuid.UUID]string)
    for worker := range workers {
        workerTaskMap[workers[worker]] = []uuid.UUID{}
    }

    return &Manager{
        Pending:        *queue.New(),
        Workers:        workers,
        TaskDb:         taskDb,
        EventDb:        eventDb,
        WorkerTaskMap:  workerTaskMap,
        TaskWorkerMap:  taskWorkerMap,
    }
}
```

With the addition of the AddTask method and New function, we've completed the initial implementation of the Cube manager. Now all that's left to do is take it for a spin!

7.4 An interlude on failures and resiliency

It's worth pausing here for a moment to identify a weakness in our implementation. While the manager can select a worker from a pool of workers and send it a task to run, it is not dealing with failures. The manager is simply recording the state of the world in its Task DB.

What we are building toward, however, is a declarative system where a user declares the desired state of a task. The manager's job is to honor that request by making a reasonable effort to bring the task into the declared state. For now, a *reasonable effort* means making a single attempt to bring the task into the desired state. We are going to revisit this topic later in chapter 9, where we will consider additional steps the manager can take in the face of failures to build a more resilient system.

7.5   *Putting it all together*

By now, the pattern we are using to build Cube should be clear. We spend the bulk of the chapter writing the core pieces we need; then, at the end of the chapter, we write or update a `main()` function in our project's `main.go` file to make use of our work. We'll continue using this same pattern here and for the next few chapters.

For this chapter, we're going to start by using the `main.go` file from chapter 6 as our starting point. Whereas in past chapters we focused exclusively on running a worker, now we want to run a worker and a manager. We want to run them both because running a manager in isolation makes no sense: the need for a manager only makes sense in the context of having one or more workers.

Let's make a copy of the `main.go` file from chapter 6. As we said, this is our starting point for running the worker and the manager. Our previous work already knows how to start an instance of the worker. As we can see in listing 7.11, we create an instance of the worker, `w`, and then we create an instance of the worker API, `api`. Next, we call the `runTasks` function, also defined in `main.go`, and pass it a pointer to our worker `w`. We make the call to `runTasks` using a goroutine, identified by the `go` keyword before the function call. Similarly, we use a second goroutine to call the worker's `Collect-Stats()` method, which periodically collects stats from the machine where the worker is running (as we saw in chapter 6). Finally, we call the API's `Start()` method, which starts up the API server and listens for requests. Here is where we make our first change. Instead of calling `api.Start()` in our main goroutine, we call it using a third goroutine, which allows us to run all the necessary pieces of the worker concurrently. We will reuse the `main()` function from the previous chapter and make one minor change to run all the worker's components in separate goroutines.

Listing 7.11   Running all the worker's components in separate goroutines

```
func main() {
    host := os.Getenv("CUBE_HOST")
    port, _ := strconv.Atoi(os.Getenv("CUBE_PORT"))

    fmt.Println("Starting Cube worker")

    w := worker.Worker{
        Queue: *queue.New(),
        Db:    make(map[uuid.UUID]*task.Task),
    }
    api := worker.Api{Address: host, Port: port, Worker: &w}

    go runTasks(&w)
    go w.CollectStats()
    go api.Start()
```

At this point, we have an instance of our worker running. Now, we want to start an instance of our manager.

To do this, we create a list of workers and assign it to a variable named `workers`. This list is a slice of strings, and we add our single worker to it. Next, we create an instance of our manager by calling the `New` function created earlier and passing it to our list of workers.

Listing 7.12 Calling the `manager.New()` function

```
workers := []string{fmt.Sprintf("%s:%d", host, port)}
    m := manager.New(workers)
```

With an instance of our worker running and an instance of a manager created, the next step is to add some tasks to the manager. In listing 7.13, we create three tasks. This is a random decision. Feel free to choose more or less. Creating the `Task` and `TaskEvent` should look familiar since it's the same thing we've done in previous chapters in working with the worker. Now, however, instead of adding the `TaskEvent` to the worker directly, we add it to the manager by calling `AddTask` on the manager `m` and passing it the task event `te`. The final step in this loop is to call the `SendWork` method on manager `m`, which will select the only worker we currently have and, using the worker's API, send the worker the task event.

Listing 7.13 Adding tasks to the manager

```
for i := 0; i < 3; i++ {
    t := task.Task{
        ID:    uuid.New(),
        Name:  fmt.Sprintf("test-container-%d", i),
        State: task.Scheduled,
        Image: "strm/helloworld-http",
    }
    te := task.TaskEvent{
        ID:    uuid.New(),
        State: task.Running,
        Task:  t,
    }
    m.AddTask(te)
    m.SendWork()
}
```

Reaching this point, let's pause for a moment and think about what has happened:

- We created an instance of the worker, and it's running and listening for API requests.
- We created an instance of the manager, and it has a list of workers containing the single worker we created earlier.
- We created three tasks and added those tasks to the manager.
- The manager selected a worker (in this case, the only one that exists) and sent it the three tasks.
- The worker received the tasks and at least attempted to start them.

From this list, it's clear there are two perspectives on the state of the tasks in this system: there is the manager's perspective, and there is the worker's perspective. From the manager's perspective, it has sent the tasks to the worker. Unless there is an error returned from the request to the worker's API, the manager's work in this process could be considered complete.

From the worker's perspective, things are more complicated. The worker has received the request from the manager. However, we must remember how we built the worker. Upon receiving the request, the worker API's request handlers don't directly perform any operations; instead, the handlers take the requests and put them on the worker's queue. In a separate goroutine, the worker performs the direct operations to start and stop tasks. As mentioned in chapter 5, this design decision allows us to separate the concern of handling API requests from the concern of performing the actual operations to start and stop tasks.

Once the worker picks a task off of its queue and attempts to perform the necessary operation, any number of things can go wrong. As we enumerated earlier, examples of things going wrong can include user errors (e.g., a user specifying a nonexisting Docker image in the task specification) or machine errors (e.g., a machine doesn't have enough disk space to download the task's Docker image).

As we can see, for the manager to be an effective component in our orchestration system, it can't just use a fire-and-forget approach to task management. It must constantly check in with the workers it is managing to reconcile its perspective with that of the workers'.

We discussed this problem earlier in the chapter, and it was our motivation for implementing the manager's `UpdateTasks` method. So, now, let's make use of our foresight. Once the manager has sent tasks off to the worker, we want to call the manager's `UpdateTasks` method.

To accomplish our objective, we'll use another goroutine, which will call an *anonymous function*. Like other programming languages, an anonymous function in Go is simply a function that is defined where it's called. Inside of this anonymous function, we use an infinite loop. Inside this loop, we print an informative log message that tells us the manager is updating tasks from its workers. Then we call the manager's `UpdateTasks` method to update its perspective on the tasks in the system. And finally, it sleeps for 15 seconds. As we've done previously, we're using sleep here purely for the purpose of slowing down the system so we can observe and understand our work.

While we're on the topic of observing our work, let's also add another infinite loop that ranges over the tasks and prints out the `ID` and `State` of each task in the system. This will allow us to observe the tasks' state changing as the `UpdateTasks` method does its job. This pattern of using an anonymous function to run a piece of code in a separate goroutine is common in the Go ecosystem.

Listing 7.14 Using an anonymous function

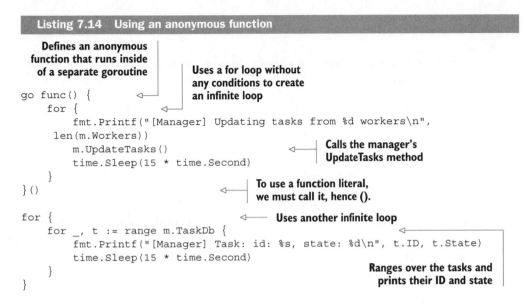

At this point, we've written all the necessary code to run our worker and manager together. So let's switch from writing code to running it.

To run our `main.go` program, call it with `go run main.go`. Also, it's important to define the `CUBE_HOST` and `CUBE_PORT` environment variables as part of the command, as this tells the worker API on what port to listen. These environment variables will also be used by the manager to populate its `Workers` field. When we start our program, the initial output should look familiar. We should see the following:

> **Our main.go program starting up the worker**
>
> **The manager pulling a task off of its pending queue (I've truncated the output for readability)**

```
$ CUBE_HOST=localhost CUBE_PORT=5555 go run main.go
Starting Cube worker
2022/01/30 14:17:12 Pulled {9f122e79-6623-4986-a9df-38a5216286fb ....
2022/01/30 14:17:12 No tasks to process currently.
2022/01/30 14:17:12 Sleeping for 10 seconds.
2022/01/30 14:17:12 Collecting stats
2022/01/30 14:17:12 Added task 9f122e79-6623-4986-a9df-38a5216286fb
```

The worker's API adds a task to the worker's queue.

The worker collects its stats.

The worker reports it doesn't have any tasks to process.

After this initial output, we should see the worker start the tasks. Then, once all three tasks are started, you should start seeing output from the `main.go` program. Our code is calling the manager's `UpdateTasks` method in one `for` loop, ranging over the manager's tasks, and printing out the `ID` and `State` of each task in a separate `for` loop:

```
[Manager] Updating tasks from 1 workers
[Manager] Task: id: 9f122e79-6623-4986-a9df-38a5216286fb, state: 2
```

```
[Manager] Updating tasks from 1 workers
[Manager] Task: id: 792427a7-e306-44ef-981a-c0b76bfaab8e, state: 2
```

Interleaved in the output, you should also see output like the following. This output is coming from our manager itself:

```
2022/01/30 14:18:57 Checking worker localhost:5555 for task updates
2022/01/30 14:18:57 Attempting to update task
➡ 792427a7-e306-44ef-981a-c0b76bfaab8e
2022/01/30 14:18:57 Attempting to update task
➡ 2507e136-7eb7-4530-aeb9-d067eeb34394
2022/01/30 14:18:57 Attempting to update task
➡ 9f122e79-6623-4986-a9df-38a5216286fb
```

While our `main.go` program is running in one terminal, open a second terminal and query the worker API. Depending on how quickly you run the `curl` command after starting up the `main.go` program, you may not see all three tasks. Eventually, though, you should see them:

```
$ curl http://localhost:5555/tasks |jq .
[
  {
    "ID": "723143b3-4cb8-44a7-8dad-df553c15bce3",
    "ContainerID":
        ➡ "14895e61db8d08ba5d0e4bb96d6bd75023349b53eb4ba5915e4e15ecda82e907",
    "Name": "test-container-0",
    "State": 2,
    [....]
  },
  {
    "ID": "a85013fb-2918-47fb-82b0-f2e8d63f433b",
    "ContainerID":
        ➡ "f307d7045a36501059092f06ff3d323e6246a7c854bfabeb5ff17b2185ffd9ec",
    "Name": "test-container-1",
    "State": 2,
    [....]
  },
  {
    "ID": "7a7eb0ef-8516-4103-84a7-9f964ba47cb8",
    "ContainerID":
        ➡ "fffc1cf5b8ca7d33eb3c725f4190b81e0978f3efc8405562f9dfe4d315decbec",
    "Name": "test-container-2",
    "State": 2,
    [....]
  }
]
```

In addition to querying the worker API, we can use the `docker` command to verify that our tasks are indeed running. Note that I've removed some of the columns from the output of `docker ps` for readability:

```
$ docker ps
CONTAINER ID    CREATED          STATUS          NAMES
fffc1cf5b8ca    5 minutes ago    Up 5 minutes    test-container-2
f307d7045a36    5 minutes ago    Up 5 minutes    test-container-1
14895e61db8d    5 minutes ago    Up 5 minutes    test-container-0
```

Summary

- The manager records user requests in the form of `task.TaskEvent` items and stores them in its `EventDB`. This task event, which includes the `task.Task` itself, serves as the user's desired state for the task.

- The manager records the "state of the world" (i.e., the actual state of a task from the perspective of a worker) in its `TaskDB`. For this initial implementation of the manager, we do not attempt to retry failed tasks and instead simply record the state. We will revisit this problem later in chapter 9.

- The manager serves a purely administrative function. It accepts requests from users, records those requests in its internal databases, selects a worker to run the task, and passes the task along to the worker. It periodically updates its internal state by querying the worker's API. It is not directly involved in any of the operations to actually run a task.

- We've used a simple, extremely naive algorithm to assign tasks to workers. This decision allowed us to code a working implementation of the manager in a relatively small number of lines of code. We will revisit this decision in chapter 10.

An API for the manager

In chapter 7, we implemented the core functionality of the manager component: pulling tasks off its queue, selecting a worker to run those tasks, sending them to the selected workers, and periodically updating the state of tasks. That functionality is just the foundation and doesn't provide a simple way for users to interact with the manager.

So, like we did with the worker in chapter 5, we're going to build an API for the manager. This API wraps the manager's core functionality and exposes it to users. In the case of the manager, `users` means *end users*, that is, developers who want to run their application in our orchestration system.

The manager's API, like the worker's, will be simple. It will provide the means for users to perform these basic operations:

- Send a task to the manager
- Get a list of tasks
- Stop a task

This API will be constructed using the same components used for the worker's API. It will comprise *handlers*, *routes*, and a *mux*.

8.1 *Overview of the manager API*

Before we get too far into our code, let's zoom out for a minute and take a more holistic view of where we're going. We've been focusing pretty tightly for the last couple of chapters, so it will be a good reminder to see how the technical details fit together.

We're not building a manager and worker just for the sake of it. The purpose of building them is to fulfill a need: developers need a way to run their applications in a reliable and resilient way. The manager and worker are abstractions that free the developer from having to think too deeply about the underlying infrastructure (whether physical or virtual) on which their applications run. Figure 8.1 reminds us of what this abstraction looks like.

With that reminder, let's zoom back to the details of constructing the manager's API. Because it will be similar to the worker's, we won't spend as much time going into

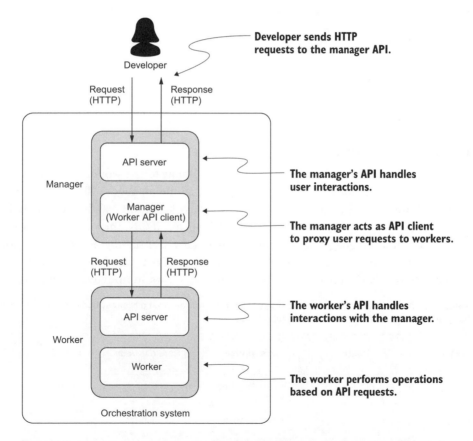

Figure 8.1   The manager comprises an API server and manager components, and similarly, the worker comprises an API server and worker components. The user communicates with the manager, and the manager communicates with one or more workers.

the details of handlers, routes, and muxes. If you need a refresher, please refer to section 5.1.

8.2 Routes

Let's start by identifying the routes that our manager API should handle. It shouldn't be too surprising that the routes are identical to that of the worker's API. In some ways, our manager is acting as a reverse proxy: instead of balancing requests for, say, web pages across a number of web servers, it's balancing requests to run tasks across a number of workers.

Thus, like the worker's, the manager's API will handle GET requests to /tasks, which will return a list of all the tasks in the system (table 8.1). This enables our users to see what tasks are currently in the system. It will handle POST requests to /tasks, which will start a task on a worker. This allows our users to run their tasks in the system. Finally, it will handle DELETE requests to /tasks/{taskID}, which will stop a task specified by the taskID in the route. This allows our users to stop their tasks.

Table 8.1   Routes used by our manager API

Method	Route	Description
GET	/tasks	Gets a list of all tasks
POST	/tasks	Creates a task
DELETE	/tasks/{taskID}	Stops the task identified by taskID

8.3 Data format, requests, and responses

If the routes we use for the manager's API are similar to the worker's, then what about the data format and the requests and responses that the manager will receive and return? Again, it should not be surprising that the manager's API will use the same data format, JSON, as the worker's API. If the worker's API speaks JSON, the manager's API should speak the same language to minimize unnecessary translation between data formats. Thus, any data sent to the manager's API must be JSON-encoded, and any data returned by the API will also be encoded as JSON. Table 8.2 shows an updated route table.

Table 8.2   An updated route table showing whether the routes send a request body and return a response body and the status code for a successful request

Method	Route	Description	Request body	Response body	Status code
GET	/tasks	Gets a list of all tasks	None	List of tasks	200
POST	/tasks	Creates a task	JSON-encoded task.TaskEvent	None	201
DELETE	/tasks/{taskID}	Stop the task identified by taskID	None	None	204

We can see how these routes are used in figure 8.2, which shows a POST request to create a new task and a GET request to get a list of tasks. The developer issues requests to the manager, and the manager returns responses. In the first example, the developer issues a POST request with a body that specifies a task to run. The manager responds with a status code of 201. In the second example, the developer issues a GET request, and the manager responds with a status code of 200 and a list of its tasks.

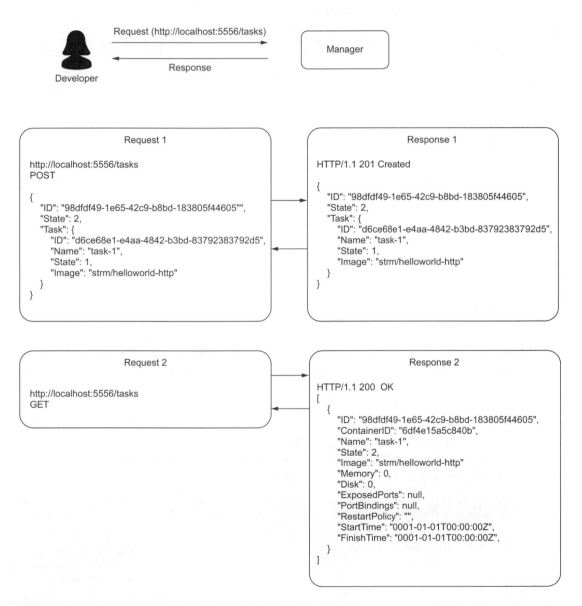

Figure 8.2   Two examples of how a developer uses the manager's API

8.4   *The API struct*

Drilling down a little further, we notice another similarity with the worker's API. The manager's API also uses an `Api` struct, which will encapsulate the necessary behavior of its API. The only difference will be swapping out a single field: the `Worker` field gets replaced by a `Manager` field, which contains a pointer to an instance of our manager. Otherwise, the `Address`, `Port`, and `Router` fields all have the same types and serve the same purposes as they did in the worker API.

Listing 8.1   The manager's `Api` struct

```
type Api struct {
    Address string
    Port    int
    Manager *Manager
    Router  *chi.Mux
}
```

8.5   *Handling requests*

Continuing to drill down, let's talk about the handlers for the manager API. These should look familiar, as they are the same three handlers we implemented for the worker:

- `StartTaskHandler(w http.ResponseWriter, r *http.Request)`
- `GetTasksHandler(w http.ResponseWriter, r *http.Request)`
- `StopTaskHandler(w http.ResponseWriter, r *http.Request)`

We'll implement these handlers in a file named `handlers.go`, which you should create in the `manager` directory next to the existing `manager.go` file. To reduce the amount of typing necessary, feel free to copy the handlers from the worker's API and paste them into the manager's `handlers.go` file. The only changes we'll need to make are to update any references to `a.Worker` and `a.Manager`.

Let's start with the `StartTaskHandler`, which works the same as its worker counterpart. It expects a request body encoded as JSON. It decodes that request body into a `task.TaskEvent`, checking for any decoding errors. Then it adds the task event to the manager's queue using the manager's `AddTask` method implemented in chapter 7. The implementation can be seen in the following listing.

Listing 8.2   The manager's `StartTaskHandler`

```
func (a *Api) StartTaskHandler(w http.ResponseWriter, r *http.Request) {
    d := json.NewDecoder(r.Body)
    d.DisallowUnknownFields()

    te := task.TaskEvent{}
    err := d.Decode(&te)
```

> Creates a json.Decoder that will read the request body from r.Body

> Decodes the body and stores the result in a task.TaskEvent

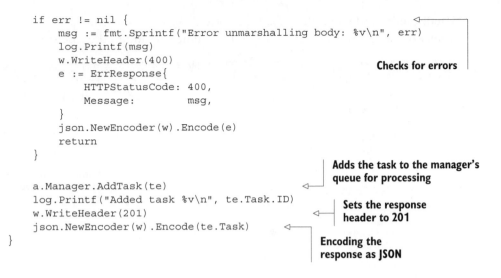

```
    if err != nil {
        msg := fmt.Sprintf("Error unmarshalling body: %v\n", err)
        log.Printf(msg)
        w.WriteHeader(400)
        e := ErrResponse{
            HTTPStatusCode: 400,
            Message:        msg,
        }
        json.NewEncoder(w).Encode(e)
        return
    }

    a.Manager.AddTask(te)
    log.Printf("Added task %v\n", te.Task.ID)
    w.WriteHeader(201)
    json.NewEncoder(w).Encode(te.Task)
}
```

Checks for errors

Adds the task to the manager's queue for processing

Sets the response header to 201

Encoding the response as JSON

Next up is the GetTasksHandler. Like the StartTaskHandler, GetTasksHandler works similarly to its counterpart in the worker API. We do, however, need to implement a helper method that will make it easy for us to get a list of the tasks from the manager. We create the GetTasks() helper on the Manager struct. The GetTasks() method is straightforward:

- Instantiate a variable named tasks as a slice of pointers to task.Task types.
- Range over the manager's TaskDb field and add each task to the tasks slice.
- Return the slice of tasks.

Listing 8.3 The GetTasks helper function returning a slice of pointers to task.Task types

```
func (m *Manager) GetTasks() []*task.Task {
    tasks := []*task.Task{}
    for _, t := range m.TaskDb {
        tasks = append(tasks, t)
    }
    return tasks
}
```

With the GetTasks() function written, we can now use it in the GetTasksHandler method. The only change we need to make from the worker's implementation is to pass the manager's GetTasks() function to the encoder.

Listing 8.4 The manager's GetTasksHandler

```
func (a *Api) GetTasksHandler(w http.ResponseWriter, r *http.Request) {
    w.Header().Set("Content-Type", "application/json")
    w.WriteHeader(200)
    json.NewEncoder(w).Encode(a.Manager.GetTasks())
}
```

Finally, let's implement the `StopTaskHandler`. Again, the method works the same way as its worker counterpart, so there isn't much new to add to the discussion.

Listing 8.5   The manager's `StopTaskHandler`

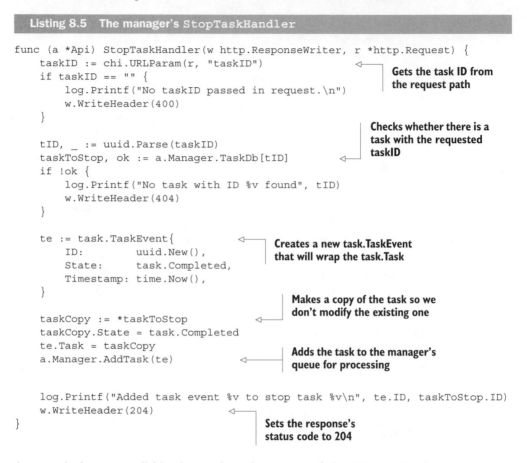

```go
func (a *Api) StopTaskHandler(w http.ResponseWriter, r *http.Request) {
    taskID := chi.URLParam(r, "taskID")                     ◁──┐ Gets the task ID from
    if taskID == "" {                                           the request path
        log.Printf("No taskID passed in request.\n")
        w.WriteHeader(400)
    }
                                                     Checks whether there is a
                                                     task with the requested
                                                     taskID
    tID, _ := uuid.Parse(taskID)
    taskToStop, ok := a.Manager.TaskDb[tID]          ◁──
    if !ok {
        log.Printf("No task with ID %v found", tID)
        w.WriteHeader(404)
    }

    te := task.TaskEvent{          ◁──  Creates a new task.TaskEvent
        ID:        uuid.New(),          that will wrap the task.Task
        State:     task.Completed,
        Timestamp: time.Now(),
    }
                                   Makes a copy of the task so we
                                   don't modify the existing one
    taskCopy := *taskToStop        ◁──
    taskCopy.State = task.Completed
    te.Task = taskCopy             ◁──  Adds the task to the manager's
    a.Manager.AddTask(te)               queue for processing

    log.Printf("Added task event %v to stop task %v\n", te.ID, taskToStop.ID)
    w.WriteHeader(204)             ◁──
}                                  Sets the response's
                                   status code to 204
```

As a reminder, as we did in the worker, the manager's handler methods are not operating directly on tasks. We have separated the concerns of responding to API requests and the operations to start and stop tasks. So the API simply puts the request on the manager's queue via the `AddTask` method, and then the manager picks up the task from its queue and performs the necessary operation.

So far, we've been able to implement the handlers in the manager's API by copying and pasting the handlers from the worker's API and making a few minor adjustments. At this point, we've implemented the meat of the API.

8.6   *Serving the API*

Now that we have implemented the manager's handlers, let's complete our work that will let us serve the API to users. We'll start by copying and pasting the `initRouter` method from the worker. This method sets up our router and creates the required endpoints, and since the endpoints will be the same as the worker's, we don't need to modify anything.

Listing 8.6   The manager API's `initRouter` method

```
func (a *Api) initRouter() {
    a.Router = chi.NewRouter()
    a.Router.Route("/tasks", func(r chi.Router) {
        r.Post("/", a.StartTaskHandler)
        r.Get("/", a.GetTasksHandler)
        r.Route("/{taskID}", func(r chi.Router) {
            r.Delete("/", a.StopTaskHandler)
        })
    })
}
```

For the icing on the cake, let's take care of starting the API by copying the `Start` method from the worker's API. The manager's API will start up in the same way, so like the `initRouter` method, we don't need to make any changes.

Listing 8.7   The manager API's `Start` method

```
func (a *Api) Start() {
    a.initRouter()
    http.ListenAndServe(fmt.Sprintf("%s:%d", a.Address, a.Port), a.Router)
}
```

8.7   A few refactorings to make our lives easier

At this point, we've implemented everything we need to have a functional API for the manager. But now that we're at a point in our journey where we have APIs for both the worker and the manager, let's make a few minor tweaks that will make it easier to run these APIs.

If you recall from chapter 5, we created the function `runTasks` in our `main.go` file. We used it as a way to continuously check for new tasks that the worker needed to run. If it found any tasks in the worker's queue, it called the workers `RunTask` method.

Instead of having this function be part of the `main.go` file, let's move it into the worker itself. This change will then encapsulate all the necessary worker behavior in the `Worker` object. Copy the `runTasks` function from the `main.go` file, and paste it into the `worker.go` file. Then, to clean everything up so the code will run, we're going to make three changes:

- Rename the existing `RunTask` method to `runTask`
- Rename the `runTasks` method from `main.go` to `RunTasks`
- Change the `RunTasks` method to call the newly renamed `runTask` method

You can see these changes in the following listing.

Listing 8.8   Moving the `runTasks` function from `main.go` to the worker

```
func (w *Worker) runTask() task.DockerResult {
}


func (w *Worker) RunTasks() {
    for {
        if w.Queue.Len() != 0 {
            result := w.runTask()
            if result.Error != nil {
                log.Printf("Error running task: %v\n", result.Error)
            }
        } else {
            log.Printf("No tasks to process currently.\n")
        }
        log.Println("Sleeping for 10 seconds.")
        time.Sleep(10 * time.Second)
    }

}
```

> Renames the worker's existing RunTask method to runTask; the body of the method stays the same

> Renames the runTasks method from main.go to RunTasks

> Calls the worker's runTask method

In a similar fashion, we're going to make some changes to the `Manager` struct that will make it easier to use the manager in our `main.go` file. For starters, let's rename the manager's `UpdateTasks` method to `updateTasks`. The method should look like this (the body of the method stays the same):

```
func (m *Manager) updateTasks() {
}
```

Next, let's create a new method on our `Manager` struct called `UpdateTasks`. This method serves a similar purpose to the `RunTasks` method we added to the worker. It runs an endless loop, inside which it calls the manager's `updateTasks` method. This change makes it possible for us to remove the anonymous function we used in the `main.go` file in chapter 7 that performed the same function.

Listing 8.9   Adding the `UpdateTasks` method to the manager

```
func (m *Manager) UpdateTasks() {
    for {
        log.Println("Checking for task updates from workers")
        m.updateTasks()
        log.Println("Task updates completed")
        log.Println("Sleeping for 15 seconds")
        time.Sleep(15 * time.Second)
    }
}
```

Finally, let's add the `ProcessTasks` method you see in the next listing to the manager. This method also works similarly to the worker's `RunTasks` method: it runs an endless loop, repeatedly calling the manager's `SendWork` method.

Listing 8.10   The manager's `ProcessTasks` method

```
func (m *Manager) ProcessTasks() {
    for {
        log.Println("Processing any tasks in the queue")
        m.SendWork()
        log.Println("Sleeping for 10 seconds")
        time.Sleep(10 * time.Second)
    }
}
```

8.8   *Putting it all together*

Alright, it's that time again—time to take what we've built in the chapter and run it. Before we do that, however, let's quickly summarize what we've built so far:

- We wrapped the manager component in an API that allows users to communicate with the manager.
- We constructed the manager's API using the same types of components we used for the worker's API: *handlers*, *routes*, and a *router*.
- The *router* listens for requests to the *routes*, and dispatches those requests to the appropriate *handlers*.

Let's start by copying and pasting the `main` function from the `main.go` file in chapter 7. This will be our starting point.

There is one major difference between our situation at the end of this chapter and that of the last: we now have APIs for both the worker and the manager. So while we will be creating instances of each, we will not be interacting with them directly as we have in the past. Instead, we will be passing these instances into their respective APIs and then starting those APIs so they are listening to HTTP requests.

In past chapters where we started instances of the worker's API, we set two environment variables: `CUBE_HOST` and `CUBE_PORT`. These were used to set up the worker API to listen for requests at `http://localhost:5555`. Now, however, we have two APIs that we need to start. To handle our new circumstances, let's set up our `main` function to extract a set of `host:port` environment variables for each API. As you can see in the following listing, these will be called `CUBE_WORKER_HOST`, `CUBE_WORKER_PORT`, `CUBE_MANAGER_HOST`, and `CUBE_MANAGER_PORT`.

Listing 8.11   Extracting the host and port for each API from environment variables

```
func main() {
    whost := os.Getenv("CUBE_WORKER_HOST")
    wport, _ := strconv.Atoi(os.Getenv("CUBE_WORKER_PORT"))
```

```
        mhost := os.Getenv("CUBE_MANAGER_HOST")
        mport, _ := strconv.Atoi(os.Getenv("CUBE_MANAGER_PORT"))
}
```

Next, after extracting the host and port values from the environment and storing them in appropriately named variables, let's start up the worker API. This process should look familiar from chapter 7. The only difference here, however, is that we're calling the `RunTasks` method on the worker object, instead of a separate `runTasks` function that we previously defined in `main.go`. As we did in chapter 7, we call each of these methods using the `go` keyword, thus running each in a separate goroutine.

```
fmt.Println("Starting Cube worker")

    w := worker.Worker{
        Queue: *queue.New(),
        Db:    make(map[uuid.UUID]*task.Task),
    }
    wapi := worker.Api{Address: whost, Port: wport, Worker: &w}

    go w.RunTasks()
    go w.CollectStats()
    go wapi.Start()
```

Finally, we'll start up the manager API. This process starts the same as it did in the last chapter. We create a list of workers that contains the single previously created worker, represented as a string by its `<host>:<port>`. Then we create an instance of our manager, passing in the list of `workers`. Next, we create an instance of the manager's API and store it in a variable called `mapi`.

The next two lines in our `main` function set up two goroutines that will run in parallel with the main goroutine running the API. The first goroutine will run the manager's `ProcessTasks` method. This ensures the manager will process any incoming tasks from users. The second goroutine will run the manager's `UpdateTasks` method. It will ensure the manager updates the state of tasks by querying the worker's API to get up-to-date states for each task.

Then comes what we've been waiting for. We start the manager's API by calling the `Start` method.

```
fmt.Println("Starting Cube manager")

    workers := []string{fmt.Sprintf("%s:%d", whost, wport)}
    m := manager.New(workers)
    mapi := manager.Api{Address: mhost, Port: mport, Manager: m}
```

```
go m.ProcessTasks()
go m.UpdateTasks()

mapi.Start()
```

}

At this point, all that's left to do is to run our main program so both the manager and worker APIs are running. As you can see, both the worker and the manager get started:

```
$ CUBE_WORKER_HOST=localhost \
CUBE_WORKER_PORT=5555 \
CUBE_MANAGER_HOST=localhost \
CUBE_MANAGER_PORT=5556 \
go run main.go
Starting Cube worker
Starting Cube manager
2022/03/06 14:45:47 Collecting stats
2022/03/06 14:45:47 Checking for task updates from workers
2022/03/06 14:45:47 Processing any tasks in the queue
2022/03/06 14:45:47 Checking worker localhost:5555 for task updates
2022/03/06 14:45:47 No work in the queue
2022/03/06 14:45:47 Sleeping for 10 seconds
2022/03/06 14:45:47 No tasks to process currently.
2022/03/06 14:45:47 Sleeping for 10 seconds.
2022/03/06 14:45:47 Task updates completed
2022/03/06 14:45:47 Sleeping for 15 seconds
```

Let's do a quick sanity check to verify that our manager does indeed respond to requests. Let's issue a GET request to get a list of the tasks it knows about. It should return an empty list:

```
$ curl -v localhost:5556/tasks
*    Trying 127.0.0.1:5556...
* Connected to localhost (127.0.0.1) port 5556 (#0)
> GET /tasks HTTP/1.1
> Host: localhost:5556
> User-Agent: curl/7.81.0
> Accept: */*
>
* Mark bundle as not supporting multiuse
< HTTP/1.1 200 OK
< Content-Type: application/json
< Date: Sun, 06 Mar 2022 19:52:46 GMT
< Content-Length: 3
<
[]
```

Cool! Our manager is listening for requests as we expected. As we can see, though, it doesn't have any tasks because we haven't told it to run any yet. Let's take the next step and send a request to the manager that instructs it to start a task for us.

For this purpose, let's create a file named `task.json` in the same directory where our `main.go` file is. Inside this file, let's create the JSON representation of a task, as seen in the next listing. This representation is similar to what we used in `main.go` in chapter 7, except we're moving it into a separate file.

Listing 8.14   JSON representation of our task

```
{
    "ID": "6be4cb6b-61d1-40cb-bc7b-9cacefefa60c",
    "State": 2,
    "Task": {
        "State": 1,
        "ID": "21b23589-5d2d-4731-b5c9-a97e9832d021",
        "Name": "test-chapter-5",
        "Image": "strm/helloworld-http"
    }
}
```

Now that we've created our `task.json` file with the task we want to send to the manager via its API, let's use `curl` to send a POST request to the manager API's `/tasks` endpoint. As expected, the manager's API responds with a `201` response code:

```
$ curl -v --request POST \
--header 'Content-Type: application/json' \
--data @task.json \
localhost:5556/tasks
*    Trying 127.0.0.1:5556...
* Connected to localhost (127.0.0.1) port 5556 (#0)
> POST /tasks HTTP/1.1
> Host: localhost:5556
> User-Agent: curl/7.81.0
> Accept: */*
> Content-Type: application/json
> Content-Length: 230
>
* Mark bundle as not supporting multiuse
< HTTP/1.1 201 Created
< Date: Sun, 06 Mar 2022 20:04:36 GMT
< Content-Length: 286
< Content-Type: text/plain; charset=utf-8
<
{
    "ID":"21b23589-5d2d-4731-b5c9-a97e9832d021",
    "ContainerID":"",
    "Name":"test-chapter-5",
    "State":1,
    "Image":"strm/helloworld-http",
    "Cpu":0,
    "Memory":0,
    "Disk":0,
    "ExposedPorts":null,
    "PortBindings":null,
```

```
    "RestartPolicy":"",
    "StartTime":"0001-01-01T00:00:00Z",
    "FinishTime":"0001-01-01T00:00:00Z"
}
```

There's one thing to note about the JSON returned by the manager's API. Notice that the ContainerID field is empty. The reason for this is that like the worker's API, the manager's API doesn't operate directly on tasks. As tasks come into the API, they are added to the manager's queue, and the manager works on them independently of the request. At the time of our request, the manager hasn't shipped the task to the worker, so it can't know what the ContainerID will be. If we make a subsequent request to the manager's API to GET /tasks, we should see a ContainerID for our task:

```
$ curl -v localhost:5556/tasks|jq
*   Trying 127.0.0.1:5556...
> GET /tasks HTTP/1.1
> Host: localhost:5556
> User-Agent: curl/7.81.0
> Accept: */*
>
* Mark bundle as not supporting multiuse
< HTTP/1.1 200 OK
< Content-Type: application/json
< Date: Sun, 06 Mar 2022 20:16:43 GMT
< Content-Length: 352
[
  {
    "ID": "21b23589-5d2d-4731-b5c9-a97e9832d021",
    "ContainerID":
    ➥ "428115c14a41243ec29e5b81feaccbf4b9632e2caaeb58f166df595726889312",
    "Name": "test-chapter-8",
    "State": 2,
    "Image": "strm/helloworld-http",
    "Cpu": 0,
    "Memory": 0,
    "Disk": 0,
    "ExposedPorts": null,
    "PortBindings": null,
    "RestartPolicy": "",
    "StartTime": "0001-01-01T00:00:00Z",
    "FinishTime": "0001-01-01T00:00:00Z"
  }
]
```

There is one minor thing to keep in mind when querying the manager's API, as we did previously. Depending on how quickly we issue our GET /tasks request after sending the initial POST /tasks request, we may still not see a ContainerID. Why is that? If you recall, the manager updates its view of tasks by making a GET /tasks request to the worker's API. It then uses the response to that request to update the state of the tasks in its own datastore. If you look back at listing 8.13, you can see that our main.go program is running the manager's `UpdateTasks` method in a separate goroutine, and that method sleeps for 15 seconds between each attempt to update tasks.

Once the manager shows the task running—that is, we get a `ContainerID` in our `GET /tasks` Response—we can further verify that the task is running using the `docker ps` command:

```
$ docker ps --format "table {{.ID}}\t{{.Image}}\t{{.Status}}\t{{.Names}}"
CONTAINER ID    IMAGE                  STATUS              NAMES
428115c14a41    strm/helloworld-http   Up About a minute   test-chapter-8
```

Now that we've seen that we can use the manager's API to start a task and to get a list of tasks, let's use it to stop our running task. To do this, we issue a `DELETE /tasks/{taskID}` request, like the following:

```
$ curl -v --request DELETE \
    'localhost:5556/tasks/21b23589-5d2d-4731-b5c9-a97e9832d021'
*    Trying 127.0.0.1:5556...
* Connected to localhost (127.0.0.1) port 5556 (#0)
> DELETE /tasks/21b23589-5d2d-4731-b5c9-a97e9832d021 HTTP/1.1
> Host: localhost:5556
> User-Agent: curl/7.81.0
> Accept: */*
>
* Mark bundle as not supporting multiuse
< HTTP/1.1 204 No Content
< Date: Sun, 06 Mar 2022 20:29:27 GMT
```

As we can see, the manager's API accepted our request, and it responded with a 204 response, as expected. You should also see it in the following output from our `main.go` program (I've truncated some of the output to make it easier to read):

```
2022/03/06 15:29:27 Added task event 937e85eb to stop task 21b23589
Found task in queue:
2022/03/06 15:29:32 attempting to transition from 2 to 3
2022/03/06 15:29:32 Attempting to stop container 442a439de
2022/03/06 15:29:43 Stopped and removed container 442a439de
➥ for task 21b23589
```

Again, we can use the `docker ps` command to confirm that our manager did what we expected it to do, which, in this case, is to stop the task:

```
$ docker ps
CONTAINER ID    IMAGE    COMMAND    CREATED    STATUS    PORTS    NAMES
```

Summary

- Like the worker's API, the manager wraps its core functionality and exposes it as an HTTP server. Unlike the worker's API, whose primary user is the manager, the primary users of the manager's API are end users—in other words, developers. Thus, the manager's API is what users interact with to run their tasks on the orchestration system.

- The manager and worker APIs provide an abstraction over our infrastructure, either physical or virtual, that removes the need for developers to concern themselves with such low-level details. Instead of thinking about how their application runs on a machine, they only have to be concerned about how their application runs in a container. If it runs as expected in a container on their machine, it can run on any machine that's also running the same container framework (i.e., Docker).

- Like the worker API, the manager's API is a simple REST-based API. It defines routes that enable users to create, query, and stop tasks. Also, when sent data, it expects that data to be encoded as JSON, and it likewise encodes any data it sends as JSON.

What could
possibly go wrong?

This chapter covers

- Enumerating potential failures
- Exploring options for recovering from failures
- Implementing task health checks to recover from task crashes

At the beginning of chapter 4, in which we started the process of implementing our worker, we talked about the scenario of running a web server that serves static pages. In that scenario, we considered how to deal with the problem of our site growing in popularity and thus needing to be resilient to failures to ensure we could serve our growing user base. The solution, we said, was to run multiple instances of our web server. In other words, we decided to scale horizontally, a common pattern for scaling. By scaling the number of web servers, we can ensure that a failure in any given instance of the web server does not bring our site completely down and, thus, unavailable to our users.

In this chapter, we're going to modify this scenario slightly. Instead of serving static web pages, we're going to serve an API. This API is very simple: it takes a POST request with a body, and it returns a response with the same body. In other words, it simply echoes the request in the response.

With that minor change to our scenario, this chapter will reflect on what we've built thus far and discuss a number of failure scenarios, both with our orchestrator and with the tasks running on it. Then we will implement several mechanisms for handling a subset of failure scenarios.

9.1 Overview of our new scenario

Our new scenario involves an API that takes the body of a request and simply returns that body in the response to the user. The format of the body is JSON, and our API defines this format in the `Message` struct:

```
type Message struct {
    Msg string
}
```

Thus, making a `curl` request to this API looks like this:

```
$ curl -X POST localhost:7777/ -d '{"Msg":"Hello, world!"}'
{"Msg":"Hello, world!"}
```

And, as you can see in the response, we get back the same body that we sent. To make this scenario simpler to use, I've gone ahead and built a Docker image that we can reuse throughout the rest of the chapter. So to run that API locally, all you have to do is this:

```
$ docker run -it --rm --name echo timboring/echo-server:latest
```

(If you're interested in the source code for this API, you can find it in the `echo` directory in the downloadable source code for this chapter.)

Now let's move on to talk about the number of ways this API can fail if we run it as a task in our orchestration system.

9.2 Failure scenarios

Failures happen all the time! As engineers, we should expect this. Failures are the norm, not the exception. More importantly, failures happen at multiple levels:

- Failures at the level of the application
- Failures at the level of individual tasks
- Failures at the level of the orchestration system

Let's walk through what failures at each of these levels might look like.

9.2.1 Application startup failure

A task can fail to start because the task's application has a bug in its startup routine. For example, we might decide to store each request our echo service receives, and to do that, we add a database as a dependency. Now, when an instance of our echo service starts up, it attempts to make a connection to the database.

What happens, however, if we can't connect to the database? Maybe it's down due to some networking problem. Or, if we're using a managed service, perhaps the administrators decided they needed to do some maintenance, and as a result, the database service is unavailable for some period of time. Or maybe the database is upset with its human overlords and has decided to go on strike.

It doesn't really matter why the database is unavailable. The fact is that our application depends on the database, and it needs to do something when it is unavailable. There are generally two options for how our application can respond:

- It can simply crash.
- It can attempt to retry connecting to the database.

In my experience, I've seen the former option used frequently. It's the default. As an engineer, I have an application that needs a database, and I attempt to connect to the database when my application starts. Maybe I check for errors, log them, and then exit gracefully.

The latter option might be the better choice, but it adds some complexity. Today, most languages have at least one third-party library that provides the framework to perform retries using exponential backoff. Using this option, I could have my application attempt to connect to the database in a separate goroutine, and until it can connect, maybe my application serves a `503` response with a helpful message explaining that the application is in the process of starting up.

9.2.2   *Application bugs*

A task can also fail after having successfully started up. For example, our echo service can start up and operate successfully for a while. But we've recently added a new feature, and we haven't tested it thoroughly because we decided it was an important feature and getting it into production would allow us to post about it on Hacker News. A user queries our service in a way that triggers our new code in an unexpected way and crashes the API. Oops!

9.2.3   *Task startup failures due to resource problems*

A task can fail to start because the worker machine doesn't have enough resources (i.e., memory, CPU, or disk). In theory, this shouldn't happen. Orchestration systems like Kubernetes and Nomad implement sophisticated schedulers that take memory and CPU requirements into account when scheduling tasks onto worker nodes.

The story for disk, however, is a little more nuanced. Container images consume disk space. Run the `docker images` command on your machine and notice the `SIZE` column in the output. On my machine, the `timboring/echo-server` we're using in this chapter is 12.3 MB in size. If I pull down the `postgres:14` image, I can see that its size is 376 MB:

```
$ docker images
REPOSITORY                TAG        IMAGE ID        CREATED         SIZE
timboring/echo-server     latest     fe039d2a9875    4 months ago    12.3MB
postgres                  14         dd21862d2f49    4 days ago      376MB
```

While there are strategies to minimize size, images still reside on disk and thus consume space. In addition to container images, the other processes running on worker nodes also use disk space—for example, they may store their logs on disk. Also, other containers running on a node may be using disk space for their own data. So it is possible that an orchestrator could schedule a task onto a worker node, and then when that worker starts up the task, the task fails because there isn't enough disk space to download the container image.

9.2.4 Task failures due to Docker daemon crashes and restarts

Running tasks can also be affected by problems with the Docker daemon. For example, if the Docker daemon crashes, then our task will be terminated. Similarly, if we stop or restart the Docker daemon, then the daemon will also stop our task. This behavior is the default for the Docker daemon. Containers can be kept alive while the daemon is down using a feature called live restore, but the usage of that feature is beyond the scope of this book. For our purposes, we will work with the default behavior.

9.2.5 Task failures due to machine crashes and restarts

The most extreme failure scenario is a worker machine crashing. In the case of an orchestration system, if a worker machine crashes, then the Docker daemon will obviously stop running, along with any tasks running on the machine.

Less extreme is the situation where a machine is restarted. Perhaps an administrator restarts it after updating some software, in which case the Docker daemon will be stopped and started back up after the machine reboots. In the process, however, any tasks will be terminated and will need to be restarted.

9.2.6 Worker failures

In addition to application and task failures, when we run the echo service on our orchestration system, the worker where the task runs can also fail. But there is a little more involved at this level. When we say *worker*, we need to clarify what exactly we're talking about. First, there is the worker component that we've written. Second, there is the machine where our worker component runs.

So when we talk about worker failures, we have two discrete types of failures at this layer of our orchestration system. Our worker component that we've written can crash due to bugs in our code. It can also crash because the machine it's running on crashes or becomes otherwise unavailable.

We already touched on machine failure, but let's talk briefly about failures with the worker component. If it fails for some reason, what happens to the running tasks? Unlike the Docker daemon, our worker going down or restarting does not terminate running containers. It does mean that the manager cannot send *new* tasks to the worker, and it means that the manager cannot query the worker to get the current state of running tasks.

So while a failure in our worker is inconvenient, it doesn't have an immediate effect on running tasks. (It could be more than inconvenient if, say, a number of workers crashed, which resulted in your team being unable to deploy a mission-critical bug fix. But that's a topic for another book.)

9.2.7   *Manager failures*

The final failure scenario to consider involves the manager component. Remember, we said the manager serves an administrative function. It receives requests from users to run their tasks, and it schedules those tasks onto workers. Unless the manager and worker components are running on the same machine (and we wouldn't do that in a production environment, would we?), any problems with the manager will only affect those administrative functions.

So if the manager component or the machine on which it is running crashes, the effect would likely be minimal. Running tasks would continue to run. Users would not, however, be able to submit new tasks to the system because the manager would not be available to receive and take action on those requests. Again, it would be inconvenient but not necessarily the end of the world.

9.3   *Recovery options*

As failures in an orchestration system can occur at multiple levels and have various degrees of effect, so too do the recovery options.

9.3.1   *Recovery from application failures*

As we previously discussed, applications can fail at startup due to external dependencies being unavailable. The only real automated recovery option here is to perform retries with exponential backoff or some other mechanism. An orchestration system cannot wave a magic wand and fix problems with external dependencies (unless, of course, that external dependency is also running on the orchestration system). An orchestrator provides us with some tools for automated recovery from these kinds of situations, but if a database is down, continually restarting the application isn't going to change the situation.

Similarly, an orchestration system can't help us with the bugs we introduce into our applications. The real solution is tools like automated testing, which can help identify bugs before they are deployed into production.

9.3.2   *Recovering from environmental failures*

An orchestration system provides a number of tools for dealing with non–application-specific failures. We can group the remaining failure scenarios together and call them *environmental* failures:

- Failures with Docker
- Failures with machines

- Failures with an orchestrator's worker
- Failures with an orchestrator's manager

Let's cover some ways in which an orchestration system can help recover from these types of failures.

9.3.3 Recovering from task-level failures

Docker has a built-in mechanism for restarting containers when they exit. This mechanism is called *restart policies* and can be specified on the command line using the `--restart` flag. In the following example command line, we run a container using the `timboring/echo-server` image and tell Docker we want it to restart the container once if it exits because of a failure:

```
$ docker run \
    --restart=on-failure:1 \
    --name echo \
    -p 7777:7777 \
    -it \
    timboring/echo-server:bad-exit
```

Docker supports four restart policies:

- `no`—Do nothing when a container exits (this is the default).
- `on-failure`—Restart the container if it exits with a nonzero status code.
- `always`—Always restart the container, regardless of the exit code.
- `unless-stopped`—Always restart the container, except if the container was stopped.

You can read more about Docker's restart policies in the docs at http://mng.bz/VRWN.

The restart policy works well when dealing with individual containers being run outside of an orchestration system. In most production situations, we run Docker itself as a systemd unit. systemd, as the initialization system for most Linux distributions, can ensure that applications that are supposed to be running are, in fact, running, especially after a reboot.

For containers running as part of an orchestration system, however, using Docker's restart policies can pose problems. The main problem is that they muddy the waters around who is responsible for dealing with failures. Is the Docker daemon ultimately responsible? Or is the orchestration system? Moreover, if the Docker daemon is involved in handling failures, this adds complexity to the orchestrator because it will need to check with the Docker daemon to see if it's in the process of restarting a container.

For Cube, we will handle task failures ourselves instead of relying on Docker's restart policy. This decision, however, does raise another question: Should the manager or worker be responsible for handling failures?

The worker is closest to the task, so it seems natural to have the worker deal with failures. But the worker is only aware of its own singular existence. Thus, it can only attempt to deal with failures in its own context. If it's overloaded, it can't make the decision to send the task to another worker because it doesn't know about any other workers.

The manager, though farther away from the actual mechanisms that control task execution, has a broader view of the whole system. It knows about all the workers in the cluster, and it knows about the individual tasks running on each of those workers. Thus, the manager has more options for recovering from failures than does an individual worker. It can ask the worker running the failed task to try to restart it. Or, if that worker is overloaded or unavailable (maybe it crashed), it can find another worker that has capacity to run the task.

9.3.4   *Recovering from worker failures*

As I previously mentioned when discussing the types of worker failures, there are two distinct types of failures when it comes to the worker. There are failures in the worker component itself and failures with the machine where the worker is running.

In the first case, when our worker component fails, we have the most flexibility. The worker itself isn't critical to existing tasks. Once a task is up and running, the worker is not involved in the task's ongoing operation. So if the worker fails, there isn't much consequence to running tasks. In such a state, however, the worker is in a degraded state. The manager won't be able to communicate with the worker, which means it won't be able to collect the task state, and it won't be able to place new tasks on the worker. It also won't be able to stop running tasks.

In this situation, we could have the manager attempt to fix the worker component. How? The obvious thing that comes to mind is for the manager to consider the worker dead and move all the tasks to another worker. This is a rather blunt force tactic, however, and could wreak more havoc. If the manager simply considers those tasks dead and attempts to restart them on another worker machine, what happens if the tasks are still running on the machine where the worker crashed? By blindly considering the worker and all of its tasks dead, the manager could be putting applications into an unexpected state. This is particularly true when there is only a single instance of a task.

The second case, where a worker machine has crashed, is also tricky. How are we defining "crashed"? Does it mean the manager cannot communicate with the worker via its API? Does it mean the manager performs some other operation to verify a worker is up—for example, by attempting an ICMP ping? Moreover, can the manager be certain that a worker machine was actually down even if it did attempt an ICMP ping and did not receive a response? What if the problem was that the worker machine's network card died, but the machine was otherwise up and operating normally? Similarly, what if the manager and worker machine were on different network segments, and a router, switch, or other piece of network equipment died, thus segmenting the two networks so the manager could not talk to the worker machine?

As we can see, trying to make our orchestration system resilient to failures in the worker component is more complex than it may initially seem. It's difficult to determine whether a machine is down—meaning it has crashed or been powered off and is otherwise not running any tasks—in which case the Docker daemon is not running, nor are any of the tasks under its control.

9.3.5 Recovering from manager failures

Finally, let's consider our options for failures in the manager component. Like the worker, there are two failure scenarios. The manager component itself could fail, and the machine on which the manager component is running could fail. While these scenarios are the same as in the worker, their effects and how we deal with them are slightly different.

First, if the manager dies, regardless of whether it's the manager component itself or the machine where it's running, there is no effect on running tasks. The tasks and the worker operate independently of the manager. In our orchestration system, if the manager dies, the worker and its tasks continue operating normally. The only difference is that the worker won't receive any new tasks.

Second, recovering from manager failures in our orchestration system will likely be less complex than recovering from failures at the worker layer. Remember, for the sake of simplicity, we have said that we will run only a single manager. So if it fails, we only need to try to recover a single instance. If the manager component crashes, we can restart it. (Ideally, we'd run it using an init system like Systemd or supervisord.) If its datastore gets corrupted, we can restore it from a backup.

While not ideal, a manager failure doesn't bring our whole system down. It does cause some pain for developers because while the manager is down, they won't be able to start new tasks or stop existing ones. So deployments of new features or bug fixes will be delayed until the manager is back online.

Obviously, the ideal state in regard to the manager would be to run multiple instances of the manager. This is what orchestrators like Borg, Kubernetes, and Nomad do. Like running multiple workers, running multiple instances of the manager adds resiliency to the system as a whole. There is, however, added complexity.

When running multiple managers, we have to think about synchronizing state across all the instances. There might be a primary instance that is responsible for handling user requests and acting on them. This instance will also be responsible for distributing the state of all the system's tasks across the other managers. If the primary instance fails, then another can take over its role. At this point, we start getting into the realm of consensus and the idea of how systems agree on the state of the world. This is where things like the Raft protocol come into play, but going farther down this road is beyond the scope of this book.

9.4 Implementing health checks

With this complexity in mind, we are going to implement a simple solution for illustration purposes. We are going to implement health checks at the task level. The basic idea here is twofold:

- An application implements a health check and exposes it on its API as `/health`. (The name of the endpoint could be anything, as long as it's well defined and doesn't change.)
- When a user submits a task, they define the health check endpoint as part of the task configuration.
- The manager calls a task's health check periodically and will attempt to start a new task for any non-200 response.

With this solution, we don't have to worry about whether the worker machine is reachable. We also don't have to figure out whether a worker component is working. We just call the health check for a task, and if it responds that it's operating as expected, we know the manager can continue about its business.

> **NOTE**   Operationally, we still care about whether the worker component is functioning as expected. But we can treat that problem separately from task health and how and when we need to attempt to restart tasks.

There are two components to health checks. First, the worker has to periodically check the state of its tasks and update them accordingly. To do this, it can call the `ContainerInspect()` method on the Docker API. If the task is in any state other than `running`, then the worker updates the task's state to `Failed`.

Second, the manager must periodically call a task's health check. If the check doesn't pass (i.e., it returns anything other than a `200` response code), it then sends a task event to the appropriate worker to restart the task.

9.4.1   Inspecting a task on the worker

Let's start with refactoring our worker so it can inspect the state of a task's Docker container. If we think back to chapter 3, we implemented the following `Docker` struct. The purpose of this struct is to hold a reference to an instance of the Docker client, which is what allows us to call the Docker API and perform various container operations. It also holds the `Config` for a task:

```
type Docker struct {
    Client *client.Client
    Config Config
}
```

To handle responses from the `ContainerInspect` API call, let's create a new struct called `DockerInspectResponse` in the `task/task.go` file. As we can see in listing 9.1, this struct will contain two fields. The `Error` field will hold an error if we encounter one when calling `ContainerInspect`. The `Container` field is a pointer to a `types.ContainerJSON` struct. This struct is defined in Docker's Go SDK (http://mng.bz/orjD). It contains all kinds of detailed information about a container, but most importantly for our purposes, it contains the field `State`. This is the current state of the container as Docker sees it.

Listing 9.1   The new `DockerInspectResponse` struct

```
type DockerInspectResponse struct {
    Error       error
    Container   *types.ContainerJSON
}
```

> ## A note about the Docker container state
>
> The concept of Docker container state can be confusing. For example, the doc (http://mng.bz/n19d) for the `docker ps` command mentions filtering by container status, where the status is one of `created`, `restarting`, `running`, `removing`, `paused`, `exited`, or `dead`.
>
> If you look at the Docker source code, however, you'll find there is a `State` struct defined in `container/state.go` (http://mng.bz/46xQ), which looks like this:
>
> ```
> type State struct {
>     Running             bool
>     Paused              bool
>     Restarting          bool
>     OOMKilled           bool
>     RemovalInProgress   bool
>     Dead                bool
>     // other fields omitted
> }
> ```
>
> As we can see, technically, there is not a state called `created`, nor is there an `exited` state. So what is going on here? It turns out there is a method on the `State` struct named `StateString` (http://mng.bz/QRj4), and this is performing some logic that results in the statuses we see in the documentation for the `docker ps` command.

In addition to adding the `DockerInspectResponse` struct, we're also going to add a new method to our existing `Docker` struct. Let's call this method `Inspect`. It should take a string that represents the container ID we want it to inspect. Then it should return a `DockerInspectResponse`. The body of the method is straightforward. It creates an instance of a Docker client called `dc`. Then we call the client's `Container-Inspect` method, passing in a context `ctx` and a `containerID`. We check for an error and return it if we find one. Otherwise, we return a `DockerInspectResponse`.

Listing 9.2   The `Inspect` method calling the Docker API

```
func (d *Docker) Inspect(containerID string) DockerInspectResponse {
    dc, _ := client.NewClientWithOpts(client.FromEnv)
    ctx := context.Background()
    resp, err := dc.ContainerInspect(ctx, containerID)
    if err != nil {
        log.Printf("Error inspecting container: %s\n", err)
```

```
        return DockerInspectResponse{Error: err}
    }

    return DockerInspectResponse{Container: &resp}
}
```

Now that we've implemented the means to inspect a task, let's move on and use it in our worker.

9.4.2 *Implementing task updates on the worker*

For the worker to update the state of its tasks, we'll need to refactor it to use the new `Inspect` method we created on the `Docker` struct. To start, let's open the `worker/worker.go` file and add the `InspectTask` method as shown in listing 9.3. This method takes a single argument `t` of type `task.Task`. It creates a task config `config` and then sets up an instance of the `Docker` type that will allow us to interact with the Docker daemon running on the worker. Finally, it calls the `Inspect` method, passing in the `ContainerID`.

Listing 9.3   The `InspectTask` method

```
func (w *Worker) InspectTask(t task.Task) task.DockerInspectResponse {
    config := task.NewConfig(&t)
    d := task.NewDocker(config)
    return d.Inspect(t.ContainerID)
}
```

Next, the worker will need to call its new `InspectTask` method. To do this, let's use the same pattern we've used in the past. We'll create a public method called `Update-Tasks`, which will allow us to run it in a separate goroutine. This method is nothing more than a wrapper that runs a continuous loop and calls the private `updateTasks` method, which does all the heavy lifting.

Listing 9.4   The worker's new `UpdateTasks` method

```
func (w *Worker) UpdateTasks() {
    for {
        log.Println("Checking status of tasks")
        w.updateTasks()
        log.Println("Task updates completed")
        log.Println("Sleeping for 15 seconds")
        time.Sleep(15 * time.Second)
    }
}
```

The `updateTasks` method performs a very simple algorithm. For each task in the worker's datastore, it does the following:

- Calls the `InspectTask` method to get the task's state from the Docker daemon
- Verifies the task is in the `running` state
- If it's not in the `running` state, or not running at all, sets the tasks' state to `failed`

The `updateTasks` method also performs one other operation. It sets the `HostPorts` field on the task. This allows us to see what ports the Docker daemon has allocated to the task's running container. Thus, the worker's new `updateTasks` method handles calling the new `InspectTask` method, which results in updating the task's state based on the state of its Docker container.

Listing 9.5 The worker's new `updateTasks` method

```go
func (w *Worker) updateTasks() {
    for id, t := range w.Db {
        if t.State == task.Running {
            resp := w.InspectTask(*t)
            if resp.Error != nil {
                fmt.Printf("ERROR: %v\n", resp.Error)
            }

            if resp.Container == nil {
                log.Printf("No container for running task %s\n", id)
                w.Db[id].State = task.Failed
            }

            if resp.Container.State.Status == "exited" {
                log.Printf("Container for task %s in non-running state %s",
                 id, resp.Container.State.Status)
                w.Db[id].State = task.Failed
            }

            w.Db[id].HostPorts =
             resp.Container.NetworkSettings.NetworkSettingsBase.Ports
        }
    }
}
```

9.4.3 Healthchecks and restarts

We've said we will have the manager perform health checks for the tasks running in our orchestration system. But how do we identify these health checks so the manager can call them? One simple way to accomplish this is to add a field called `HealthCheck` to the `Task` struct, and by convention, we can use this new field to include a URL that the manager can call to perform a health check.

In addition to the `HealthCheck` field, let's also add a field called `RestartCount` to the `Tasks` struct. This field will be incremented each time the task is restarted, as we will see later in this chapter.

Listing 9.6 Adding the `HealthCheck` and `RestartCount` fields

```go
type Task struct {
    // existing fields omitted
    HealthCheck   string
```

```
    RestartCount   int
}
```

The benefit of this approach to health checks is that it makes it the responsibility of the task to define what it means to be healthy. Indeed, the definition of *healthy* can vary wildly from task to task. Thus, by having the task define its health check as a URL that can be called by the manager, all the manager has to do then is to call that URL. The result of calling the task's health check URL then determines a task's health: if the call returns a 200 status, the task is healthy; otherwise, it is not.

Now that we've implemented the necessary bits to enable our health check strategy, let's write the code necessary for the manager to make use of that work. Let's start with the lowest-level code first. Open the manager/manager.go file in your editor, and add the checkTaskHealth method as shown in listing 9.7. This method implements the necessary steps that allow the manager to check the health of an individual task. It takes a single argument t of type task.Task, and it returns an error if the health check is not successful.

There are a couple of things to note about this method. First, recall that when the manager schedules a task onto a worker, it adds an entry in its TaskWorkerMap field that maps the task's ID to the worker where it has been scheduled. That entry is a string and will be the IP address and port of the worker (e.g., 192.168.1.100:5555). Thus, it's the address of the worker's API. The task will, of course, be listening on a different port from the worker API. Thus, it's necessary to get the task's port that the Docker daemon assigned to it when the task started, and we accomplish this by calling the getHostPort helper method. Then, using the worker's IP address, the port on which the task is listening, and the health check defined in the task's definition, the manager can build a URL like http://192.168.1.100:49847/health.

Listing 9.7 The manager's new checkTaskHealth method

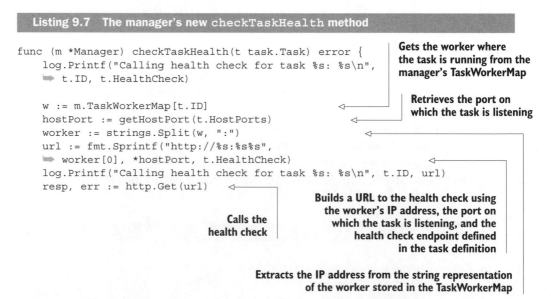

```
func (m *Manager) checkTaskHealth(t task.Task) error {
    log.Printf("Calling health check for task %s: %s\n",
    ⇒ t.ID, t.HealthCheck)

    w := m.TaskWorkerMap[t.ID]
    hostPort := getHostPort(t.HostPorts)
    worker := strings.Split(w, ":")
    url := fmt.Sprintf("http://%s:%s%s",
    ⇒ worker[0], *hostPort, t.HealthCheck)
    log.Printf("Calling health check for task %s: %s\n", t.ID, url)
    resp, err := http.Get(url)
```

Gets the worker where the task is running from the manager's TaskWorkerMap

Retrieves the port on which the task is listening

Builds a URL to the health check using the worker's IP address, the port on which the task is listening, and the health check endpoint defined in the task definition

Calls the health check

Extracts the IP address from the string representation of the worker stored in the TaskWorkerMap

```
    if err != nil {
        msg := fmt.Sprintf("Error connecting to health check %s", url)
        log.Println(msg)
        return errors.New(msg)        ◁──────── Handles connection errors
    }
                                                    │ Handles non-200 responses
    if resp.StatusCode != http.StatusOK {    ◁──┘
        msg := fmt.Sprintf("Error health check for task %s did not
    ➥ return 200\n", t.ID)
        log.Println(msg)
        return errors.New(msg)
    }

    log.Printf("Task %s health check response: %v\n", t.ID, resp.StatusCode)

    return nil
}
```

The `getHostPort` method is a helper that returns the host port where the task is listening.

Listing 9.8 The `getHostPort` method

```
func getHostPort(ports nat.PortMap) *string {
    for k, _ := range ports {
        return &ports[k][0].HostPort
    }
    return nil
}
```

Now that our manager knows how to call individual task health checks, let's create a new method that will use that knowledge to operate on all the tasks in our system. It's important to note that we want the manager to check the health of tasks only in `Running` or `Failed` states. Tasks in `Pending` or `Scheduled` states are in the process of being started, so we don't want to attempt calling their health checks at this point. And the `Completed` state is terminal, meaning the task has stopped normally and is in the expected state.

The process we'll use to check the health of individual tasks will involve iterating over the tasks in the manager's `TaskDb`. If a task is in the `Running` state, it will call the task's health check endpoint and attempt to restart the task if the health check fails. If a task is in the `Failed` state, there is no reason to call its health check, so we move on and attempt to restart the task. We can summarize this process like this:

- If the task is in the `Running` state, call the manager's `checkTaskHealth` method, which, in turn, will call the task's health check endpoint.
- If the task's health check fails, attempt to restart the task.
- If the task is in the `Failed` state, attempt to restart the task.

This process is coded as you see in the `doHealthChecks` method in listing 9.9. Notice that we are only attempting to restart failed tasks if their `RestartCount` field is less than 3. We are arbitrarily choosing to only attempt to restart failed tasks three times. If we were writing a production-quality system, we would likely do something smarter and much more sophisticated.

Listing 9.9   The manager's `doHealthChecks` method

```go
func (m *Manager) doHealthChecks() {
    for _, t := range m.GetTasks() {
        if t.State == task.Running && t.RestartCount < 3 {
            err := m.checkTaskHealth(*t)
            if err != nil {
                if t.RestartCount < 3 {
                    m.restartTask(t)
                }
            }
        } else if t.State == task.Failed && t.RestartCount < 3 {
            m.restartTask(t)
        }
    }
}
```

The `doHealthChecks` method calls the `restartTask` method, which is responsible for restarting tasks that have failed, as shown in listing 9.10. Despite the number of lines involved, this code is fairly straightforward. Because our manager is naively attempting to restart the task on the same worker where the task was originally scheduled, it looks up that worker in its `TaskWorkerMap` using the task's `task.ID` field. Next, it changes the task's state to `Scheduled` and increments the task's `RestartCount`. Then it overwrites the existing task in the `TaskDb` datastore to ensure the manager has the correct state of the task. At this point, the rest of the code should look familiar. It creates a `task.TaskEvent`, adds the `task` to it, and then marshals the `TaskEvent` into JSON. Using the JSON-encoded `TaskEvent`, it sends a POST request to the worker's API to restart the task.

Listing 9.10   The manager's new `restartTask` method

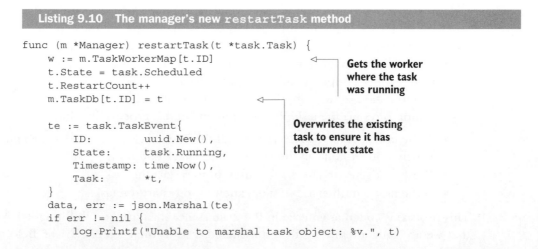

```go
func (m *Manager) restartTask(t *task.Task) {
    w := m.TaskWorkerMap[t.ID]          ◁──── Gets the worker
    t.State = task.Scheduled                   where the task
    t.RestartCount++                           was running
    m.TaskDb[t.ID] = t          ◁────
                                       Overwrites the existing
    te := task.TaskEvent{              task to ensure it has
        ID:        uuid.New(),         the current state
        State:     task.Running,
        Timestamp: time.Now(),
        Task:      *t,
    }
    data, err := json.Marshal(te)
    if err != nil {
        log.Printf("Unable to marshal task object: %v.", t)
```

```
            return
    }

    url := fmt.Sprintf("http://%s/tasks", w)
    resp, err := http.Post(url, "application/json", bytes.NewBuffer(data))
    if err != nil {
        log.Printf("Error connecting to %v: %v", w, err)
        m.Pending.Enqueue(t)
        return
    }

    d := json.NewDecoder(resp.Body)
    if resp.StatusCode != http.StatusCreated {
        e := worker.ErrResponse{}
        err := d.Decode(&e)
        if err != nil {
            fmt.Printf("Error decoding response: %s\n", err.Error())
            return
        }
        log.Printf("Response error (%d): %s", e.HTTPStatusCode, e.Message)
        return
    }

    newTask := task.Task{}
    err = d.Decode(&newTask)
    if err != nil {
        fmt.Printf("Error decoding response: %s\n", err.Error())
        return
    }
    log.Printf("%#v\n", t)
}
```

With the low-level details implemented, we can wrap the necessary coding for the manager by writing the `DoHealthChecks` method, as in the following listing. This method will be used to run the manager's health checking functionality in a separate goroutine.

Listing 9.11 The `DoHealthChecks` method wrapping the `doHealthChecks` method

```
func (m *Manager) DoHealthChecks() {
    for {
        log.Println("Performing task health check")
        m.doHealthChecks()
        log.Println("Task health checks completed")
        log.Println("Sleeping for 60 seconds")
        time.Sleep(60 * time.Second)
    }
}
```

9.5 *Putting it all together*

To test our code and see it work, we'll need a task that implements a health check. Also, we'll want a way to trigger it to fail so our manager will attempt to restart it. We can use the echo service mentioned at the beginning of the chapter for this purpose.

To run it, use this command:

```
$ docker run -p 7777:7777 --name echo timboring/echo-server:latest
```

The echo service implements three endpoints. Calling the root endpoint / with a POST and a JSON-encoded request body will simply echo a JSON request body back in a response body:

```
$ curl -X POST http://localhost:7777/ -d '{"Msg": "hello world"}'
{"Msg":"hello world"}
```

Calling the /health endpoint with a GET will return an empty body with a 200 OK response:

```
$ curl -v http://localhost:7777/health
*    Trying 127.0.0.1:7777...
* Connected to localhost (127.0.0.1) port 7777 (#0)
> GET /health HTTP/1.1
> Host: localhost:7777
> User-Agent: curl/7.83.1
> Accept: */*
>
* Mark bundle as not supporting multiuse
< HTTP/1.1 200 OK
< Date: Sun, 12 Jun 2022 16:17:02 GMT
< Content-Length: 2
< Content-Type: text/plain; charset=utf-8
<
* Connection #0 to host localhost left intact
OK
```

Finally, calling the /healthfail endpoint with a GET will return an empty body with a 500 Internal Server Error response:

```
$ curl -v http://localhost:7777/healthfail
*    Trying 127.0.0.1:7777...
* Connected to localhost (127.0.0.1) port 7777 (#0)
> GET /healthfail HTTP/1.1
> Host: localhost:7777
> User-Agent: curl/7.83.1
> Accept: */*
>
* Mark bundle as not supporting multiuse
< HTTP/1.1 500 Internal Server Error
< Date: Sun, 12 Jun 2022 16:17:45 GMT
< Content-Length: 21
< Content-Type: text/plain; charset=utf-8
<
* Connection #0 to host localhost left intact
Internal server error
```

At this point, we can start up our worker and manager locally. We only need to make two tweaks to the code in the `main.go` file from chapter 8. The first is to call the new `UpdateTasks` method on our worker. The second is to call the new `DoHealthChecks` method on our manager. The rest of the code remains the same and results in the worker and manager starting up.

> **Listing 9.12 Adding `UpdateTasks` and `DoHealthChecks` methods to `main.go`**

```go
func main() {
    w := worker.Worker{
        Queue: *queue.New(),
        Db:    make(map[uuid.UUID]*task.Task),
    }
    wapi := worker.Api{Address: whost, Port: wport, Worker: &w}

    go w.RunTasks()
    go w.CollectStats()
    go w.UpdateTasks()
    go wapi.Start()

    m := manager.New(workers)
    mapi := manager.Api{Address: mhost, Port: mport, Manager: m}

    go m.ProcessTasks()
    go m.UpdateTasks()
    go m.DoHealthChecks()

    mapi.Start()

}
```

When we start up the worker and manager, we should see familiar output like this:

```
2022/06/12 12:25:52 Sleeping for 15 seconds
2022/06/12 12:25:52 Collecting stats
2022/06/12 12:25:52 Checking for task updates from workers
2022/06/12 12:25:52 Checking worker localhost:5555 for task updates
2022/06/12 12:25:52 No tasks to process currently.
2022/06/12 12:25:52 Sleeping for 10 seconds.
2022/06/12 12:25:52 Processing any tasks in the queue
2022/06/12 12:25:52 No work in the queue
2022/06/12 12:25:52 Sleeping for 10 seconds
2022/06/12 12:25:52 Performing task health check
2022/06/12 12:25:52 Task health checks completed
2022/06/12 12:25:52 Sleeping for 60 seconds
2022/06/12 12:25:52 Task updates completed
2022/06/12 12:25:52 Sleeping for 15 seconds
```

We can verify that the worker and manager are indeed working as expected by sending requests to their APIs:

```
# querying the worker API
$ curl localhost:5555/tasks
[]

# querying the manager API
$ curl localhost:5556/tasks
[]
```

As we'd expect, both the worker and manager return empty lists for their respective
/tasks endpoints.

Let's create a task so the manager can start it up. To simplify the process, create a
file called task1.json, and add the JSON in the following listing. We can store a task
in JSON format in a file and pass the file to the curl command, thus saving us time
and confusion.

Listing 9.13   Storing a task in a file

```
{
    "ID": "a7aa1d44-08f6-443e-9378-f5884311019e",
    "State": 2,
    "Task": {
        "State": 1,
        "ID": "bb1d59ef-9fc1-4e4b-a44d-db571eeed203",
        "Name": "test-chapter-9.1",
        "Image": "timboring/echo-server:latest",
        "ExposedPorts": {
            "7777/tcp": {}
        },
        "PortBindings": {
            "7777/tcp": "7777"
        },
        "HealthCheck": "/health"
    }
}
```

Next, let's make a POST request to the manager using this JSON as a request body:

```
$ curl -v -X POST localhost:5556/tasks -d @task1.json
```

When we submit the task to the manager, we should see the manager and worker
going through their normal paces to create the task. Ultimately, we should see the task
in a running state if we query the manager:

```
$ curl http://localhost:5556/tasks|jq
[
  {
    "ID": "bb1d59ef-9fc1-4e4b-a44d-db571eeed203",
    "ContainerID":
      "fbdcb43461134fc20cafdfcdadc4cc905571c386908b15428d2cba4fa09be270",
    "Name": "test-chapter-9.1",
    "State": 2,
    "Image": "timboring/echo-server:latest",
```

```
    "Cpu": 0,
    "Memory": 0,
    "Disk": 0,
    "ExposedPorts": {
      "7777/tcp": {}
    },
    "HostPorts": {
      "7777/tcp": [
        {
          "HostIp": "0.0.0.0",
          "HostPort": "49155"
        },
        {
          "HostIp": "::",
          "HostPort": "49154"
        }
      ]
    },
    "PortBindings": {
      "7777/tcp": "7777"
    },
    "RestartPolicy": "",
    "StartTime": "0001-01-01T00:00:00Z",
    "FinishTime": "0001-01-01T00:00:00Z",
    "HealthCheck": "/health",
    "RestartCount": 0
  }
]
```

And we should eventually see output from the manager showing it calling the task's health check:

```
2022/06/12 13:17:13 Performing task health check
2022/06/12 13:17:13 Calling health check for task
➡ bb1d59ef-9fc1-4e4b-a44d-db571eeed203: /health
2022/06/12 13:17:13 Calling health check for task
➡ bb1d59ef-9fc1-4e4b-a44d-db571eeed203: http://localhost:49155/health
2022/06/12 13:17:13 Task bb1d59ef-9fc1-4e4b-a44d-db571eeed203
➡ health check response: 200
2022/06/12 13:17:13 Task health checks completed
```

This is good news. We can see that our health-checking strategy is working. Well, at least in the case of a healthy task! What happens in the case of an unhealthy one?

To see what happens if a task's health check fails, let's submit another task to the manager. This time, we're going to set the task's health check endpoint to /healthfail. The JSON definition for our second task includes a health check that will result in a non-200 response.

> **Listing 9.14 The JSON definition for our second task**

```
{

    "ID": "6be4cb6b-61d1-40cb-bc7b-9cacefefa60c",
    "State": 2,
```

```
    "Task": {
        "State": 1,
        "ID": "21b23589-5d2d-4731-b5c9-a97e9832d021",
        "Name": "test-chapter-9.2",
        "Image": "timboring/echo-server:latest",
        "ExposedPorts": {
            "7777/tcp": {}
        },
        "PortBindings": {
            "7777/tcp": "7777"
        },
        "HealthCheck": "/healthfail"
    }
}
```

If we watch the output in the terminal where our worker and manager are running, we should eventually see the call to this task's /healthfail endpoint return a non-200 response:

```
2022/06/12 13:37:30 Calling health check for task
➥ 21b23589-5d2d-4731-b5c9-a97e9832d021: /healthfail
2022/06/12 13:37:30 Calling health check for task
➥ 21b23589-5d2d-4731-b5c9-a97e9832d021: http://localhost:49160/healthfail
2022/06/12 13:37:30 Error health check for task
➥ 21b23589-5d2d-4731-b5c9-a97e9832d021 did not return 200
```

As a result of this health check failure, we should see the manager attempt to restart the task:

```
2022/06/12 13:37:30 Added task 21b23589-5d2d-4731-b5c9-a97e9832d021
```

This process should continue until the task has been restarted three times, after which the manager will stop trying to restart the task, thus leaving it in the Running state. We can see this by querying the manager's API and looking at the task's State and RetryCount fields:

```
{
    "ID": "21b23589-5d2d-4731-b5c9-a97e9832d021",
    "ContainerID":
    ➥ "acb37c0c2577461cae93c50b894eccfdbc363a6c51ea2255c8314cc35c91e702",
    "Name": "test-chapter-9.2",
    "State": 2,
    "Image": "timboring/echo-server:latest",
    // other fields omitted
    "RestartCount": 3
}
```

In addition to restarting tasks when their health check fails, this strategy also works in the case where a task dies. For example, we can simulate the situation of a task dying by stopping the task's container manually using the docker stop command. Let's do this for the first task we created, which should still be running:

```
2022/06/12 14:14:08 Performing task health check
2022/06/12 14:14:08 Calling health check for task
➡ bb1d59ef-9fc1-4e4b-a44d-db571eeed203: /health
2022/06/12 14:14:08 Calling health check for task
➡ bb1d59ef-9fc1-4e4b-a44d-db571eeed203: http://localhost:49169/health
2022/06/12 14:14:08 Error connecting to health check
➡ http://localhost:49169/health
2022/06/12 14:14:08 Added task bb1d59ef-9fc1-4e4b-a44d-db571eeed203
```

We should then see the container running again:

```
$ docker ps
CONTAINER ID    IMAGE                          CREATED          STATUS
1d75e69fa804    timboring/echo-server:latest   36 seconds ago   Up 36 seconds
```

And if we query the manager's API, we should see that the task has a `RestartCount` of 1:

```
$ curl http://localhost:5556/tasks|jq
[
  {
    "ID": "bb1d59ef-9fc1-4e4b-a44d-db571eeed203",
    "ContainerID":
    ➡ "1d75e69fa80431b39980ba605bccdb2e049d39d44afa32cd3471d3d987209bf3",
    "Name": "test-chapter-9.1",
    "State": 2,
    "Image": "timboring/echo-server:latest",
    // other fields omitted
    "RestartCount": 1
  }
]
```

Summary

- Failures happen all the time, and the causes can be numerous.
- Handling failures in an orchestration system is complex. We can implement task-level health checking as a strategy to handle a small number of failure scenarios.
- An orchestration system can automate the process of recovering from task failures up to a certain point. Past a certain point, however, the best it can do is provide useful debugging information that helps administrators and application owners troubleshoot the problem further. (Note that we did not do this for our orchestration system. If you're curious, you can try to implement something like task logging.)

Part 4

Refactorings

The fourth part of the book walks you through two refactoring exercises.

In chapter 10, we will design a scheduler interface that we can use to implement multiple concrete schedulers. We will then implement two schedulers: a round-robin scheduler to replace the version of it we implemented in chapter 7 and a more sophisticated scheduler called E-PVM. Then we will refactor the `Manager` object to use this interface.

In chapter 11, we will design a storage interface that allows us to implement multiple concrete storage components. Using this interface, we will implement in-memory and persistent storage components, and then we will refactor the worker and manager to use them.

Implementing a more sophisticated scheduler

10

This chapter covers

- Describing the scheduling problem
- Defining the phases of scheduling
- Re-implementing the round-robin scheduler
- Discussing the enhanced parallel virtual machine (E-PVM) concept and algorithm
- Implementing the E-PVM scheduler

We implemented a simple round-robin scheduler in chapter 7. Now let's return and dig a little deeper into the general problem of scheduling and see how we might implement a more sophisticated scheduler.

10.1 The scheduling problem

Whether we realize it or not, the scheduling problem lives with us in our daily lives. In our homes, we have work to do, like sweeping the floors, cooking meals, washing clothes, mowing the grass, and so on. Depending on the size of our family, we have one or more people to perform the necessary work. If you live by yourself, then you have a single worker, yourself. If you live with a partner, you have two workers. If you live with a partner and children, you have three or more workers.

Now, how do we assign our housework to our workers? Do you take it all on yourself because your partner is taking the kids to soccer practice? Do you mow the grass and wash the clothes, while your partner will sweep the floors and cook dinner after returning from taking the kids to soccer practice? Do you take the kids to soccer practice while your partner cooks dinner, and when you return, your oldest child will mow the grass, and the youngest will do the laundry while your partner sweeps the floors?

In chapter 6, we described the scheduling problem using the scenario of a host seating customers at a busy restaurant on a Friday night. The host has six servers waiting on customers sitting at tables spread across the room. Each customer at each of those tables has different requirements. One customer might be there to have drinks and appetizers with a group of friends they haven't seen in a while. Another customer might be there for a full dinner, complete with an appetizer and dessert. Yet another customer might have strict dietary requirements and only eat plant-based food.

Now a new group of customers walks in. It's a family of four: two adults and two teenage children. Where does the host seat them? Do they place them at the table in the section being served by John, who already has three tables with four customers each? Do they place them at the table in Jill's section, which has six tables with a single customer each? Or do they place them in Willie's section, which has a single table with three customers?

The same scheduling problem also exists in our work lives. Most of us work on a team, and we have work that needs to get done: writing documentation for a new feature or a new piece of infrastructure, fixing a critical bug that a customer reported over the weekend, drafting team goals for the next quarter. How do we divvy up this work among ourselves? As we can see from the previous examples, scheduling is all around us.

10.2   *Scheduling considerations*

When we implemented the round-robin scheduler in chapter 7, we didn't take much into consideration. We just wanted a simple implementation of a scheduler that we could implement quickly so we could focus on other areas of our orchestration system.

There are, however, a wide range of things to consider if we take the time. What goals are we trying to achieve?

- Seating customers as quickly as possible to avoid a large queue of customers having to wait
- Distributing customers evenly across our servers so they get the best service
- Getting customers in and out as quickly as possible because we want high volume

The same considerations exist in an orchestration system. Instead of seating customers at tables, we're placing tasks on machines:

- Do we want the task to be placed and running as quickly as possible?
- Do we want to place the task on a machine that is best capable of meeting the unique needs of the task?
- Do we want to place the task on a machine that will distribute the load evenly across all of our workers?

10.3 Scheduler interface

Unfortunately, there is no one-size-fits-all approach to scheduling. How we schedule tasks depends on the goals we want to achieve. For this reason, most orchestrators support multiple schedulers. Kubernetes achieves this through scheduling *Profiles* (see https://kubernetes.io/docs/reference/scheduling/config/), while Nomad achieves it through four scheduler types (see https://developer.hashicorp.com/nomad/docs/schedulers).

Like Kubernetes and Nomad, we want to support more than one type of scheduler. We can accomplish this by using an interface. In fact, we already defined such an interface in chapter 2:

```
type Scheduler interface {
    SelectCandidateNodes()
    Score()
    Pick()
}
```

Our interface is simple. It has three methods:

- `SelectCandidateNodes`
- `Score`
- `Pick`

We can think of these methods as the different phases of the scheduling problem, as seen in figure 10.1.

Using just these three methods, we can implement any number of schedulers. However, before we dive into writing any new code, let's revise our `Scheduler` interface with a few more details.

To start, we want our `SelectCandidateNodes` method to accept a task and a list of nodes. As we will soon see, this method acts as a filter early in the scheduling process, reducing the number of possible workers to only those we are confident can run the task. For example, if our task needs 1 GB of disk space because we haven't taken the time to reduce the size of our Docker image, then we only want to consider scheduling the task onto workers that have at least 1 GB of disk space available to download our image. As a result, `SelectCandidateNodes` returns a list of nodes that will, at a minimum, meet the resource requirements of the task.

Next, we want our `Score` method to also accept a task and list of nodes as parameters. This method performs the heavy lifting. Depending on the scheduling algorithm we're implementing, this method assigns a score to each candidate node it receives. Then it returns a `map[string]float64`, where the map key is the name of the node and the value is its score.

Finally, our `Pick` method needs to accept a map of scores (i.e., the output of the `Score` method) and a list of candidate nodes. Then it picks the node with the best score. The definition of *best* is left as an implementation detail.

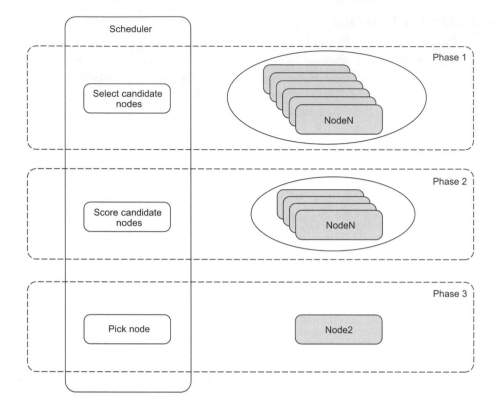

Figure 10.1   The scheduling problem can be broken down into three phases: selecting candidate nodes, scoring candidate nodes, and finally, picking one of the nodes.

Listing 10.1   The updated `Scheduler` interface

```
type Scheduler interface {
    SelectCandidateNodes(t task.Task, nodes []*node.Node) []*node.Node
    Score(t task.Task, nodes []*node.Node) map[string]float64
    Pick(scores map[string]float64, candidates []*node.Node) *node.Node
}
```

10.4   *Adapting the round-robin scheduler to the scheduler interface*

Since we have already implemented a round-robin scheduler, let's adapt that code to our scheduler interface. The sequence diagram in figure 10.2 illustrates how our manager will interact with the `Scheduler` interface to select a node for running a task.

Let's start by opening the `scheduler.go` file and creating the `RoundRobin` struct seen in listing 10.2. Our struct has two fields: `Name`, which allows us to give it a descriptive name, and `LastWorker`, which will take over the role of the field with the same name from the `Manager` struct.

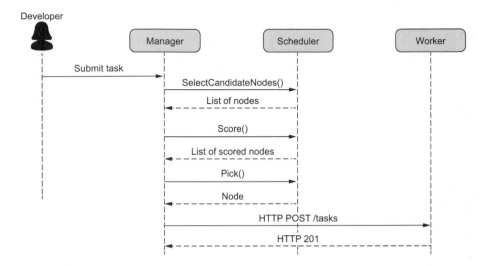

Figure 10.2   Sequence diagram showing the interactions between the manager, scheduler, and worker

---

Listing 10.2   The `RoundRobin` struct

```
type RoundRobin struct {
    Name       string
    LastWorker int
}
```

Next, let's implement the `SelectCandidateNodes` method for our round-robin scheduler. Because we are adapting our original implementation, not improving upon it, we're going to simply return the list of nodes that are passed in as one of the two method parameters. While it might seem a bit silly for this method to just return what it received, the `RoundRobin` scheduler needs to implement this method to meet the contract of the `Scheduler` interface.

Listing 10.3   The `SelectCandidateNodes` method for the round-robin scheduler

```
func (r *RoundRobin) SelectCandidateNodes(t task.Task, nodes []*node.Node)
    []*node.Node {
    return nodes
}
```

Now let's implement the `Score` method for our round-robin implementation. Here we're effectively taking the code from the existing manager's `SelectWorker` method and pasting it into the `Score` method. We do, however, need to make a few modifications.

First, we define the `nodeScores` variable, which is of type `map[string]float64`. This variable will hold the scores we assign to each node. Depending on the number of nodes we're using, the resulting map will look something like this:

```
{
    "node1": 1.0,
    "node2": 0.1,
    "node3": 1.0,
}
```

Second, we iterate over the list of `nodes` that are passed into the method and build our map of `nodeScores`. Notice that our method of scoring is not that sophisticated. We check whether the index is equal to the `newWorker` variable, and if it is, we assign the node a score of `0.1`. If the index is not equal to the `newWorker`, we give it a score of `1.0`. Once we have built our map of `nodeScores`, we return it. Thus, the `Score` method adapts the original code from the manager's `SelectWorker` method to the `Score` method of the `Scheduler` interface.

Listing 10.4   The `Score` method

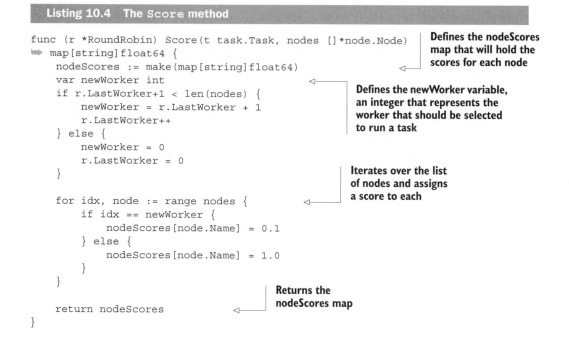

```
func (r *RoundRobin) Score(t task.Task, nodes []*node.Node)
    map[string]float64 {
    nodeScores := make(map[string]float64)
    var newWorker int
    if r.LastWorker+1 < len(nodes) {
        newWorker = r.LastWorker + 1
        r.LastWorker++
    } else {
        newWorker = 0
        r.LastWorker = 0
    }

    for idx, node := range nodes {
        if idx == newWorker {
            nodeScores[node.Name] = 0.1
        } else {
            nodeScores[node.Name] = 1.0
        }
    }

    return nodeScores
}
```

Defines the nodeScores map that will hold the scores for each node

Defines the newWorker variable, an integer that represents the worker that should be selected to run a task

Iterates over the list of nodes and assigns a score to each

Returns the nodeScores map

With the `SelectCandidateNodes` and `Score` methods implemented, let's turn our attention to the final method of the `Scheduler` interface, the `Pick` method. As its name suggests, this method picks the best node to run a task. It accepts a `map[string]float64`, which will be the scores returned from the `Score` method. It also accepts a list of candidate nodes. It returns a single type of a pointer to a `node.Node`.

For the purposes of the round-robin implementation, the best score is the lowest score. So if we had a list of three nodes with scores of 0.1, 1.0, and 1.0, the node with the 0.1 score would be selected.

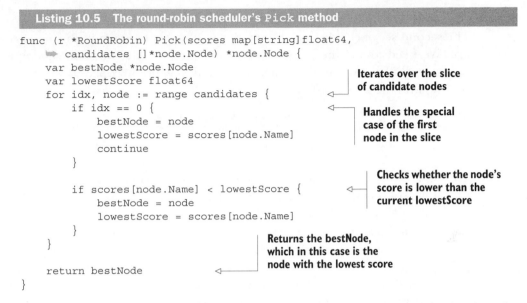

Listing 10.5 The round-robin scheduler's `Pick` method

```
func (r *RoundRobin) Pick(scores map[string]float64,
    candidates []*node.Node) *node.Node {
    var bestNode *node.Node
    var lowestScore float64
    for idx, node := range candidates {
        if idx == 0 {
            bestNode = node
            lowestScore = scores[node.Name]
            continue
        }

        if scores[node.Name] < lowestScore {
            bestNode = node
            lowestScore = scores[node.Name]
        }
    }

    return bestNode
}
```

Iterates over the slice of candidate nodes

Handles the special case of the first node in the slice

Checks whether the node's score is lower than the current lowestScore

Returns the bestNode, which in this case is the node with the lowest score

With the implementation of the `Pick` method, we have completed adapting the round-robin scheduler to the `Scheduler` interface. Now let's see how we can use it.

10.5 Using the new scheduler interface

To use the new `Scheduler` interface, there are a few changes we need to make to the manager. There are three types of changes:

- Adding new fields to the `Manager` struct
- Modifying the `New` helper function in the `manager` package
- Modifying several of the manager's methods to use the scheduler

10.5.1 Adding new fields to the Manager struct

The first set of changes to make is to add two new fields to our `Manager` struct. As you can see in listing 10.6, the first is a field named `WorkerNodes`. This field is a slice of pointers of `node.Node`. It will hold instances of each worker node. The second field we need to add is `Scheduler`, which is our new interface type `scheduler.Scheduler`. As you will see later, defining the `Scheduler` field type as the `Scheduler` interface allows the manager to use any scheduler that implements the interface.

Listing 10.6 Adding the `WorkerNodes` and `Scheduler` fields to the `Manager` struct

```
type Manager struct {
    // previous code not shown

    WorkerNodes    []*node.Node
    Scheduler      scheduler.Scheduler
}
```

10.5.2 *Modifying the New helper function*

The second set of changes involves modifying the New function in the manager package. We need to add the schedulerType parameter to the function signature. This parameter will allow us to create a manager with one of the concrete scheduler types, starting with the RoundRobin type.

Listing 10.7   The New helper function, modified to take a new argument, schedulerType

```
func New(workers []string, schedulerType string) *Manager {
```

The next change to the function happens in the body. We define the variable nodes to hold a slice of pointers to the node.Node type. We're going to perform this work inside the existing loop over the workers slice. Inside this loop, we create a node by calling the node.NewNode function, passing it the name of the worker, the address for the worker's API (e.g., http://192.168.33.17:5556), and the node's role. All three values passed in to the NewNode function are strings. Once we have created the node, we add it to the slice of nodes by calling the built-in append function.

After creating the list of nodes, we can move on to the next-to-last change in the function body. Depending on the schedulerType passed in, we need to create a scheduler of the appropriate type. To do this, we create the variable s to hold the scheduler. Then we use a switch statement to initialize the appropriate scheduler. We start out with only a single case to support the "roundrobin" scheduler. If schedulerType is not "roundrobin" or is the empty string "", then we hit the default case and set a reasonable default. Since we only have a single scheduler right now, we'll just use it.

The final changes to the function are simple. We need to add our list of nodes and our scheduler s to the Manager that we're returning at the end of the function. We do this by adding the slice of nodes to the WorkerNodes field and the scheduler s to the Scheduler field.

Listing 10.8   Changing the New helper function to use the new Scheduler interface

```
func New(workers []string, schedulerType string) *Manager {
    // previous code not shown

    var nodes []*node.Node
    for worker := range workers {
        workerTaskMap[workers[worker]] = []uuid.UUID{}

        nAPI := fmt.Sprintf("http://%v", workers[worker])
        n := node.NewNode(workers[worker], nAPI, "worker")
        nodes = append(nodes, n)
    }

    var s scheduler.Scheduler
    switch schedulerType {
    case "roundrobin":
        s = &scheduler.RoundRobin{Name: "roundrobin"}
```

```
        default:
            s = &scheduler.RoundRobin{Name: "roundrobin"}
        }

        return &Manager{
            Pending:        *queue.New(),
            Workers:        workers,
            TaskDb:         taskDb,
            EventDb:        eventDb,
            WorkerTaskMap:  workerTaskMap,
            TaskWorkerMap:  taskWorkerMap,
            WorkerNodes:    nodes,
            Scheduler:      s,
        }
    }
```

With these changes to the New function, we can now create our manager with different types of schedulers. But we still have more work to do on our manager before it can actually use the scheduler.

The next piece of the Manager type we need to change is the SelectWorker method. We're going to scrap the previous implementation of this method and replace it. Why? Because the previous implementation was specifically geared toward the round-robin scheduling algorithm. With the creation of the Scheduler interface and the RoundRobin implementation of that interface, we need to refactor the SelectWorker method to operate on the scheduler interface.

As you can see in listing 10.9, the SelectWorker method becomes more straightforward. It does the following:

- Calls the manager's Scheduler.SelectCandidateNodes method, passing it the task t and the slice of nodes in the manager's WorkerNodes field. If the call to SelectCandidateNodes results in the candidates variable being nil, we return an error.
- Calls the manager's Scheduler.Score method, passing it the task t and slice of candidates.
- Calls the manager's Scheduler.Pick method, passing it the scores from the previous step and the slice of candidates.
- Returns the selectedNode.

> **Listing 10.9 The SelectWorker method using the Scheduler interface**

```
func (m *Manager) SelectWorker(t task.Task) (*node.Node, error) {
    candidates := m.Scheduler.SelectCandidateNodes(t, m.WorkerNodes)
    if candidates == nil {
        msg := fmt.Sprintf("No available candidates match resource request
    ➥ for task %v", t.ID)
        err := errors.New(msg)
        return nil, err
    }
```

```
    scores := m.Scheduler.Score(t, candidates)
    selectedNode := m.Scheduler.Pick(scores, candidates)

    return selectedNode, nil
}
```

Now let's move on to the `SendWork` method of the manager. In the original version, the beginning of the method looked like that shown in listing 10.10. Notice that we called the `SelectWorker` method first, and we didn't pass it a task. We need to rework the beginning of this method to account for the previous changes we made to the `SelectWorker` method.

Listing 10.10   The original `SendWork` method

```
func (m *Manager) SendWork() {
    if m.Pending.Len() > 0 {
        w := m.SelectWorker()

        e := m.Pending.Dequeue()
        te := e.(task.TaskEvent)
        t := te.Task
        log.Printf("Pulled %v off pending queue\n", t)

        m.EventDb[te.ID] = &te
        m.WorkerTaskMap[w] = append(m.WorkerTaskMap[w], te.Task.ID)
        m.TaskWorkerMap[t.ID] = w
```

Instead of calling the `SelectWorker` method first, we now want to pop a task off the manager's pending queue as the first step. Then we do some accounting work, notably adding the `task.TaskEvent` te to the manager's `EventDb` map. It's only after pulling a task off the queue and doing the necessary accounting work that we then call the new version of `SelectWorker`. Moreover, we pass the task t to the new `SelectWorker` method. Thus, the new `SendWork` method re-orders the steps in the process of sending a task to a worker.

Listing 10.11   The new `SendWork` method

```
func (m *Manager) SendWork() {
    if m.Pending.Len() > 0 {
        e := m.Pending.Dequeue()
        te := e.(task.TaskEvent)
        m.EventDb[te.ID] = &te
        log.Printf("Pulled %v off pending queue", te)

        t := te.Task
        w, err := m.SelectWorker(t)
        if err != nil {
            log.Printf("error selecting worker for task %s: %v\n", t.ID, err)
        }
```

One important thing to note about the previous changes: the type returned from the new implementation of `SelectWorker` is no longer a string. `SelectWorker` now returns a type of `node.Node`. To make this more concrete, the old version of `SelectWorker` returned a string that looked like `192.168.13.13:1234`. So we need to make a few minor adjustments throughout the remainder of the `SendWork` method to replace any usage of the old string value held in the variable `w` with the value of the node's `Name` field. The following listing shows that the `w` variable has changed from a string to a `node.Node` type, so we need to use the `w.Name` field.

Listing 10.12 Using the `w.Name` field

```
m.WorkerTaskMap[w.Name] = append(m.WorkerTaskMap[w.Name], te.Task.ID)
m.TaskWorkerMap[t.ID] = w.Name

url := fmt.Sprintf("http://%s/tasks", w.Name)
}
```

With that, we've completed all the necessary changes to our manager. Well, sort of.

10.6 *Did you notice the bug?*

Up until this chapter, we've been working with a single instance of the worker. This choice made it easier for us to focus on the bigger picture. In the next section, however, we're going to modify our `main.go` program to start three workers.

There is a problem lurking in the manager's `SendWork` method. Notice that it's popping a task off its queue and then selecting a worker where it will send that task. What happens, however, when the task popped off the queue is for an already existing task? The most obvious case for this behavior is stopping a running task. In such a case, the manager already knows about the running task and the associated task event, so we shouldn't create new ones. Instead, we need to check for an existing task and update it as necessary.

Our code in the previous chapters was working by chance. Since we were running a single worker, the `SelectWorker` method only had one choice when it encountered a task intended to stop a running task. Since we're now running three workers, there is a 67% chance that the existing code will select a worker where the existing task to be stopped is *not* running. Let's fix this problem!

To start, let's introduce a new method to our manager, called `stopTask`. This method takes two arguments: a `worker` of type `string` and a `taskID` also of type `string`. From the name of the method and the names of the parameters, it's obvious what the method will do. It uses the `worker` and `taskID` arguments to build a URL to the worker's `/tasks/{taskID}` endpoint. Then it creates a request by calling the `NewRequest` function in the `http` package. Next, it executes the request.

Listing 10.13 The new `stopTask` method

```
func (m *Manager) stopTask(worker string, taskID string) {
    client := &http.Client{}
    url := fmt.Sprintf("http://%s/tasks/%s", worker, taskID)
```

```
req, err := http.NewRequest("DELETE", url, nil)
if err != nil {
    log.Printf("error creating request to delete task %s: %v\n", taskID, err)
    return
}

resp, err := client.Do(req)
if err != nil {
    log.Printf("error connecting to worker at %s: %v\n", url, err)
    return
}

if resp.StatusCode != 204 {
    log.Printf("Error sending request: %v\n", err)
    return
}

log.Printf("task %s has been scheduled to be stopped", taskID)
}
```

Now let's use the `stopTask` method by calling it from the `SendWork` method. We're going to add new code near the beginning of the first `if` statement, which checks the length of the manager's `Pending` queue. Just after the log statement that prints `"Pulled %v off pending queue"`, add a new line, and enter the code after the `//` `new code` comment, as seen in the following listing.

Listing 10.14   Checking for existing tasks and calling the new `stopTask` method

```
// existing code
if m.Pending.Len() > 0 {
    e := m.Pending.Dequeue()
    te := e.(task.TaskEvent)
    m.EventDb[te.ID] = &te
    log.Printf("Pulled %v off pending queue\n", te)

    // new code
    taskWorker, ok := m.TaskWorkerMap[te.Task.ID]
    if ok {
        persistedTask := m.TaskDb[te.Task.ID]
        if te.State == task.Completed &&
        ➡ task.ValidStateTransition(persistedTask.State, te.State) {
            m.stopTask(taskWorker, te.Task.ID.String())
            return
        }

        log.Printf("invalid request: existing task %s is in state %v and
    ➡ cannot transition to the completed state\n",
    ➡ persistedTask.ID.String(), persistedTask.State)
        return
    }
```

Uses the "comma ok" idiom to check for an existing task in the manager's TaskDb

Assigns the existing task to the persistedTask variable

If the state of the task from the Pending queue is task.Completed and the running task can be transitioned from its current state to the completed state, calls the new stopTask method

10.7 Putting it all together

Now that we've made the changes to the manager so it can make use of the new scheduler interface, we're ready to make several changes to our `main.go` program. As I mentioned, in previous chapters, we used a single worker. That choice was mostly one of convenience. However, given that we've implemented a more sophisticated `Scheduler` interface, it'll be more interesting to start up several workers. This will better illustrate how our scheduler works.

The first change in our main program is to create three workers. To do this, we take the same approach as in previous chapters but repeat it three times to create workers `w1`, `w2`, and `w3`, as seen in listing 10.15. After creating each worker, we then create an API for it. Notice that for the first worker, we use the existing `wport` variable for the `Port` field of the `API`. Then, to start multiple APIs, we increment the value of the `wport` variable so each API has a unique port to run on. This saves us from having to specify three different variables when we run the program from the command line.

Listing 10.15 Creating three workers and their APIs

```
w1 := worker.Worker{
        Queue: *queue.New(),
        Db:    make(map[uuid.UUID]*task.Task),
    }
    wapi1 := worker.Api{Address: whost, Port: wport, Worker: &w1}

    w2 := worker.Worker{
        Queue: *queue.New(),
        Db:    make(map[uuid.UUID]*task.Task),
    }
    wapi2 := worker.Api{Address: whost, Port: wport + 1, Worker: &w2}

    w3 := worker.Worker{
        Queue: *queue.New(),
        Db:    make(map[uuid.UUID]*task.Task),
    }
    wapi3 := worker.Api{Address: whost, Port: wport + 2, Worker: &w3}
```

Now that we have our three workers and their APIs, let's start everything up. The process is the same as in past chapters, just doing it once for each worker/API combo.

Listing 10.16 Starting up each worker in the same way as we did for a single worker

```
go w1.RunTasks()
go w1.UpdateTasks()
go wapi1.Start()

go w2.RunTasks()
go w2.UpdateTasks()
go wapi2.Start()
```

```
go w3.RunTasks()
go w3.UpdateTasks()
go wapi3.Start()
```

The next change is to build a slice that contains all three of our workers:

```
workers := []string{
    fmt.Sprintf("%s:%d", whost, wport),
    fmt.Sprintf("%s:%d", whost, wport+1),
    fmt.Sprintf("%s:%d", whost, wport+2),
}
```

Now we need to update the existing call to the manager package's `New` function to specify the type of scheduler we want the manager to use. As you can see, we're going to start by using the `"roundrobin"` scheduler:

```
func main() {
    m := manager.New(workers, "roundrobin")
}
```

With these changes, we can now start up our `main` program. Notice that we start up in the same way, by passing in the necessary environment variables for the worker and manager and then using the command `go run main.go`. Also notice that the output we see looks the same as it has. We see that the program starts up the worker, then it starts up the manager, and then it starts cycling through, checking for new tasks, collecting stats, checking the status of tasks, and attempting to update any existing tasks:

```
$ CUBE_WORKER_HOST=localhost CUBE_WORKER_PORT=5556
➥ CUBE_MANAGER_HOST=localhost CUBE_MANAGER_PORT=5555 go run main.go
Starting Cube worker
Starting Cube manager
2022/11/12 11:28:48 No tasks to process currently.
2022/11/12 11:28:48 Sleeping for 10 seconds.
2022/11/12 11:28:48 Collecting stats
2022/11/12 11:28:48 Checking status of tasks
2022/11/12 11:28:48 Task updates completed
2022/11/12 11:28:48 Sleeping for 15 seconds
2022/11/12 11:28:48 Processing any tasks in the queue
2022/11/12 11:28:48 No work in the queue
2022/11/12 11:28:48 Sleeping for 10 seconds
2022/11/12 11:28:48 Checking for task updates from workers
2022/11/12 11:28:48 Checking worker localhost:5556 for task updates
2022/11/12 11:28:48 Checking worker localhost:5557 for task updates
2022/11/12 11:28:48 Checking worker localhost:5558 for task updates
2022/11/12 11:28:48 Performing task health check
2022/11/12 11:28:48 Task health checks completed
2022/11/12 11:28:48 Sleeping for 60 seconds
```

Next, let's send a task to our manager. We'll use the same command that we have in past chapters to start up an instance of the echo server. The output from the `curl` command looks like what we're used to seeing from previous chapters:

```
$ curl -X POST localhost:5555/tasks -d @task1.json
{
    "ID":"bb1d59ef-9fc1-4e4b-a44d-db571eeed203",
    "ContainerID":"",
    "Name":"test-chapter-9.1",
    "State":1,
    "Image":"timboring/echo-server:latest",
    "Cpu":0,
    "Memory":0,
    "Disk":0,
    "ExposedPorts": {
        "7777/tcp": {}
    },
    "HostPorts":null,
    "PortBindings": {
        "7777/tcp":"7777"
    },
    "RestartPolicy":"",
    "StartTime":"0001-01-01T00:00:00Z",
    "FinishTime":"0001-01-01T00:00:00Z",
    "HealthCheck":"/health",
    "RestartCount":0
}
```

After sending the task to the manager, we should see something like the following in the output of our main program. This should look familiar. The manager is checking its pending queue for tasks, and it finds the task we sent it:

```
2022/11/12 11:40:18 Processing any tasks in the queue
2022/11/12 11:40:18 Pulled {a7aa1d44-08f6-443e-9378-f5884311019e 2
➥ 0001-01-01 00:00:00 +0000 UTC {bb1d59ef-9fc1-4e4b-a44d-db571eeed203
➥ test-chapter-9.1 1 timboring/echo-server:latest 0 0 0 map[7777/tcp:{}]
➥ map[] map[7777/tcp:7777]  0001-01-01 00:00:00 +0000 UTC 0001-01-01
➥ 00:00:00 +0000 UTC /health 0}} off pending queue
```

The following output is from the worker. It shows that the manager selected it when it called its `SelectWorker` method, which calls the `SelectCandidateNodes`, `Score`, and `Pick` methods on the scheduler:

```
Found task in queue: {bb1d59ef-9fc1-4e4b-a44d-db571eeed203  test-chapter-9.1
➥ 1 timboring/echo-server:latest 0 0 0 map[7777/tcp:{}] map[]
➥ map[7777/tcp:7777]  0001-01-01 00:00:00 +0000 UTC 0001-01-01 00:00:00
➥ +0000 UTC /health 0}: 2022/11/12 11:40:28 attempting to transition
➥ from 1 to 1
```

Once the task is running, we can see the manager check it for any updates:

```
2022/11/12 11:40:33 Checking for task updates from workers
2022/11/12 11:40:33 Checking worker localhost:5556 for task updates
2022/11/12 11:40:33 [manager] Attempting to update task
➥ bb1d59ef-9fc1-4e4b-a44d-db571eeed203
2022/11/12 11:40:33 Task updates completed
```

At this point, we can start the other two tasks we've been using in past chapters. Using the `RoundRobin` scheduler, you should notice the manager selecting each of the other two workers in succession.

We can see that the round-robin scheduler works. Now let's implement a second scheduler.

10.8   *The E-PVM scheduler*

The next type of scheduler we're going to implement is more sophisticated than our round-robin scheduler. For our new scheduler, our goal is to spread the tasks across our cluster of worker machines so we minimize the CPU load of each node. In other words, we would rather each node in our cluster do some work and have overhead for any bursts of work.

10.8.1   *The theory*

To accomplish our goal of spreading the load across our cluster, we're going to use an opportunity cost approach to scoring our tasks. It is one of the approaches that Google used for its Borg orchestrator in its early days and is based on the work presented in the paper "An Opportunity Cost Approach for Job Assignment in a Scalable Computing Cluster" (https://mosix.cs.huji.ac.il/pub/ocja.pdf). According to the paper, "the key idea . . . is to convert the total usage of several heterogeneous resources . . . into a single homogeneous "cost." Jobs are then assigned to the machine where they have the lowest cost." The heterogenous resources are CPU and memory. The authors call this method *Enhanced PVM* (where *PVM* stands for *Parallel Virtual Machine*).

The main idea here is that when a new task enters the system and needs to be scheduled, this algorithm will calculate a `marginal_cost` for each machine in our cluster. What does *marginal cost* mean? If each machine has a homogeneous cost that represents the total usage of all its resources, then the marginal cost is the amount by which that homogeneous cost will increase if we add a new task to its workload.

The paper provides us with the pseudocode for this algorithm, as seen in listing 10.17. If the `marginal_cost` of assigning the job to a machine is less than the `MAX_COST`, we assign the machine to `machine_pick`. Once we've iterated through our list of machines, `machine_pick` will contain the machine with the lowest marginal cost. We will slightly modify our implementation of this pseudocode to fit our own purposes.

> Listing 10.17   Pseudocode describing the algorithm used in the E-PVM scheduling method

```
max_jobs = 1;

while () {
    machine_pick = 1; cost = MAX_COST
    repeat {} until (new job j arrives)
    for (each machine m) {
        marginal_cost = power(n, percentage memory utilization on
        ➥ m if j was added) +
```

```
        power(n, (jobs on m + 1/max_jobs) - power(n, memory use on m)
    ➥    - power(n, jobs on m/max_jobs));

        if (marginal_cost < cost) { machine_pick = m; }
    }

    assign job to machine_pick;
    if (jobs on machine_pick > max_jobs) max_jobs = max_jobs * 2;
}
```

10.8.2 *In practice*

Implementing our new scheduler, which we'll call the E-PVM scheduler, will follow a path similar to the one we used to adapt the round-robin algorithm to our scheduler interface. We start by defining the `Epvm` struct. Notice that we're only defining a single field, `Name`, because we don't need to keep track of the last selected node as we did for the round-robin scheduler:

```
type Epvm struct {
    Name string
}
```

Next, we implement the `SelectCandidateNodes` method of the E-PVM scheduler. Unlike the round-robin scheduler, in this version of `SelectCandidateNodes`, we attempt to narrow the list of potential candidates. We do this by checking that the resources the task is requesting are less than the resources the node has available. For our purposes, we're only checking disk because we want to ensure the selected node has the available disk space to download the task's Docker image. The `Epvm` scheduler's `SelectCandidateNodes` method filters out any nodes that can't meet the task's disk requirements.

Listing 10.18 The `Epvm` scheduler's `SelectCandidateNodes` method

```
func (e *Epvm) SelectCandidateNodes(t task.Task, nodes []*node.Node)
    ➥   []*node.Node {
    var candidates []*node.Node
    for node := range nodes {
        if checkDisk(t, nodes[node].Disk-nodes[node].DiskAllocated) {
            candidates = append(candidates, nodes[node])
        }
    }

    return candidates
}

func checkDisk(t task.Task, diskAvailable int64) bool {
    return t.Disk <= diskAvailable
}
```

Now let's dive into the meat of the E-PVM scheduler. It's time to implement the `Score` method based on the E-PVM pseudocode.

We start by defining a couple of variables that we'll use later in the method. The first variable we define is `nodeScores`, which is a type of `map[string]float64` and will hold the scores of each node. Next we define the `maxJobs` variable. We are randomly setting it to the value of `4.0`, meaning each node can handle four tasks at most. I chose this value because I initially developed the code for this book using a cluster of several Raspberry Pis, and it seemed like a reasonable guess as to how many tasks each Pi could handle. In a production system, we would tune this value based on an analysis of observed metrics from our running production system.

The next step is to iterate over each of our `nodes` passed into the method and calculate the marginal cost of assigning the task to the node. This process involves eight steps.

To calculate the node's current CPU usage, we use the `calculateCpuUsage` helper function defined later. Then we call the `calculateLoad` helper function. This function takes two parameters, `usage` and `capacity`. The `usage` value we get from the previous call to `calculateCpuUsage`, and for the capacity, we use a fraction of what we think our max load will be. This definition of usage comes from the E-PVM paper, which assumes that the maximum possible load is "the smallest integer power of two greater than the largest load we have seen at any given time." Again, given that I originally developed this code using Raspberry Pis, and only three of them at that, I guessed that the highest load seen on any of the nodes was 80%.

The E-PVM scheduler's `Score` has the same signature as the one in the `RoundRobin` scheduler, but it calculates scores in a more complicated way.

Listing 10.19 Signature of the E-PVM scheduler's `Score`

```
const (
    // LIEB square ice constant
    // https://en.wikipedia.org/wiki/Lieb%27s_square_ice_constant
    LIEB = 1.53960071783900203869
)

func (e *Epvm) Score(t task.Task, nodes []*node.Node) map[string]float64 {
    nodeScores := make(map[string]float64)
    maxJobs := 4.0

    for _, node := range nodes {
        cpuUsage := calculateCpuUsage(node)
        cpuLoad := calculateLoad(cpuUsage, math.Pow(2, 0.8))

        memoryAllocated := float64(node.Stats.MemUsedKb()) +
        ➥ float64(node.MemoryAllocated)
        memoryPercentAllocated := memoryAllocated / float64(node.Memory)

        newMemPercent := (calculateLoad(memoryAllocated +
        ➥ float64(t.Memory/1000), float64(node.Memory)))

        memCost := math.Pow(LIEB, newMemPercent) + math.Pow(LIEB,
        ➥ (float64(node.TaskCount+1))/maxJobs) -
        ➥ math.Pow(LIEB, memoryPercentAllocated) -
        ➥ math.Pow(LIEB, float64(node.TaskCount)/float64(maxJobs))
```

```
      cpuCost := math.Pow(LIEB, cpuLoad) +
⮕         math.Pow(LIEB, (float64(node.TaskCount+1))/maxJobs) -
⮕         math.Pow(LIEB, cpuLoad) -
⮕         math.Pow(LIEB, float64(node.TaskCount)/float64(maxJobs))

      nodeScores[node.Name] = memCost + cpuCost
          nodeScores[node.Name] = marginalCost
      }
   }
   return nodeScores
}
```

Our score method uses two helper functions to calculate CPU usage and load. The
first of these helpers, `calculateCpuUsage`, is itself a multistep process. The code for
this function is based on the algorithm presented in the Stack Overflow post at
https://stackoverflow.com/a/23376195. I won't go into more details about this algorithm because the post does a good job of covering the topic. I'd urge you to read it if
you are interested.

Listing 10.20   The `calculateCpuUsage` helper function

```
func calculateCpuUsage(node *node.Node) *float64 {
    stat1 := getNodeStats(node)
    time.Sleep(3 * time.Second)
    stat2 := getNodeStats(node)

    stat1Idle := stat1.CpuStats.Idle + stat1.CpuStats.IOWait
    stat2Idle := stat2.CpuStats.Idle + stat2.CpuStats.IOWait

    stat1NonIdle := stat1.CpuStats.User + stat1.CpuStats.Nice +
⮕      stat1.CpuStats.System + stat1.CpuStats.IRQ +
⮕      stat1.CpuStats.SoftIRQ + stat1.CpuStats.Steal

    stat2NonIdle := stat2.CpuStats.User + stat2.CpuStats.Nice +
⮕      stat2.CpuStats.System + stat2.CpuStats.IRQ +
⮕      stat2.CpuStats.SoftIRQ + stat2.CpuStats.Steal

    stat1Total := stat1Idle + stat1NonIdle
    stat2Total := stat2Idle + stat2NonIdle

    total := stat2Total - stat1Total
    idle := stat2Idle - stat1Idle

    var cpuPercentUsage float64
    if total == 0 && idle == 0 {
        cpuPercentUsage = 0.00
    } else {
        cpuPercentUsage = (float64(total) - float64(idle)) / float64(total)
    }
    return &cpuPercentUsage
}
```

Note that this function uses a second helper function, getNodeStats. This function, seen in the following listing, is calling the /stats endpoint on the worker node and retrieving the worker's stats at that point in time.

Listing 10.21 The getNodeStats helper function returning the stats for a given node

```
func getNodeStats(node *node.Node) *stats.Stats {
    url := fmt.Sprintf("%s/stats", node.Api)
    resp, err := http.Get(url)
    if err != nil {
        log.Printf("Error connecting to %v: %v", node.Api, err)
    }

    if resp.StatusCode != 200 {
        log.Printf("Error retrieving stats from %v: %v", node.Api, err)
    }

    defer resp.Body.Close()
    body, _ := ioutil.ReadAll(resp.Body)
    var stats stats.Stats
    json.Unmarshal(body, &stats)
    return &stats
}
```

The third helper function used by our Score method is the calculateLoad function. This function is much simpler than the calculateCpuUsage function. It takes two parameters: usage, which is of type float64, and capacity, also a float64 type. Then it simply divides usage by capacity and returns the result:

```
func calculateLoad(usage float64, capacity float64) float64 {
    return usage / capacity
}
```

The final method of our E-PVM scheduler to implement is the Pick method. This method is similar to the same method in the round-robin scheduler. It differs only in changing the name of the lowestScore variable to minCost to reflect the shift to the E-PVM scheduler's focus on marginal cost. Otherwise, the method performs the same basic purpose: to select the node with the minimum, or lowest, cost. The E-PVM scheduler's Pick method, as shown in the following listing, is almost identical to the one in the RoundRobin scheduler.

Listing 10.22 The E-PVM scheduler's Pick method

```
func (e *Epvm) Pick(scores map[string]float64, candidates []*node.Node)
    *node.Node {
    minCost := 0.00
    var bestNode *node.Node
    for idx, node := range candidates {
        if idx == 0 {
            minCost = scores[node.Name]
```

```
            bestNode = node
            continue
        }

        if scores[node.Name] < minCost {
            minCost = scores[node.Name]
            bestNode = node
        }
    }
    return bestNode
}
```

With the implementation of the `Pick` method, we have completed the implementation of our second scheduler. This scheduler, like the round-robin scheduler, implements the `Scheduler` interface. As a result, we can use either scheduler in our manager. Before we change our `main.go` program to use this new scheduler, however, let's take a minor detour and take care of some unfinished business.

10.9 Completing the Node implementation

Earlier, we implemented a helper function named `getNodeStats`. This function takes a variable `node`, which is a pointer to a `node.Node` type. As the name of the function suggests, it communicates with the node by making a GET call to the node's `/stats` endpoint. It then returns the resulting stats from the node as a pointer to a `stats.Stats` type. This function is part of the scheduler, so it's awkward to have it handle the lower-level details of calling the node's `/stats` endpoint, checking the response, and decoding the response from JSON.

Let's factor this code out of the scheduler and put it where it really belongs—in the `Node` type. We implemented the `Node` type back in chapter 2, so let's review what it looks like since it has been a while since we've seen it.

The `Node` type is pretty straightforward, as we can see in the next listing. Its fields hold the values that represent various attributes of our physical or virtual machine that's performing the role of the worker.

Listing 10.23 The `Node` type defined in chapter 2

```
type Node struct {
    Name            string
    Ip              string
    Cores           int64
    Memory          int64
    MemoryAllocated int64
    Disk            int64
    DiskAllocated   int64
    Stats           stats.Stats
    Role            string
    TaskCount       int
}
```

Before we actually move the getNodesStats function, let's implement another helper function. We'll name this helper function HTTPWithRetry, and we're going to use it from the getNodesStats function. HTTPWithRetry will ensure we can (eventually) get the stats from a worker even in the case where a worker experiences transient problems—say, for example, the node rebooted or there is a temporary network problem. So rather than simply failing after a single attempt to call the /stats endpoint, we make several attempts before giving up.

HTTPWithRetry will take a function f(string) and a string url as arguments. The f(string) argument will be an HTTP method from the net/http package (e.g., http.Get). The function returns a pointer to the HTTP response and potentially an error. When we call HTTPWithRetry, it will look like this:

```
result, err := utils.HTTPWithRetry(http.Get, "http://localhost:5556/stats")
```

In the body of the function, we initialize a counter, count, to 10. Then we use the counter in a for loop, where we call the function f(string) and check the response. If the function returns an error, we sleep for 5 seconds and then try again. If the function is successful, we break out of the loop. Finally, we return the HTTP response and an error.

We're going to place the HTTPWithRetry function in its own package. Create a new directory in your project called utils, and inside that directory, create a file named retry.go. Inside this file, let's add the code from the following listing.

> Listing 10.24   The HTTPWithRetry helper function in the new utils package

```
package utils

import (
    "fmt"
    "net/http"
    "time"
)

func HTTPWithRetry(f func(string) (*http.Response, error), url string)
    (*http.Response, error) {
    count := 10
    var resp *http.Response
    var err error
    for i := 0; i < count; i++ {
        resp, err = f(url)
        if err != nil {
            fmt.Printf("Error calling url %v\n", url)
            time.Sleep(5 * time.Second)
        } else {
            break
        }
    }
    return resp, err
}
```

With the `HTTPWithRetry` helper defined, let's return to the `getNodesStats` function. Remove it from our `scheduler.go` file, and add it to the `node.go` file in the `node/` package directory. As part of this moving process, let's also change the name to `Get-Stats` and make it a method of the `node.Node` type.

Listing 10.25 Renaming the `getNodeStats` helper function

```
func (n *Node) GetStats() (*stats.Stats, error) {
    var resp *http.Response
    var err error

    url := fmt.Sprintf("%s/stats", n.Api)
    resp, err = utils.HTTPWithRetry(http.Get, url)
    if err != nil {
        msg := fmt.Sprintf("Unable to connect to %v. Permanent failure.\n",
        ⮩ n.Api)
        log.Println(msg)
        return nil, errors.New(msg)
    }

    if resp.StatusCode != 200 {
        msg := fmt.Sprintf("Error retrieving stats from %v: %v", n.Api, err)
        log.Println(msg)
        return nil, errors.New(msg)
    }

    defer resp.Body.Close()
    body, _ := ioutil.ReadAll(resp.Body)
    var stats stats.Stats
    err = json.Unmarshal(body, &stats)
    if err != nil {
        msg := fmt.Sprintf("error decoding message while getting stats for
        ⮩ node %s", n.Name)
        log.Println(msg)
        return nil, errors.New(msg)
    }

    n.Memory = int64(stats.MemTotalKb())
    n.Disk = int64(stats.DiskTotal())

    n.Stats = stats

    return &n.Stats, nil
}
```

With the `GetStats` method now implemented on the `Node` type, we can remove the old `getNodeStats` helper function from `scheduler.go`. And finally, we can update the `calculateCpuUsage` helper function to use the `node.GetStats` method. In addition to using the `node.GetStats` method, let's also change the function signature to return a pointer to a `float64` and an `error`. The changed function looks like this:

```
func calculateCpuUsage(node *node.Node) (*float64, error) {
    //stat1 := getNodeStats(node)
    stat1, err := node.GetStats()
    if err != nil {
        return nil, err
    }
    time.Sleep(3 * time.Second)
    //stat2 := getNodeStats(node)
    stat2, err := node.GetStats()
    if err != nil {
        return nil, err
    }

    // unchanged code

    return &cpuPercentUsage, nil
```

The `GetStats` helper calls a node's worker API, so we need to expose the `/stats` endpoint on the worker `Api` type. This change is simple:

```
func (a *Api) initRouter() {
    // previous code unchanged

    a.Router.Route("/stats", func(r chi.Router) {
        r.Get("/", a.GetStatsHandler)
    })
}
```

With these changes, we have completed our detour. Now let's return to our fancy new E-PVM scheduler and take it for a spin!

10.10 *Using the E-PVM scheduler*

At this point, we have all the work completed on our shiny new scheduler interface. We have two types of schedulers we can use in our manager: the round-robin scheduler and the E-PVM scheduler. We have already made most of the necessary changes to use the scheduler interface, but we have a few minor tweaks to make that will allow us to easily switch between the `RoundRobin` and `Epvm` scheduler types implemented previously.

The first change to make involves adding a new `case` to the `switch` statement in the manager's `New` function. The new case adds support for the `Epvm` scheduler.

Listing 10.26   Adding a new "epvm" case to the `switch` statement

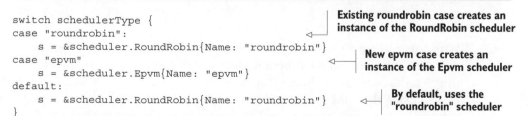

```
switch schedulerType {
case "roundrobin":
    s = &scheduler.RoundRobin{Name: "roundrobin"}
case "epvm"
    s = &scheduler.Epvm{Name: "epvm"}
default:
    s = &scheduler.RoundRobin{Name: "roundrobin"}
}
```

Existing roundrobin case creates an instance of the RoundRobin scheduler

New epvm case creates an instance of the Epvm scheduler

By default, uses the "roundrobin" scheduler

The second and final change happens in our `main.go` program. If you recall, we previously created a new instance of the manager with the `"roundrobin"` scheduler using the `New` function:

```
func main() {
    m := manager.New(workers, "roundrobin")
}
```

Now, however, we want to create an instance of the manager that will use the `Epvm` scheduler. To do this, we can simply change the string in the call to `New` from roundrobin to epvm:

```
func main() {
    m := manager.New(workers, "epvm")
}
```

That's it! We can now run our main program, and it will use the `Epvm` scheduler instead of the `RoundRobin` scheduler. Give it a try!

Summary

- The scheduling problem exists all around us, from home chores to seating customers in a restaurant.
- Scheduling does not have a one-size-fits-all solution. There are multiple solutions, and each one makes tradeoffs based on what we are trying to achieve. It can be as simple as using a round-robin algorithm to select each node in turn. Or it can be as complex as devising a method to calculate a score for each node based on some set of data—for example, the current CPU load and memory usage of each node.
- For the purposes of scheduling tasks in an orchestration system, we can generalize the process to three functions: selecting candidate nodes, which involves reducing the number of possible nodes based on some selection criteria (e.g., does the node have enough disk space to pull the task's container image?); scoring the set of candidate nodes; and finally, picking the best candidate node.
- We can use these three functions to create a general framework to allow us to implement multiple schedulers. In Go, the `interface` is what allows us to create this framework.
- In this chapter, we started three workers, in contrast to a single one in past chapters. Using three workers allowed us to see a more realistic example of how the scheduling process works. However, it's not the same as a more real-world scenario of using multiple physical or virtual machines.

Implementing persistent
storage for tasks

11

This chapter covers

- Describing the purpose of a datastore in an orchestration system
- Defining the requirements for our persistent datastore
- Defining the `Store` interface
- Introducing BoltDB
- Implementing the persistent datastore using the `Store` interface
- Discussing the special concerns that exist for the manager's datastore

The fundamental unit of our orchestration system is the `task`. Up until now, we have been keeping track of this fundamental unit by storing it in Go's built-in `map` type. Both our worker and our manager store their respective tasks in a map. This strategy has served us well, but you may have noticed a major problem with it: any time we restart the worker or the manager, they lose all their tasks. The reason they lose their tasks is that Go's built-in map is an in-memory data structure and is not persisted to disk.

Similar to how we revisited our earlier decisions around scheduling tasks, we're now going to return to our decision about how we store them. We're going to talk briefly about the purpose of a datastore in an orchestration system, and then we're going to start the process of replacing our previous in-memory map datastore with a persistent one.

11.1   The storage problem

Why do we need to store the tasks in our orchestration system? While we haven't talked much about the problem, the storage of tasks is crucial to a working orchestration system. Storing tasks in some kind of datastore enables the higher-level functionality of our system:

- It enables the system to keep track of each task's current state.
- It enables the system to make informed decisions about scheduling.
- It enables the system to help tasks recover from failures.

As we mentioned earlier, our current implementation uses Go's built-in map type, which means we're storing tasks in memory. If we stop the manager and then start it back up because, say, we made a code change, the manager loses the state of all its tasks. We then have no way to recover the system as a whole. If we start our system with three workers and a manager, restarting the manager means we can't gracefully stop running tasks by calling the manager's API. For example, we can't call `curl -X DELETE http:localhost:5555/tasks/1234567890`. The manager no longer has any knowledge of that task.

At a basic level, the solution to the problem is to replace the in-memory map with a persistent datastore. Such a solution will write the task state to disk, thus enabling the manager and worker to be restarted without any loss of state.

11.2   The Store interface

Before jumping directly to a persistent storage solution, let's follow the same process we used in the last chapter. Remember, we didn't just jump straight to the E-PVM scheduler. Instead, we started by creating the `Scheduler` interface, and then we adapted the existing round-robin scheduler to the interface.

The mental model of our store interface looks like that shown in figure 11.1. At the top of the model, we have the `Manager` and `Worker`, each using the same `Store` interface. That interface is abstract, but as we can see, it sits on top of two concrete implementations: an `In-memory Store` and a `Persistent Store`.

If we think about the operations we have been using to store and retrieve tasks and task events, we can identify four methods to create an interface. Those four methods are

- `Put(key string, value interface{})`
- `Get(key)`
- `List()`
- `Count()`

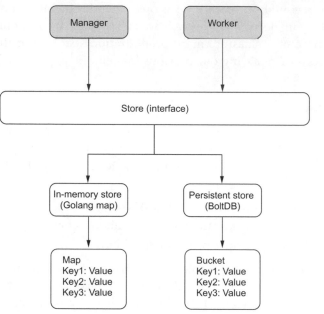

Figure 11.1   **The mental model of our store interface**

NOTE   You might be wondering why the list doesn't include a `Remove` or `Delete` method. Theoretically, the datastore serves as a historical record of the tasks in an orchestration system, so it doesn't make sense to provide a method to remove history. In practice, however, it could be useful to provide such a method. For example, over time, an orchestration system would build up a datastore containing tens of thousands of tasks, if not hundreds of thousands or more. If the datastore supports the `Remove` operation, it could be used to perform maintenance on the datastore itself.

The `Put` method, as its name suggests, puts an item, identified by a `key`, into the store. Until now, we have been interacting with our store by saving tasks and task events directly in a map. For example, in the manager's `SendWork` method, we can see several examples of interacting directly with the `TaskDb` and `EventDb` stores. In the first example, we pop a task event off the manager's `Pending` queue, convert it to the `task .TaskEvent` type, and then store a pointer to the `task.TaskEvent` in the `EventDb` using the task event's ID as the key. In the second example, we extract the task from the task event and then store a pointer to it in the `TaskDb` using the task's ID as the key.

Listing 11.1   Examples of using Go's built-in map to store tasks and events

```
e := m.Pending.Dequeue()
te := e.(task.TaskEvent)
m.EventDb[te.ID] = &te

t := te.Task
```

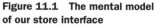

Putting a task event directly into the EventDb map

```
// code hidden for the sake of brevity

t.State = task.Scheduled
                                          ┌─ Putting a task directly
m.TaskDb[t.ID] = &t    ⊲─────────────────┘   into the TaskDb map
```

There is nothing technically wrong with how we've implemented the task and task event stores up to now. It is quick and easy. More importantly, it just works. One downside to this implementation, however, is that it is dependent on the underlying data structure underpinning the store. In this case, the manager must know how to put items into and retrieve them from Go's built-in map. In other words, we have tightly coupled the manager to the built-in map type. We cannot easily change out this implementation of the store for some other implementation. For example, what if we wanted to use SQLite, a popular SQL-based embedded datastore?

To make it easier for us to use different implementations of a datastore, let's create the `Store` interface seen in the next listing. The interface includes the four methods we listed previously, `Put`, `Get`, `List`, and `Count`.

Listing 11.2 The `Store` interface

```
type Store interface {
    Put(key string, value interface{}) error
    Get(key string) (interface{}, error)
    List() (interface{}, error)
    Count() (int, error)
}
```

One thing to note in our `Store` interface is that we have declared several values in the method signatures as being of type `interface{}`. The *empty interface*, as this is called, means that the value can be of any type. For example, the `Put` method takes a `key` that is a string and a `value` that is an empty interface or any type. This means the `Put` method can accept a `value` that is a `task.Task`, `task.TaskEvent`, or some other type.

With the `Store` interface defined, let's move on and implement an in-memory store that can replace our existing one.

11.3 *Implementing an in-memory store for tasks*

We're going to start with an implementation of the task store, and then we'll move on to the task events store. Both the manager and worker use task stores, but only the manager uses an event store. The new implementations of the task and event stores will both wrap Go's built-in map type. By wrapping the built-in map type, we can remove the manager's coupling to the underlying data structure. Instead of needing to understand the mechanics of a map, the manager will simply call the methods of the `Store` interface, and the implementation of the interface will handle all the lower-level details of how to interact with the underlying data structure.

For our purposes, we're going to implement separate types for the task and event stores. We could create a generate store that is able to operate on both tasks and events, but that is more complex and would involve additional concepts that are beyond the scope of this book.

The first implementation is the `InMemoryTaskStore`, which provides a wrapper around Go's built-in map type for the purpose of storing tasks. We start by defining a struct and giving it a single field called `Db`. Not surprisingly, this field is of type `map[string]*task.Task`, the same as the current implementation. Next, let's define a helper function that will return an instance of the `InMemoryTaskStore`. We'll call this helper function `NewInMemoryTaskStore`, and it takes no arguments and returns a pointer to an `InMemoryTaskStore` that has its `Db` field initialized to an empty map of type `map[string]*task.Task`.

Listing 11.3   The `InMemoryTaskStore` struct

```go
type InMemoryTaskStore struct {
    Db map[string]*task.Task
}

func NewInMemoryTaskStore() *InMemoryTaskStore {
    return &InMemoryTaskStore{
        Db: make(map[string]*task.Task),
    }
}
```

Let's move on and implement the `Put` method. The sequence diagram in figure 11.2 shows how the `Put` method will be used. When a user calls the manager's API to start a task (`POST /tasks`), the manager will call the `Put` method to store the task in its own datastore. Then the manager sends the task to the worker by calling the worker's API. The worker, in turn, calls the `Put` method to store the task in its datastore.

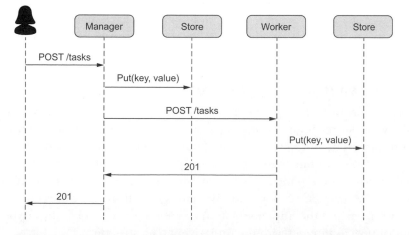

Figure 11.2   Sequence diagram illustrating how the manager and worker save tasks to their respective datastores using the `Put` method

The implementation of the `Put` method, seen in listing 11.4, is fairly straightforward. The method takes two arguments: a `key` that is of type string and a `value` that is of the empty interface type. In the body of the method, we first attempt to convert the `value` to a concrete type using a *type assertion*. What we are doing is asserting that `value` is not `nil` and that the value in `value` is a pointer to a `task.Task`. We also capture a Boolean named `ok`, which tells us whether the assertion was successful. If the assertion is not successful, we return an error; otherwise, we store the task `t` in the map.

Listing 11.4 The `Put` method

```
func (i *InMemoryTaskStore) Put(key string, value interface{}) error {
    t, ok := value.(*task.Task)
    if !ok {
        return fmt.Errorf("value %v is not a task.Task type", value)
    }
    i.Db[key] = t
    return nil
}
```

Next, we'll implement the `Get` method. The sequence diagram in figure 11.3 shows how the `Get` method will be used. When a user calls the manager's API to get a task (`Get /tasks/{taskID}`), the manager will call the `Get` method to retrieve the task from its datastore and return it.

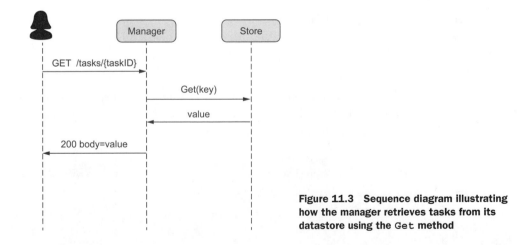

Figure 11.3 Sequence diagram illustrating how the manager retrieves tasks from its datastore using the `Get` method

The implementation of the `Get` method takes a `key` of type string and returns an empty interface and potentially an error. We start by looking for the `key` in the store's `Db`. Notice that we're using the "comma ok" idiom here too. If the `key` exists in `Db`, `t` will contain the task identified by the `key`, and we will return it. If it does not exist, `t` will be `nil`, `ok` will be `false`, and we will return an error.

Listing 11.5   The `Get` method

```go
func (i *InMemoryTaskStore) Get(key string) (interface{}, error) {
    t, ok := i.Db[key]
    if !ok {
        return nil, fmt.Errorf("task with key %s does not exist", key)
    }

    return t, nil
}
```

The next method we'll implement is the `List` method. The `List` method builds up a slice of tasks by ranging over the map. This method always returns `nil` for the `error` value. This is necessary in order to conform to the contract specified by the `Store` interface.

Unlike the `Get` method, which returns a single task, this method returns all the tasks in the store. As you can see in listing 11.6, we start by creating a variable called `tasks` as a slice of pointers to `task.Task`. This slice will hold all the tasks in the store. Then we range over the map in the `Db` field and append each task to the `tasks` slice. Once we've ranged over all the tasks and appended them to the slice, we return it.

Listing 11.6   The `List` method

```go
func (i *InMemoryTaskStore) List() (interface{}, error) {
    var tasks []*task.Task
    for _, t := range i.Db {
        tasks = append(tasks, t)
    }
    return tasks, nil
}
```

The final method in our task store is `Count`. As its name implies, this method returns the number of tasks contained in the store's `Db` field. Because `Db` is a map, we can get the count of items using the built-in `len` function.

Listing 11.7   The `Count` function

```go
func (i *InMemoryTaskStore) Count() (int, error) {
    return len(i.Db), nil
}
```

Now that we've implemented an in-memory version of the task store, let's move on and do the same thing for task events.

11.4 Implementing an in-memory store for task events

The store for the task events will be identical to the one for tasks. The obvious difference will be that the task events store will operate on the `task.TaskEvent` type and not `task.Task`. Because the differences are minor, we won't go into the details.

Listing 11.8 The `InMemoryTaskEventStore`

```go
type InMemoryTaskEventStore struct {
    Db map[string]*task.TaskEvent
}

func NewInMemoryTaskEventStore() *InMemoryTaskEventStore {
    return &InMemoryTaskEventStore{
        Db: make(map[string]*task.TaskEvent),
    }
}

func (i *InMemoryTaskEventStore) Put(key string, value interface{}) error {
    e, ok := value.(*task.TaskEvent)
    if !ok {
        return fmt.Errorf("value %v is not a task.TaskEvent type", value)
    }
    i.Db[key] = e
    return nil
}

func (i *InMemoryTaskEventStore) Get(key string) (interface{}, error) {
    e, ok := i.Db[key]
    if !ok {
        return nil, fmt.Errorf("task event with key %s does not exist", key)
    }

    return e, nil
}

func (i *InMemoryTaskEventStore) List() (interface{}, error) {
    var events []*task.TaskEvent
    for _, e := range i.Db {
        events = append(events, e)
    }
    return events, nil
}

func (i *InMemoryTaskEventStore) Count() (int, error) {
    return len(i.Db), nil
}
```

11.5   *Refactoring the manager to use the new in-memory stores*

At this point, we have defined an interface that will allow us to store tasks and events. We have also implemented two concrete types of our store interface, both of which wrap Go's built-in map type and remove the need for the manager and worker to interact with it directly. Let's make some changes to the manager and worker so they can make use of our new code.

Starting with the manager, we need to update the `TaskDb` and `EventDb` fields on the `Manager` struct. Instead of these fields being of type `map[uuid.UUID]*task.Task` and `map[uuid.UUID]*task.TaskEvent`, let's change them both to be of type `store.Store`. With this change, our manager can now use any kind of store that implements the `store.Store` interface:

```
type Manager struct {
    // fields omitted for convenience
    TaskDb        store.Store
    EventDb       store.Store
    // fields omitted
```

Changing the `TaskDb` and `EventDb` fields to an interface type should look familiar to you. If you remember, in chapter 10, we did something similar when we introduced the `Scheduler` field, which was of type `scheduler.Scheduler`, also an interface. That change allowed us to configure the manager to use different types of schedulers, and now we have configured it to use different types of stores.

Next, let's modify the `New` function in the manager package. In the last chapter, we updated it so it accepted a `schedulerType` in addition to a slice of `workers`. Now let's add another argument to the `New` function, one called `dbType`. The new signature will look like the following:

```
func New(workers []string, schedulerType string, dbType string) *Manager
```

There are several changes to the body of the `New` function that we'll need to make next. The first of these changes is to remove the initialization of the `taskDb` and `eventDb` variables using the `make()` built-in function. Just delete those two lines for now. We're going to do something slightly different here in a bit.

Now we want to change how we're returning from the function. We are currently returning a pointer to the `Manager` type like this:

```
return &Manager{ ... }
```

Instead of returning a pointer using what's called a *struct literal*, let's assign it to a variable named `m`. It will look like the following listing.

Listing 11.9   Assigning a struct literal to the `m` variable instead of returning it

```
m := Manager{
    Pending:       *queue.New(),
    Workers:       workers,
    WorkerTaskMap: workerTaskMap,
    TaskWorkerMap: taskWorkerMap,
    WorkerNodes:   nodes,
    Scheduler:     s,
}
```

At this point, we have an instance of our `Manager` type, but it does not have any stores for tasks and events. We're going to use the `dbType` variable we added to the `New` function's signature as part of a `switch` statement to allow us to set up different types of datastores based on the value of `dbType`. Because we've only implemented in-memory stores, we're going to start by only supporting the case where the value of `dbType` is `memory`. In this case, we call the `NewInMemoryTaskStore` function to create an instance of our in-memory task store, and we call the `NewInMemoryTaskEventStore` function to create an instance of our in-memory event store.

All that's left to do now is to assign the value of the `ts` variable to the manager's `TaskDb` field and assign the `es` value to the manager's `EventDb` field. Then return a pointer to the manager:

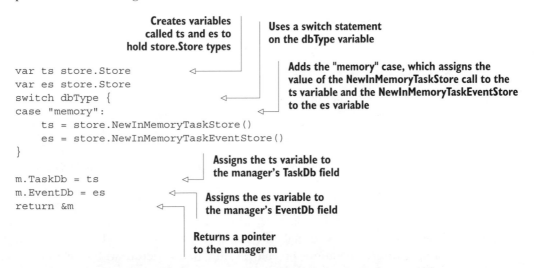

Now we're ready for the substantive changes! We need to change the manager's methods so it interacts with the datastore using the methods of our new `Store` interface instead of operating directly on the map structures. The first method we'll work on is `updateTasks`.

All of the changes we need to make in the `updateTasks` method occur inside the `for` loop that ranges over a slice of pointers to `task.Task` types. The first change to make involves replacing the block of code that checks whether an individual task reported by a worker exists in the manager's task store. The current code uses the "comma ok" idiom to perform this check. We'll replace this block with a call to the store interface's Get method and check the err value to indicate that the task doesn't exist in the manager's store.

We can see this change in listing 11.10. The existing code is commented out, and its replacement follows just afterward. Now our updated code is calling the Get method on the manager's TaskDb store, passing it the ID of the task as a string. If the task exists in the manager's store, it will be assigned to the result variable, and if there is an error, it will be assigned to the err variable. Next, we perform the usual error checking, and if there is an error, we log it and move on to the next task using the continue statement. Finally, we use a type assertion to convert the result, which is of type interface{} to the concrete task.Task type (actually a pointer to a task.Task). If the type assertion fails, we log a message and continue to the next task.

Listing 11.10 Using the new datastore interface to get a task from TaskDb

```
for _, t := range tasks {

    // previous code omitted for convenience

    // existing code to be replaced
    // _, ok := m.TaskDb[t.ID]
    // if !ok {
    //     log.Printf("[manager] Task with ID %s not found\n", t.ID)
    //     continue
    // }

    result, err := m.TaskDb.Get(t.ID.String())
    if err != nil {
            log.Printf("[manager] %s\n", err)
            continue
    }
    taskPersisted, ok := result.(*task.Task)
    if !ok {
            log.Printf("cannot convert result %v to task.Task type\n",
     result)
            continue
    }
```

The last set of changes to make in the updateTasks method involves replacing the remaining direct operations on the existing map structure with calls to the appropriate methods of the Store interface. The existing code can be seen in the next listing. Here we are modifying a task by directly changing its fields in the map.

Listing 11.11 Existing code directly accessing the TaskDB map

```
if m.TaskDb[t.ID].State != t.State {

    m.TaskDb[t.ID].State = t.State

}
```

```
m.TaskDb[t.ID].StartTime = t.StartTime

m.TaskDb[t.ID].FinishTime = t.FinishTime

m.TaskDb[t.ID].ContainerID = t.ContainerID

m.TaskDb[t.ID].HostPorts = t.HostPorts
```

We want to replace the previous code with that shown in listing 11.12. Since we have already retrieved the task from the manager's task store and converted it from an empty interface type to a pointer to the concrete `task.Task` type, we can simply update the necessary fields on the `taskPersisted` variable. Then we finish up by calling the store's `Put` method to save the updated task.

Listing 11.12 Using the new datastore interface to put a task in the TaskDb

```
if taskPersisted.State != t.State {
        taskPersisted.State = t.State
}

taskPersisted.StartTime = t.StartTime
taskPersisted.FinishTime = t.FinishTime
taskPersisted.ContainerID = t.ContainerID
taskPersisted.HostPorts = t.HostPorts

m.TaskDb.Put(taskPersisted.ID.String(), taskPersisted)
```

The `GetTasks` method is the next method we need to update. It uses a `for` loop to range over all the tasks in the manager's task store. Up to now, this method has been ranging directly over the map of tasks. So we need to change `GetTasks` to use the `Store` interface's `List` method, convert the result from a slice of empty interfaces to a slice of pointers to `task.Task` types, and return that slice.

Listing 11.13 The `GetTasks` method

```
func (m *Manager) GetTasks() []*task.Task {
    taskList, err := m.TaskDb.List()
    if err != nil {
        log.Printf("error getting list of tasks: %v\n", err)
        return nil
    }

    return taskList.([]*task.Task)
}
```

> Calls the List method on the manager's TaskDb, assigning the returned value to taskList and any error to the err variable

> Handles any errors from the List method

> Returns the slice of tasks, converting from the empty interface returned by List to a slice of pointers to the task.Task type

The next method that needs updating is the `restartTask` method. This one is easy. It currently has a single interaction with the map built-in, so all we need to do is replace it with a call to the store's `Put` method. So it's just a matter of replacing the first line with the second:

```
// m.TaskDb[t.ID] = t
m.TaskDb.Put(t.ID.String(), t)
```

The final method to update is the `SendWork` method. Despite being a long method that encompasses a multistep process to send tasks to workers, we have only a few updates to make here. The first update involves our first interaction with the new `EventDb` store. We want to change from interacting directly with the old task events map to using the new `EventDb` store. Early on in the `SendWork` method, we popped an event off the manager's `Pending` queue and converted it to `task.TaskEvent` type. Now we want to call the `Put` method on the events store, passing it the event `ID` as a string and a pointer to the task event `te`. If the call to `Put` returns an error, we log it and return.

Listing 11.14 **The first change to the `SendWork` method, using the new `Put` method**

```
e := m.Pending.Dequeue()
te := e.(task.TaskEvent)
err := m.EventDb.Put(te.ID.String(), &te)
if err != nil {
        log.Printf("error attempting to store task event %s: %s\n",
    ➡ te.ID.String(), err)
        return
}
```

The second update involves this method's use of the tasks store. In listing 11.15, we can see the existing code where we are again interacting directly with the `TaskDb` map. Since this code is getting a task from the map, we want to convert the code to use the store interface's `Get` method as we've done previously.

Listing 11.15 **Existing code that gets a task from the store by operating directly on the map**

```
taskWorker, ok := m.TaskWorkerMap[te.Task.ID]
if ok {
        persistedTask := m.TaskDb[te.Task.ID]
        if te.State == task.Completed && task.ValidStateTransition(
    ➡ persistedTask.State, te.State) {
            m.stopTask(taskWorker, te.Task.ID.String())
            return
        }
}
```

To change the code to use our new `Get` method on the store interface, we need to rearrange our code a little:

```
result, err := m.TaskDb.Get(te.Task.ID.String())    ◄─┐
if err != nil {    ◄───┐
```

| | Calls the task store's Get method and assigns the returned task and any error to appropriately named variables |

Handles any errors returned from the call to Get

```
        log.Printf("unable to schedule task: %s", err)
        return
}

persistedTask, ok := result.(*task.Task)
if !ok {
        log.Printf("unable to convert task to task.Task type")
        return
}
```

Uses a type assertion to convert the result to a pointer to a task.Task

Checks that the type assertion was successful

The final update to the SendWork method, and our final update to the manager, involves another change to use the task store's Put method instead of inserting a task directly in a map:

```
t.State = task.Scheduled
// m.TaskDb[t.ID] = &t
m.TaskDb.Put(t.ID.String(), &t)
```

In addition to the changes we just made on the Manager struct, we need to make one small change to the manager's StopTaskHandler method on the API struct. There is one line where we are accessing the manager's TaskDb map directly. Instead, we simply need to change this line to use the Store interface's Get method.

Listing 11.16 Calling the Store interface's Get method

```
// taskToStop, ok := a.Manager.TaskDb[tID]
taskToStop, err := a.Manager.TaskDb.Get(tID.String())
```

11.6 *Refactoring the worker*

At this point, our manager is using the new Store interface. Our worker, however, is not. It's still operating directly on the built-in map type. Let's perform the same refactoring on the worker so it, too, uses the Store interface.

Like the manager, the first order of business is to change the worker's Db type from a map[uuid.UUID]*task.Task to the store.Store interface type. By doing so, it can use any type of store that implements the store.Store interface:

```
type Worker struct {
    // fields omitted
    Db      store.Store
    // fields omitted
}
```

Next, we need to update the New helper function in the worker package. Let's update its function signature to take another argument. This new argument is named taskDbType and is a string. We then create a variable s that is of the new store.Store type. Now we use a switch statement on the taskDbType argument and assign the result of the NewInMemoryTaskStore function call to the variable s. Finally, we assign s to the worker's `Db` field. We can then return a pointer to the worker `w`, which will include the store interface.

Listing 11.17   The `New` helper function creating an instance of the `InMemoryTaskStore`

```
func New(name string, taskDbType string) *Worker {
    w := Worker{
        Name:  name,
        Queue: *queue.New(),
    }

    var s store.Store
    switch taskDbType {
    case "memory":
        s = store.NewInMemoryTaskStore()
    }
    w.Db = s
    return &w
}
```

With the change to the `New` helper function, let's move on to the worker's methods. The first to modify is the `GetTasks` method. Remember, this method was previously operating directly on the worker's `Db` map field. Since we've moved the logic that operates directly on the underlying store (in this case, a built-in map), we want `Get-Tasks` to use the store interface instead. We want to replace the body of `GetTasks` with the simplified version seen in the following listing.

Listing 11.18   The `GetTasks` method using the store interface's `List` method

```
func (w *Worker) GetTasks() []*task.Task {
    taskList, err := w.Db.List()
    if err != nil {
        log.Printf("error getting list of tasks: %v\n", err)
        return nil
    }

    return taskList.([]*task.Task)
}
```

Next, we need to modify the `runTask` method. Like all of the previous code, it has been operating directly on the `Db` map. The beginning steps of this method are the following:

1 Pop a task off the worker's `Queue`.
2 Convert the task from an empty interface to a `task.Task` type.
3 Get the task from the `Db` map.
4 If the task doesn't exist, create it.

Notice steps 3 and 4. The process attempts to get the task from the map by looking it up using the task's `ID`. This operation, however, doesn't return an error if the task isn't in the map. Our `InMemoryTaskStore` implements the `Store` interface's `Get` method, which returns an `error`. That error could be due to any number of factors. It could be because the task simply didn't exist in the store or because there was some problem with interacting with the underlying store itself. So if we were to use the same order of operations when we switch to using the new `Store` interface, we'd have a problem. If the call to the store's `Get` method returns an error, how do we distinguish whether it's because the task didn't exist or there was an error with the underlying store itself? In the former case, we want to create the task; in the latter case, we want to return an error.

As we've done in the past, our solution is making a tradeoff. We're going to switch the order of operations so that we call the store's `Put` method first, which will effectively overwrite the task if it exists. If the call to `Put` does not return an error, then we call the store's `Get` method to retrieve the task from the store. The `runTask` method changes the order of operations to account for our `Store` interface, including errors in return values.

Listing 11.19   The modified `runTask` method

```
func (w *Worker) runTask() task.DockerResult {
    // previous code omitted

    err := w.Db.Put(taskQueued.ID.String(), &taskQueued)
    if err != nil {
        msg := fmt.Errorf("error storing task %s: %v",
    ➥ taskQueued.ID.String(), err)
        log.Println(msg)
        return task.DockerResult{Error: msg}
    }

    queuedTask, err := w.Db.Get(taskQueued.ID.String())
    if err != nil {
        msg := fmt.Errorf("error getting task %s from database: %v",
    ➥ taskQueued.ID.String(), err)
        log.Println(msg)
        return task.DockerResult{Error: msg}
    }

    taskPersisted := *queuedTask.(*task.Task)

    // code omitted
```

The `StartTask` method is the next one that requires changes. It performs two operations on the task store. Each one is updating the state of the task and storing the updated task in the `Db`. In these cases, we can simply swap the direct operation on the map with a call to the new `Put` method, as seen in the following listing.

Listing 11.20   Using the `Put` method instead of directly operating on a map

```
func (w *Worker) StartTask(t task.Task) task.DockerResult {
    config := task.NewConfig(&t)
```

```
d := task.NewDocker(config)
result := d.Run()
if result.Error != nil {
    log.Printf("Err running task %v: %v\n", t.ID, result.Error)
    t.State = task.Failed
    w.Db.Put(t.ID.String(), &t)
    return result
}

t.ContainerID = result.ContainerId
t.State = task.Running
w.Db.Put(t.ID.String(), &t)
```

Next, the `StopTask` method operates on the task store just once. Similar to the `Start-Task` method, it updates the state of the task and saves it to the map. Again, we can simply swap out the direct interaction with the map and replace it with a call to the store's `Put` method:

```
func (w *Worker) StopTask(t task.Task) task.DockerResult {
    config := task.NewConfig(&t)
    d := task.NewDocker(config)

    stopResult := d.Stop(t.ContainerID)
    if stopResult.Error != nil {
        log.Printf("%v\n", stopResult.Error)
    }
    removeResult := d.Remove(t.ContainerID)
    if removeResult.Error != nil {
        log.Printf("%v\n", removeResult.Error)
    }

    t.FinishTime = time.Now().UTC()
    t.State = task.Completed
    w.Db.Put(t.ID.String(), &t)
    log.Printf("Stopped and removed container %v for task %v\n",
➥    t.ContainerID, t.ID)

    return removeResult
}
```

Finally, the `updateTasks` method operates on the task store four times. The first operation is a `for` loop that ranges over the worker's `Db` map. Because Go supports iterating over a map, we were able to loop over the store directly. Go doesn't support iterating over function call—it only returns once:

```
func (w *Worker) updateTasks() {               Calls the List method and
    tasks, err := w.Db.List()        ◁┐        assigns the results to variables
    if err != nil {
        log.Printf("error getting list of tasks: %v\n", err)
        return
    }
```

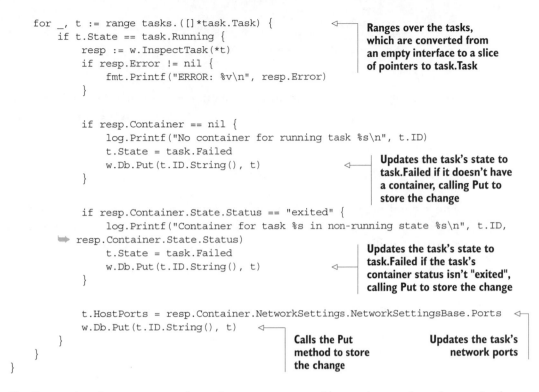

```
    for _, t := range tasks.([]*task.Task) {
        if t.State == task.Running {
            resp := w.InspectTask(*t)
            if resp.Error != nil {
                fmt.Printf("ERROR: %v\n", resp.Error)
            }

            if resp.Container == nil {
                log.Printf("No container for running task %s\n", t.ID)
                t.State = task.Failed
                w.Db.Put(t.ID.String(), t)
            }

            if resp.Container.State.Status == "exited" {
                log.Printf("Container for task %s in non-running state %s\n", t.ID,
    resp.Container.State.Status)
                t.State = task.Failed
                w.Db.Put(t.ID.String(), t)
            }

            t.HostPorts = resp.Container.NetworkSettings.NetworkSettingsBase.Ports
            w.Db.Put(t.ID.String(), t)
        }
    }
}
```

Ranges over the tasks, which are converted from an empty interface to a slice of pointers to task.Task

Updates the task's state to task.Failed if it doesn't have a container, calling Put to store the change

Updates the task's state to task.Failed if the task's container status isn't "exited", calling Put to store the change

Calls the Put method to store the change

Updates the task's network ports

Similar to the changes we made to the manager, we also need to update the worker's API handlers to use the `Store` interface. There are two changes we need to make, one to the `InspectTaskHandler` and one to the `StopTaskHandler`.

In the `InspectTaskHandler`, we need to call the `Store` interface's `Get` method instead of directly accessing the task map:

```
// t, ok := a.Worker.Db[tID]
t, err := a.Worker.Db.Get(tID.String())
```

We need to make a similar change in the `StopTaskHandler`:

```
// taskToStop, ok := a.Worker.Db[tID]
taskToStop, err := a.Worker.Db.Get(tID.String())
```

With those last two changes, we have completed the refactoring of the worker and the manager. Both now use the methods from our new `Store` interface.

11.7 Putting it all together

At this point, we're almost ready to spin up our manager and workers and have them use the new `Store` interface. All that's needed are a few minor tweaks to our `main.go` program.

The first tweak to make involves how we create our workers. If you recall, we had been creating them by assigning a struct literal to a variable:

```
w1 := worker.Worker{
        Queue: *queue.New(),
        Db:     store.NewInMemoryTaskStore(),
}
```

Now, however, we can simplify this part of our code by using the New helper function in the worker package. We'll replace the three lines with a single call to the New function:

```
w1 := worker.New("worker-1", "memory")
w2 := worker.New("worker-2", "memory")
w3 := worker.New("worker-3", "memory")
```

The second tweak involves how we're creating the manager. We already had a New helper function that we were using. We now need to add an argument to our call to New that specifies what type of datastore the manager should use:

```
m := manager.New(workers, "epvm", "memory")
```

With these changes, we can now run our main program and see what we get:

```
$ CUBE_WORKER_HOST=localhost CUBE_WORKER_PORT=5556
  ➡ CUBE_MANAGER_HOST=localhost CUBE_MANAGER_PORT=5555 go run main.go
Starting Cube worker
Starting Cube manager
2023/03/04 16:19:38 No tasks to process currently.
2023/03/04 16:19:38 Sleeping for 10 seconds.
2023/03/04 16:19:38 Checking status of tasks
2023/03/04 16:19:38 Task updates completed
2023/03/04 16:19:38 Sleeping for 15 seconds
2023/03/04 16:19:38 Checking status of tasks
2023/03/04 16:19:38 Task updates completed
2023/03/04 16:19:38 Sleeping for 15 seconds
2023/03/04 16:19:38 Processing any tasks in the queue
2023/03/04 16:19:38 No work in the queue
2023/03/04 16:19:38 Sleeping for 10 seconds
2023/03/04 16:19:38 No tasks to process currently.
2023/03/04 16:19:38 Sleeping for 10 seconds.
2023/03/04 16:19:38 Checking for task updates from workers
2023/03/04 16:19:38 Checking worker localhost:5556 for task updates
```

As you can see, not much has changed. The workers and manager start up as expected and do their respective jobs.

Let's send a task to the manager:

```
$ curl -X POST localhost:5555/tasks -d @task1.json

2023/03/04 16:19:42 Add event {a7aa1d44-08f6-443e-9378-f5884311019e
2023/03/04 16:19:48 Pulled {a7aa1d44-08f6-443e-9378-f5884311019e
2023/03/04 16:19:57 [manager] selected worker localhost:5556 for task
  ➡ bb1d59ef-9fc1-4e4b-a44d-db571eeed203
```

```
2023/03/04 16:19:57 [worker] Added task bb1d59ef-9fc1-4e4b-a44d-db571eeed203
2023/03/04 16:19:57 [manager] received response from worker
[worker] Found task in queue: {bb1d59ef-9fc1-4e4b-a44d-db571eeed203
2023/03/04 21:19:59 Listening on http://localhost:7777
```

It works! We have successfully refactored the manager and worker to use an interface representing a datastore instead of operating directly on the datastore itself. There is still one problem. If we stop and restart either the manager or the worker, they will forget about any tasks they have previously seen. We can solve this problem by implementing a persistent datastore.

11.8 Introducing BoltDB

In moving from an in-memory datastore to a persistent one, there are some high-level questions we have to ask ourselves. First, do we need a *server-based* datastore? A server-based datastore is like PostgreSQL, MySQL, Cassandra, Mongo, or any other datastore that runs as its own process. For our purposes, a server-based datastore is overkill. It would be another process we'd have to start and then manage, and most server-based systems can get complex quickly.

Instead, we're going to choose an *embedded* datastore. It's called an *embedded* datastore because it uses a library that you embed directly in your application.

The second question involves the data model that we want to use. The most popular data model is the relational model, which systems like PostgreSQL and MySQL use. There is even an embedded relational datastore, SQLite. While such datastores are popular and robust, they also require the use of the *Structured Query Language*, or SQL, to insert and query data. SQL datastores are highly structured and require strict schemas defining tables and columns.

Another data model that has become popular in the last decade is the key–value datastore, sometimes also referred to as NoSQL. Popular open source key–value datastores include Cassandra and Redis.

If you recall our in-memory datastore using Go's built-in `map` type, it had a simple interface: we *put* data into the datastore, and we *got* data out of it. The main mechanism by which we put or got tasks into this datastore was the `key`—in our case, a `UUID`. Our tasks are the *values* to which the *keys* refer.

Because we are already using a key-value datastore, it makes sense to pick a persistent datastore that uses the same paradigm. And to keep this as simple as possible, we're going to use an embedded library called BoltDB (https://github.com/boltdb/ bolt). As mentioned in BoltDB's README, it is "a pure Go key/value store" and the "goal of the project is to provide a simple, fast, and reliable database for projects that don't require a full database server such as Postgres or MySQL."

To use the BoltDB library, we will need to install it. From your project directory, install the library using the following command:

```
$ go get github.com/boltdb/bolt/...
```

As we did with the in-memory version of the task and event datastores, we are now going to implement persistent versions of each store.

11.9 *Implementing a persistent task store*

The first persistent store we will implement is the `TaskStore`. It will implement the `Store` interface, the same as the in-memory stores do. The only difference will be in the implementation details.

The first thing to do is to create the `TaskStore` struct, as shown in listing 11.21. There are several differences from the in-memory version to note. The first is that the `TaskStore` struct uses a different type for its `Db` field. Whereas the `InMemoryTaskStore` used a `map[string]*task.Task` type, here the field is a pointer to the `bolt.DB` type. This type is defined in the BoltDB library. Next, the `TaskStore` struct defines the `DbFile` and `FileMode` fields. BoltDB uses a file on disk to persist data, the `DbFile` field tells BoltDB the name of the file it will operate on, and the `FileMode` ensures we have the necessary permissions to read and write to the file. In BoltDB, key–value pairs are stored in collections called *buckets*, so the struct's `Bucket` field defines the name of the bucket we want to use for the `TaskStore`.

Listing 11.21 The persistent version of our task store, called `TaskStore`

```
import (
        // previous imports omitted

        "github.com/boltdb/bolt"
)

type TaskStore struct {
    Db       *bolt.DB
    DbFile   string
    FileMode os.FileMode
    Bucket   string
}
```

The next thing to do is to create a helper function to create an instance of our persistent datastore. We did the same thing with our in-memory datastores. The `NewTaskStore` helper takes three arguments: a string `file` that provides the name of the file we want to use, the `mode` of the file as an `os.FileMode` type, and a string that provides the name of the bucket in which we want to store our tasks.

Listing 11.22 The `NewTaskStore` helper function

```
func NewTaskStore(file string, mode os.FileMode, bucket string)
➥  (*TaskStore, error) {
    db, err := bolt.Open(file, mode, nil)          ◁─── Creates a datastore
    if err != nil {                                       by calling the BoltDB
        return nil, fmt.Errorf("unable to open %v", file)   library's Open function,
    }                                                     passing in the file, mode,
                                                          and bucket from our
                                                          function signature, and
                                                          checks for any errors
```

```
t := TaskStore{
    DbFile:   file,
    FileMode: mode,
    Db:       db,
    Bucket:   bucket,
}

err = t.CreateBucket()
if err != nil {
    log.Printf("bucket already exists, will use it instead
➥ of creating new one")
}

return &t, nil
}
```

Creates an instance of the
TaskStore and assigns it
to the variable t

Creates the bucket by calling
the CreateBucket method and
checks for any errors

Returns a pointer to the
newly created task store

With the `TaskStore` struct defined and our helper function created, let's turn our attention to the methods of the `TaskStore`. In addition to the methods defined by the `Store` interface—`Put`, `Get`, `List`, and `Count`—we're going to define a `Close` method. Why do we need such a method? Remember, our persistent datastore is writing its data to a file on disk. Moreover, in the `NewTaskStore` helper function, we called the `Open` function to open the file. The `Close` method will close the file when we're done with it:

```
func (t *TaskStore) Close() {
    t.Db.Close()
}
```

The first method of the `Store` interface to implement is `Count`. As with the in-memory stores, the persistent version will return the number of tasks in the datastore. Unlike the in-memory versions, this one is a little more involved.

Similar to relational datastores like PostgreSQL and MySQL, BoltDB supports transactions. Per the BoltDB README, each transaction in BoltDB "has a consistent view of the data as it existed when the transaction started." BoltDB supports three types of transactions:

- Read-write
- Read-only
- Batch read-write

For our purposes, we will only be using the first two.

Since our `Count` method needs to get the number of tasks, we can use a read-only transaction. Unlike the in-memory stores, where we were able to use Go's built-in `len` method on Go's map type, here we have to iterate over all the keys in the bucket to construct our count. BoltDB provides the `ForEach` method to simplify this process.

To perform a read-only transaction, we use Bolt's `View` function. This method takes a function, which itself takes an argument of a pointer to a `bolt.Tx` type and returns an error. This is the mechanism that provides the transaction. Inside the transaction, we identify the bucket on which we want to operate, then iterate over each key in that bucket and increment the `taskCount` value. After iterating over all the keys, we check for any errors before finally returning the `taskCount`:

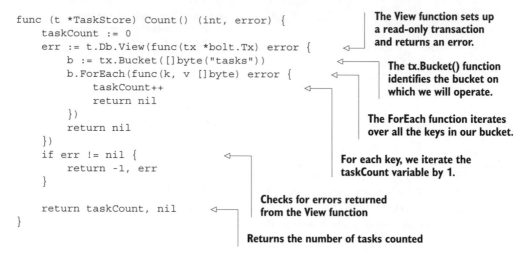

```
func (t *TaskStore) Count() (int, error) {
    taskCount := 0
    err := t.Db.View(func(tx *bolt.Tx) error {
        b := tx.Bucket([]byte("tasks"))
        b.ForEach(func(k, v []byte) error {
            taskCount++
            return nil
        })
        return nil
    })
    if err != nil {
        return -1, err
    }

    return taskCount, nil
}
```

The View function sets up a read-only transaction and returns an error.

The tx.Bucket() function identifies the bucket on which we will operate.

The ForEach function iterates over all the keys in our bucket.

For each key, we iterate the taskCount variable by 1.

Checks for errors returned from the View function

Returns the number of tasks counted

Let's move on and implement another method that is specific to the persistent store and is thus not part of the `Store` interface. The method, `CreateBucket`, as seen in listing 11.22, is a wrapper around a function of the same name in the BoltDB library. It takes no arguments and returns an error. In this method, we create the bucket that will hold all of our tasks as key–value pairs. Because we are creating a bucket, we need to use a read-write transaction, and we do this with the `Update` function. Using `Update` works similarly to `View`. It takes a function that takes a pointer to a `bolt.Tx` type and returns an error. We then call the `CreateBucket` function and pass in the name of the bucket to create. We then check for any errors. Our `CreateBucket` method is shown in the next listing.

Listing 11.23   The `CreateBucket` method

```
func (t *TaskStore) CreateBucket() error {
    return t.Db.Update(func(tx *bolt.Tx) error {
        _, err := tx.CreateBucket([]byte(t.Bucket))
        if err != nil {
            return fmt.Errorf("create bucket %s: %s", t.Bucket, err)
        }
        return nil
    })
}
```

Now let's return to the methods of the `Store` interface and implement the second of these methods, `Put`. The signature of this `Put` method is the same as for the in-memory versions, so there is nothing new here. What is new is how we store the key–value pair. As we did in the `CreateBucket` method, we will use the `Update` function to get a read-write transaction. We identify the bucket where we will store the key–value pair using the tx.Bucket function, passing it the name as a string. To store the value in the BoltDB bucket, we have to convert the value to a slice of bytes. We do this by calling the Marshal function from the json package and passing it the value converted to a pointer to the task.Task type. Once the value has been converted to a slice of bytes, we call the Put function on the bucket, passing it the key and value (both as slices of bytes), as shown in the following listing.

Listing 11.24   The Put method for the persistent task store

```
func (t *TaskStore) Put(key string, value interface{}) error {
    return t.Db.Update(func(tx *bolt.Tx) error {
        b := tx.Bucket([]byte(t.Bucket))

        buf, err := json.Marshal(value.(*task.Task))
        if err != nil {
            return err
        }

        err = b.Put([]byte(key), buf)
        if err != nil {
            return err
        }
        return nil
    })
}
```

The third method of the Store interface to implement is the Get method. It takes a string, which is the key we want to retrieve. It returns an interface{}, which is the task we wanted, and an error. We start by defining the variable task of type task.Task. Next, we use a read-only transaction by way of the View function, which we've previously seen. Again, we identify the bucket on which we want to operate. Then we look up the task using the Get function, passing it the key as a slice of bytes. Notice that we do not check the Get call for any errors. The reason for this is that the BoltDB library guarantees Get will work unless there is a system failure (e.g., the datastore file is deleted from disk). If there is no task in the bucket for the key, Get returns nil. Once we have the task, we have to decode it from a slice of bytes back into a task.Type, which we do using the Unmarshal function from the json package. Finally, we do some error checking and then return a pointer to the task.

Listing 11.25   The Get method for the persistent task store

```
func (t *TaskStore) Get(key string) (interface{}, error) {
    var task task.Task
    err := t.Db.View(func(tx *bolt.Tx) error {
        b := tx.Bucket([]byte(t.Bucket))
        t := b.Get([]byte(key))
        if t == nil {
            return fmt.Errorf("task %v not found", key)
        }
```

```
        err := json.Unmarshal(t, &task)
        if err != nil {
            return err
        }
        return nil
    })
    if err != nil {
        return nil, err
    }
    return &task, nil
}
```

The fourth and final method to implement is the List method. Like Get, List uses a read-only transaction. Instead of getting a single task, however, it iterates over all the tasks in the bucket and creates a slice of tasks. In this, it is similar to the Count method:

```
func (t *TaskStore) List() (interface{}, error) {
    var tasks []*task.Task
    err := t.Db.View(func(tx *bolt.Tx) error {
        b := tx.Bucket([]byte(t.Bucket))
        b.ForEach(func(k, v []byte) error {
            var task task.Task
            err := json.Unmarshal(v, &task)
            if err != nil {
                return err
            }
            tasks = append(tasks, &task)
            return nil
        })
        return nil
    })
    if err != nil {
        return nil, err
    }

    return tasks, nil
}
```

11.10 *Implementing a persistent task event store*

The persistent store for task events will look almost the same as the one for tasks. The obvious differences will be in naming. Our struct is named EventStore instead of TaskStore, and it will operate on the task.TaskEvent type instead of task.Task.

The EventStore struct and NewEventStore helper functions should look familiar. There isn't much to discuss here:

```
type EventStore struct {
    DbFile   string
    FileMode os.FileMode
    Db       *bolt.DB
    Bucket   string
}
```

```
func NewEventStore(file string, mode os.FileMode, bucket string)
    (*EventStore, error) {
    db, err := bolt.Open(file, mode, nil)
    if err != nil {
        return nil, fmt.Errorf("unable to open %v", file)
    }
    e := EventStore{
        DbFile:   file,
        FileMode: mode,
        Db:       db,
        Bucket:   bucket,
    }

    err = e.CreateBucket()
    if err != nil {
        log.Printf("bucket already exists, will use it instead
        of creating new one")
    }

    return &e, nil
}
```

Likewise, the `Close` and `CreateBucket` methods on the `EventStore` type should also look familiar. The former is closing the datastore file opened in `NewEventStore`, and the latter is creating a bucket to store events:

```
func (e *EventStore) Close() {
    e.Db.Close()
}

func (e *EventStore) CreateBucket() error {
    return e.Db.Update(func(tx *bolt.Tx) error {
        _, err := tx.CreateBucket([]byte(e.Bucket))
        if err != nil {
            return fmt.Errorf("create bucket %s: %s", e.Bucket, err)
        }
        return nil
    })
}
```

The `Count` method counts the number of events in the persistent store, returning the `Count`:

```
func (e *EventStore) Count() (int, error) {
    eventCount := 0
    err := e.Db.View(func(tx *bolt.Tx) error {
        b := tx.Bucket([]byte(e.Bucket))
        b.ForEach(func(k, v []byte) error {
            eventCount++
            return nil
        })
        return nil
    })
```

```
    if err != nil {
        return -1, err
    }

    return eventCount, nil
}
```

The Put and Get methods are also identical to their counterparts in the TaskStore type. Put takes a key and a value, writes it to the datastore, and returns any errors. Get takes a key, looks it up in the datastore, and returns the value if found:

```
func (e *EventStore) Put(key string, value interface{}) error {
    return e.Db.Update(func(tx *bolt.Tx) error {
        b := tx.Bucket([]byte(e.Bucket))

        buf, err := json.Marshal(value.(*task.TaskEvent))
        if err != nil {
            return err
        }

        err = b.Put([]byte(key), buf)
        if err != nil {
            log.Printf("unable to save item %s", key)
            return err
        }
        return nil
    })
}

func (e *EventStore) Get(key string) (interface{}, error) {
    var event task.TaskEvent
    err := e.Db.View(func(tx *bolt.Tx) error {
        b := tx.Bucket([]byte(e.Bucket))
        t := b.Get([]byte(key))
        if t == nil {
            return fmt.Errorf("event %v not found", key)
        }
        err := json.Unmarshal(t, &event)
        if err != nil {
            return err
        }
        return nil
    })

    if err != nil {
        return nil, err
    }
    return &event, nil
}
```

And last but not least, the List method builds a list of all the events in the datastore and returns it:

```
func (e *EventStore) List() (interface{}, error) {
    var events []*task.TaskEvent
    err := e.Db.View(func(tx *bolt.Tx) error {
        b := tx.Bucket([]byte(e.Bucket))
        b.ForEach(func(k, v []byte) error {
            var event task.TaskEvent
            err := json.Unmarshal(v, &event)
            if err != nil {
                return err
            }
            events = append(events, &event)
            return nil
        })
        return nil
    })
    if err != nil {
        return nil, err
    }

    return events, nil
}
```

With the persistent versions of our task and event stores implemented, we can change our main program to use them instead of their in-memory counterparts.

11.11 Switching out the in-memory stores for permanent ones

We need to make a couple of minor changes in our manager and worker code to use the new persistent stores. Both changes involve adding cases for creating persistent datastores in the New helper functions in the manager and worker packages.

Let's start with the manager. We need to add the persistent case to our switch statement, seen in listing 11.26. Thus, when a caller of the New function passes in persistent as the value of dbType, we call the NewTaskStore and NewEventStore functions instead of their in-memory equivalents. Notice that each function takes three arguments: the name of the file to use for the datastore, the filemode of the file, and the name of the bucket that will store the key–value pairs. The 0600 in the function calls represents the filemode argument, which means only the owner of the file can read and write it.

> **Listing 11.26 Adding the persistent case to the manager's New function**

```
var err error
switch dbType {
case "memory":
    ts = store.NewInMemoryTaskStore()
    es = store.NewInMemoryTaskEventStore()
case "persistent":
    ts, err = store.NewTaskStore("tasks.db", 0600, "tasks")
```

```
    es, err = store.NewEventStore("events.db", 0600, "events")
}
```

The changes in the worker's `New` function are similar. We add a `persistent` case, which calls the `NewTaskStore` helper function. We're starting three workers, so we use the `filename` variable to create a unique filename for each worker. Because the worker only operates on tasks, there is no need to set up an event store.

Listing 11.27   Changing workers to use the `persistent` store

```
case "persistent":
    filename := fmt.Sprintf("%s_tasks.db", name)
    s, err = store.NewTaskStore(filename, 0600, "tasks")
}
```

At this point, changing our main program to use the new persistent store is just a matter of changing four lines of existing code. In all four lines, we simply change the string `memory` to `persistent`:

```
//w1 := worker.New("worker-1", "memory")
w1 := worker.New("worker-1", "persistent")

//w2 := worker.New("worker-2", "memory")
w2 := worker.New("worker-2", "persistent")

// w3 := worker.New("worker-3", "memory")
w3 := worker.New("worker-3", "persistent")

//m := manager.New(workers, "epvm", "memory")
m := manager.New(workers, "epvm", "persistent")
```

With these changes, start up the main program and perform the same operations we performed earlier in the chapter. You should notice that everything looks the same from the outside as when we used the in-memory stores. The only difference is that you will now see several files with the `.db` extension in the working directory. These are the files BoltDB is using to persist the system's tasks and events. The files you should see are

- `tasks.db`
- `worker-1_tasks.db`
- `worker-2_tasks.db`
- `worker-3_tasks.db`

Summary

- Storing the orchestrator's tasks and events in persistent datastores allows the system to keep track of task and event state, to make informed decisions about scheduling, and to help recover from failures.

- The `store.Store` interface lets us swap out datastore implementations based on our needs. For example, while doing development work, we can use an in-memory store, while we use a persistent store for production.
- While we adapted our old stores that were based on Go's built-in map type to the new `store.Store` interface, these in-memory implementations suffer the same problem—that is, the manager and worker will still lose their tasks when they restart.
- With the `store.Store` interface and a concrete implementation, we made changes to the manager and worker to remove their operating directly on the datastore. For example, instead of operating on a map of `map[uuid.UUID]*task.Task`, we changed them to operate on the `store.Store` interface. In doing this, we decoupled the manager and worker from the underlying datastore implementation. They no longer needed to know the internal workings of the specific datastore; they only needed to know how to call the methods of the interface while all the technical details were handled by an implementation.
- The BoltDB library provides an embedded key–value datastore on top of which we built our `TaskStore` and `EventStore` stores. These datastores persist their data to files on disk, thus allowing the manager and worker to gracefully restart without losing their tasks.
- Once we created the `store.Store` interface and two implementations (one in-memory, one persistent), we could switch between the implementations by simply passing a string of either `memory` or `persistent` to the `New` helper functions.

Part 5

CLI

The fifth and final part of the book implements a command-line interface (CLI) for Cube. The CLI replaces the `main.go` program that we've been using to operate Cube in previous parts of the book.

Chapter 12 implements commands for starting the manager and worker, starting and stopping tasks, and getting the status of tasks.

Chapter 13 provides a summary of what we've accomplished and provides some suggestions for where to go from here.

12

Building
a command-line interface

This chapter covers

- Core components of command-line interfaces
- Introducing the Cobra framework
- Creating command skeletons
- Producing a CLI that replaces the combined use of the `main.go` and `curl` programs

Throughout the book, we have been using a crude main program to operate our orchestration system (figure 12.1). This program is a single monolith that does it all: starts the workers, starts the workers' API servers, starts the manager, and starts the manager's API server. If we want to stop the manager for any reason, we also stop the workers, and vice versa. When we want to interact with the orchestrator, however, we do this separately via the `curl` command.

Now that we have our orchestration system implemented, let's turn our attention to how we operate it. Popular orchestration systems like Kubernetes and Nomad are operated by command-line interfaces (CLIs). Kubernetes uses multiple binaries to implement its CLI:

- `kubeadm` bootstraps a Kubernetes cluster.
- `kubelet` performs the same function as our worker (i.e., it runs tasks).
- `kubectl` provides an interface to interact with the cluster.

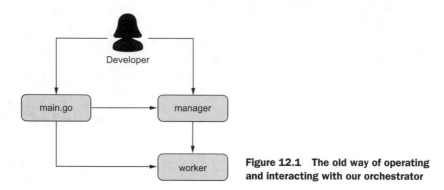

Figure 12.1 **The old way of operating and interacting with our orchestrator**

Nomad, on the other hand, implements its CLI with a single binary called `nomad` but otherwise provides a similar interface.

Our task in this chapter will be to implement a CLI for the Cube orchestrator. This CLI will support the following operations:

- Starting the worker
- Starting the manager
- Starting and stopping tasks
- Getting the status of tasks

12.1 *The core components of CLIs*

Many of the best CLIs are made up of common elements. They use a consistent pattern for each command and provide built-in help messages. The pattern we'll use for our CLI takes the form of APPNAME COMMAND ARG --FLAG. For example, the worker command implemented later in this chapter will look like this:

```
$ cube worker --name worker-1 --dbtype memory
```

Built-in help messages make it easy for a user to get contextual help by passing a `--help` or `-h` flag along with the command. The output from passing `--help` typically consists of a short summary of the command, a more detailed description that provides deeper explanations and possible examples, and a list of the flags the command accepts. In the case of our worker, passing the `--help` flag will result in this message:

```
$ cube worker --help
cube worker command.

The worker runs tasks and responds to the manager's requests about task
➡ state.

Usage:
  cube worker [flags]

Flags:
  -d, --dbtype string   Type of datastore to use for tasks ("memory" or
➡ "persistent") (default "memory")
```

```
-h, --help              help for worker
-H, --host string       Hostname or IP address (default "0.0.0.0")
-n, --name string       Name of the worker (default
➡ "worker-9a385171-f980-47c4-a250-75736d3eb6f0")
-p, --port int          Port on which to listen (default 5556)
```

Each command we'll implement in this chapter will follow this pattern and provide a similarly useful help message (figure 12.2).

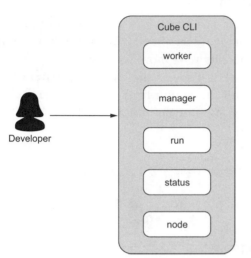

Figure 12.2 The new way of operating and interacting with our orchestrator

12.2 Introducing the Cobra framework

We are going to use a framework to implement our CLI. Specifically, we will use the Cobra framework (https://github.com/spf13/cobra). Cobra powers popular projects like Kubernetes, Helm, Hugo, Moby (Docker), and the GitHub CLI. (For a fuller list of projects using Cobra, see http://mng.bz/XqBE.)

Why use a framework? Technically, we don't need a framework. We could build our CLI from the ground up using just the Go standard library.

In its most basic form, a CLI performs these functions:

- Parses arguments and flags passed on the command line
- Calls a handler that matches the command, passing the arguments and flags as parameters
- Presents any output from the handler to the user

While this list is short and appears simple, there is quite a bit of work involved. Just handling flags, for example, can turn into thousands of lines of code (see `flag.go` in the `flag` package in Go's standard library or `flag.go` in the pflag library). A CLI framework provides standard building blocks, similar to web frameworks.

Let's get started by installing Cobra:

```
go get -u github.com/spf13/cobra@latest
```

We also want to install the `cobra-cli`:

```
go install github.com/spf13/cobra-cli@latest
```

12.3 *Setting up our Cobra application*

We have now installed the Cobra library, which provides the framework we will use in our CLI, and the `cobra-cli` tool, which gives us some handy shortcuts for initializing our CLI application and adding commands as we move forward.

Before we get started, make a backup copy of the `main.go` program from past chapters. We will be overwriting it with the output from the `cobra-cli` tool. Then, from the root of your project directory, let's initialize our Cobra CLI:

```
$ cobra-cli init
Your Cobra application is ready at
/home/t/workspace/personal/manning/code/ch12
```

The `init` command performs several tasks for us:

- Generates a new `main.go`
- Creates a `cmd` directory in our project
- Create a `root.go` file inside the new `cmd` directory

The new `cmd` directory should look like this:

```
$ tree cmd
cmd
└── root.go
```

At this point, we have bootstrapped everything we need to build our CLI. We can run the main program to see what we have to start with:

```
$ go run main.go
A longer description that spans multiple lines and likely contains
examples and usage of using your application. For example:

Cobra is a CLI library for Go that empowers applications.
This application is a tool to generate the needed files
to quickly create a Cobra application.
```

12.4 *Understanding the new main.go*

After running `cobra-cli init`, we should have a new `main.go` file in the root of our project. As we can see in listing 12.1, this new version of our main program is much smaller, and it performs the following functions:

- Declares the `main` package
- Imports the `cube/cmd` package
- Defines the `main` function, which runs the `Execute` function from the `cmd` package

Listing 12.1 The new `main.go` generated by `cobra-cli`

```
/*
Copyright © 2023 NAME HERE <EMAIL ADDRESS>

*/
package main

import "cube/cmd"

func main() {
    cmd.Execute()
}
```

12.5 Understanding root.go

Let's explore the `cmd/root.go` file before delving into our own commands. At the top of the file, the `cobra-cli init` command has added a copyright notice. This is convenient if you're planning to publish your CLI as open source software, but it's not necessary for our purposes. Feel free to remove it. Next, there is the package declaration, which gives the package the name `cmd`. Then there are a couple of imports, notably the importing of the Cobra library, `github.com/spf13/cobra`:

```
/*
Copyright © 2023 NAME HERE <EMAIL ADDRESS>

*/
package cmd

import (
    "os"

    "github.com/spf13/cobra"
)
```

The meat of the file comes next, and it contains the `rootCmd`. As its name suggests, this is the *root* of our CLI. The important thing to note is how commands are built with Cobra. Each command is a pointer to the `cobra.Command` type, and we're creating an instance of it and assigning it to a variable.

In creating this instance of `cobra.Command` to assign to the `rootCmd` variable, several fields are defined. The `Use` field provides a one-line usage message. The `Short` field defines a brief description of the CLI. Finally, the `Long` field provides a more detailed description of the CLI. All three of these fields are used in the CLIs help system (i.e., when running `go run main.go --help`). The most important field, commented out in the generated `root.go`, is the `Run` field. It is defined as a function type that takes two arguments: a pointer to a `Command` type and a slice of strings. This function performs the work when a user invokes the command. We will see this function in action shortly:

```
// rootCmd represents the base command when called without any subcommands
var rootCmd = &cobra.Command{
    Use:   "cube",
    Short: "A brief description of your application",
    Long: `A longer description that spans multiple lines and likely
➥ contains
examples and usage of using your application. For example:

Cobra is a CLI library for Go that empowers applications.
This application is a tool to generate the needed files
to quickly create a Cobra application.`,
    // Uncomment the following line if your bare application
    // has an action associated with it:
    // Run: func(cmd *cobra.Command, args []string) { },
}
```

The next piece of the generated `root.go` file is the `Execute` command. As the comment above the function says, this function is called by `main.main()` and occurs only once:

```
// Execute adds all child commands to the root command and sets flags
➥ appropriately.
// This is called by main.main(). It only needs to happen once to the
➥ rootCmd.
func Execute() {
    err := rootCmd.Execute()
    if err != nil {
        os.Exit(1)
    }
}
```

The final piece of `root.go` is the definition of the `init` function. The `init` function is special in Go. It is predefined by the Go language and is used to perform configuration. In Cobra applications, the definition of flags and other configuration settings are done in an `init` function.

In the Cobra framework, there are two types of flags: *persistent* and *local*. Persistent flags persist from the parent command where they are defined through to any children. Local flags exist only for the command where they are defined. The `init` function in the generated `root.go` file includes one of each type of flag:

```
func init() {
    // Here you will define your flags and configuration settings.
    // Cobra supports persistent flags, which, if defined here,
    // will be global for your application.

    // rootCmd.PersistentFlags().StringVar(&cfgFile, "config", "",
    ➥ "config file (default is $HOME/.cube.yaml)")
```

```
        // Cobra also supports local flags, which will only run
        // when this action is called directly.
        rootCmd.Flags().BoolP("toggle", "t", false, "Help message for toggle")
}
```

12.6 Implementing the worker command

Now that we have a basic understanding of the Cobra framework, let's start implementing our commands. The first command we'll build is the `worker` command. To get started, we can use the `cobra-cli` command to create a skeleton for us:

```
$ cobra-cli add worker
```

This command creates the `worker.go` file in the `cmd` directory:

```
$ tree cmd
cmd
├── root.go
└── worker.go
```

The skeleton created by the `cobra-cli add` command should look like that shown in listing 12.2. One thing to note in this skeleton is that the `add` command included a functional `Run` field. The field value is a function that simply prints out `worker called`. And as we saw with the root command, the skeleton includes an `init` function where we can define flags. Also, note that the init function calls the `rootCmd.AddCommand` method, passing it the `workerCmd`. This call, as its name suggests, adds our worker command to the root, thus making it available to the CLI application.

> **Listing 12.2 The skeleton worker command created by the `cobra-cli add` command**

```
/*
Copyright © 2023 NAME HERE <EMAIL ADDRESS>

*/
package cmd

import (
    "fmt"

    "github.com/spf13/cobra"
)

// workerCmd represents the worker command
var workerCmd = &cobra.Command{
    Use:   "worker",
    Short: "A brief description of your command",
    Long: `A longer description that spans multiple lines and likely
➥ contains examples
and usage of using your command. For example:

Cobra is a CLI library for Go that empowers applications.
This application is a tool to generate the needed files
```

```
to quickly create a Cobra application.`,
    Run: func(cmd *cobra.Command, args []string) {
        fmt.Println("worker called")
    },
}

func init() {
    rootCmd.AddCommand(workerCmd)

    // Here you will define your flags and configuration settings.

    // Cobra supports Persistent Flags which will work for this command
    // and all subcommands, e.g.:
    // workerCmd.PersistentFlags().String("foo", "", "A help for foo")

    // Cobra supports local flags which will only run when this command
    // is called directly, e.g.:
    // workerCmd.Flags().BoolP("toggle", "t", false, "Help message for
    ➥ toggle")
}
```

Once we have this skeleton in place, we can run it and see that it works. If we run it with the `--help` flag, we see the usage message:

```
$ go run main.go worker --help
A longer description that spans multiple lines and likely contains examples
and usage of using your command. For example:

Cobra is a CLI library for Go that empowers applications.
This application is a tool to generate the needed files
to quickly create a Cobra application.

Usage:
  cube worker [flags]

Flags:
  -h, --help   help for worker
```

And if we run the command, we see the output `worker called`:

```
$ go run main.go worker
worker called
```

Let's start modifying this skeleton by defining the necessary flags for the worker command. If we recall our old `main.go` program, we were reading environment variables to get the hostname and the port on which the worker would listen.

> **Listing 12.3 Getting the worker's `host` and `port` from environment variables**

```
whost := os.Getenv("CUBE_WORKER_HOST")
wport, _ := strconv.Atoi(os.Getenv("CUBE_WORKER_PORT"))
```

Instead of reading environment variables, let's use flags. In listing 12.4, we add the `host` and `port` flags. We create the `host` flag using the `StringP` method, and we create the `port` flag using the `IntP` method. Both methods take the following arguments (all as strings):

- The name of the flag
- A shorthand letter that can be used after a single dash
- A default value
- A description of the flag's usage

Listing 12.4 Defining the `host` and `port` flags in the generated `init` method

```
package cmd

import (
    "cube/worker"
    "fmt"
    "log"

    "github.com/google/uuid"
    "github.com/spf13/cobra"
)

func init() {
    rootCmd.AddCommand(workerCmd)
    workerCmd.Flags().StringP("host", "H", "0.0.0.0",
        "Hostname or IP address")
    workerCmd.Flags().IntP("port", "p", 5556, "Port on
        which to listen")
}
```

The host flag can be used as either --host or -H.

The port flag can be used as either --port or -p.

> **NOTE** Under the hood, Cobra uses the `pFlag` (https://github.com/spf13/pflag) library. It is written by the same author as Cobra and is advertised as a "drop-in replacement for Go's flag package."

Next, let's add two more flags. The `name` flag will be used as the name of the worker. Once again, we are creating it using the `StringP` method, and we're using the `Sprintf` function from the `fmt` package to build a string that creates a unique name as a default. The `dbytpe` flag will be used to create the worker with the specified type of task storage, either `memory` or `persistent`, with `memory` being the default. The `name` flag can be used as either `--name` or `-n`, and the `dbtype` flag can be used as either `--dbtype` or `-d`.

Listing 12.5 The `name` flag

```
workerCmd.Flags().StringP("name", "n", fmt.Sprintf("worker-%s",
    uuid.New().String()), "Name of the worker")
    workerCmd.Flags().StringP("dbtype", "d", "memory", "Type of datastore
    to use for tasks (\"memory\" or \"persistent\")")
}
```

At this point, we have a functional `worker` command. Let's check the help message:

```
$ go run main.go worker --help
A longer description that spans multiple lines and likely contains examples
and usage of using your command. For example:

Cobra is a CLI library for Go that empowers applications.
This application is a tool to generate the needed files
to quickly create a Cobra application.

Usage:
  cube worker [flags]

Flags:
  -d, --dbtype string    Type of datastore to use for tasks ("memory" or
➥ "persistent") (default "memory")
  -h, --help             help for worker
  -H, --host string      Hostname or IP address (default "0.0.0.0")
  -n, --name string      Name of the worker
➥ (default "worker-ed9b23bf-3070-4da6-a163-ef16bdae8c22")
  -p, --port int         Port on which to listen (default 5556)
```

As we can see, running `worker --help` prints out a message about the command, and it lists the flags we defined with their individual usage messages.

We can also call the command:

```
$ go run main.go worker
worker called
```

Calling the `worker` command doesn't do anything useful. It does, however, demonstrate a working command printing out `worker called`.

With our flags defined, we can move on to the `workerCmd`. As we saw when we ran the command with the `--help` flag, the usage message was about Cobra itself. Let's customize the help message to be more relevant. To do this, we modify the `Use`, `Short`, and `Long` fields on the `workerCmd`, as seen in the following listing.

Listing 12.6 Modifying the `workerCmd` for a more useful help message

```
var workerCmd = &cobra.Command{
    Use:   "worker",
    Short: "Worker command to operate a Cube worker node.",
    Long: `cube worker command.

The worker runs tasks and responds to the manager's requests about task
➥ state.`,
```

Now, if we run the command with the `--help` flag, we should see a more useful help message:

```
$ go run main.go worker --help
cube worker command.

The worker runs tasks and responds to the manager's requests about task
➡ state.

Usage:
  cube worker [flags]

Flags:
  -d, --dbtype string   Type of datastore to use for tasks ("memory" or
  ➡ "persistent") (default "memory")
  -h, --help            help for worker
  -H, --host string     Hostname or IP address (default "0.0.0.0")
  -n, --name string     Name of the worker
  ➡ (default "worker-bd7dc7dc-abf7-4cea-943b-11f13f128208")
  -p, --port int        Port on which to listen (default 5556)
```

That looks much better!

Finally, let's modify the `Run` field of our `workerCmd`. The first thing we need to do is get the values of the command's flags. We do this by calling the appropriate method on the `cmd` passed into the function. In our case, we call `GetString` to get the `host`, `name`, and `dbtype` flags, and we call `GetInt` to get the `port` flag. Notice that we are using the blank identifier in each of these calls. Each call returns two values: the value of the flag and an error. In our case, we are not storing the error because we have set default values for each of the flags.

Listing 12.7   The `Run` field, the core of a Cobra command

```
Run: func(cmd *cobra.Command, args []string) {
    host, _ := cmd.Flags().GetString("host")
    port, _ := cmd.Flags().GetInt("port")
    name, _ := cmd.Flags().GetString("name")
    dbType, _ := cmd.Flags().GetString("dbtype")
},
```

Next, we need to create the worker and its API and then start everything up. When we performed these tasks in our old `main.go` program, we were doing it for three workers. If you recall, it looked like this:

```
w1 := worker.New("worker-1", "persistent")
wapi1 := worker.Api{Address: whost, Port: wport, Worker: w1}

w2 := worker.New("worker-2", "persistent")
wapi2 := worker.Api{Address: whost, Port: wport + 1, Worker: w2}

w3 := worker.New("worker-3", "persistent")
wapi3 := worker.Api{Address: whost, Port: wport + 2, Worker: w3}

go w1.RunTasks()
go w1.UpdateTasks()
go wapi1.Start()
```

```
go w2.RunTasks()
go w2.UpdateTasks()
go wapi2.Start()

go w3.RunTasks()
go w3.UpdateTasks()
go wapi3.Start()
```

Because we're creating a command that can be run multiple times, we only need to perform these tasks once. The `workerCmd` starts a worker using a simplified version of the code in our old `main.go` program.

Listing 12.8   The `workerCmd` starting a worker

```
Run: func(cmd *cobra.Command, args []string) {
    // previous code omitted

    log.Println("Starting worker.")
    w := worker.New(name, dbType)
    api := worker.Api{Address: host, Port: port, Worker: w}
    go w.RunTasks()
    go w.CollectStats()
    go w.UpdateTasks()
    log.Printf("Starting worker API on http://%s:%d", host, port)
    api.Start()
},
```

Now, if we run our command, we should end up with a running, fully functioning worker:

```
$ go run main.go worker
2023/04/29 14:36:34 Starting worker.
2023/04/29 14:36:34 Starting worker API on http://0.0.0.0:5556
2023/04/29 14:36:34 No tasks to process currently.
2023/04/29 14:36:34 Sleeping for 10 seconds.
2023/04/29 14:36:34 Checking status of tasks
2023/04/29 14:36:34 Task updates completed
2023/04/29 14:36:34 Sleeping for 15 seconds.
2023/04/29 14:36:34 Collecting stats
2023/04/29 14:36:44 No tasks to process currently.
2023/04/29 14:36:44 Sleeping for 10 seconds.
```

Before moving on, try to start two more workers in separate terminals. You will need to specify a different port for each one using the `--port` flag, but otherwise the defaults should work.

12.7 Implementing the manager command

With the worker command complete, let's move on and implement the manager command. We'll follow a similar process used for the worker command. We'll start by creating our skeleton using the `cobra-cli add` command:

```
$ cobra-cli add manager
manager created at /home/t/workspace/personal/manning/code/ch12
```

Again, the `add` command will create a skeleton for us in the `cmd` directory:

```
$ tree cmd
cmd
├── manager.go
├── root.go
└── worker.go
```

Let's start modifying our `manager` skeleton by defining the flags we'll need in the `init` function. As with the `worker` command, we need to define the `host` and `port` flags to tell the manager where it should listen for traffic. Next, we define the `workers` flag, which is a list of workers identified by strings in the form of `host:port`. We did something similar in our old `main.go` program, but we built up the list of workers manually. Here, we can use the `StringSliceP` method that will allow a user to specify the workers on the command line as a string. With the `workers` flag defined, we move on and define the `scheduler` flag. Finally, we define the `dbType` flag, which will identify the type of datastore the manager will use for its tasks and events.

> **Listing 12.9 Customizing the `init` method of the `managerCmd` to define flags**

```go
package cmd

import (
    "cube/manager"
    "log"

    "github.com/spf13/cobra"
)

func init() {
    rootCmd.AddCommand(managerCmd)
    managerCmd.Flags().StringP("host", "H", "0.0.0.0",
        "Hostname or IP address")
    managerCmd.Flags().IntP("port", "p", 5555, "Port on which to listen")
    managerCmd.Flags().StringSliceP("workers", "w",
        []string{"localhost:5556"}, "List of workers on which the manager
        will schedule tasks.")
    managerCmd.Flags().StringP("scheduler", "s", "epvm", "Name
        of scheduler to use.")
    managerCmd.Flags().StringP("dbType", "d", "memory", "Type of datastore
        to use for events and tasks (\"memory\" or \"persistent\")")
}
```

The next step to modifying the `manager` skeleton is to customize the usage message that gets displayed when running the command with the `--help` flag:

```
var managerCmd = &cobra.Command{
    Use:   "manager",
    Short: "Manager command to operate a Cube manager
 ➡ node.",
    Long: `cube manager command.

The manager controls the orchestration system and is responsible for:
- Accepting tasks from users
- Scheduling tasks onto worker nodes
- Rescheduling tasks in the event of a node failure
- Periodically polling workers to get task updates`,
```

Changes the Use field to "manager"

Changes the Short field to a more informative short version of the help message

Changes the Long field to a more descriptive help message

At this point, we have a functioning `manager` command. If we run the `manager` command now with the `--help` flag, we see the following output:

```
$ go run main.go manager --help
cube manager command.

The manager controls the orchestration system and is responsible for:
- Accepting tasks from users
- Scheduling tasks onto worker nodes
- Rescheduling tasks in the event of a node failure
- Periodically polling workers to get task updates

Usage:
  cube manager [flags]

Flags:
  -d, --dbType string      Type of datastore to use for events and tasks
 ➡ ("memory" or "persistent") (default "memory")
  -h, --help               help for manager
  -H, --host string        Hostname or IP address (default "0.0.0.0")
  -p, --port int           Port on which to listen (default 5555)
  -s, --scheduler string   Name of scheduler to use. (default "epvm")
  -w, --workers strings    List of workers on which the manager will schedule
 ➡ tasks. (default [localhost:5556])
```

As with the `worker` command, the only thing left to implement now is the `Run` field of our `managerCmd`. Again, we start by getting the values of the flags passed on the command line. And once again, we don't check for errors because we have set default values for all our flags. Notice that the functions we use to retrieve the flag values are a combination of the word `Get` and the type, so a flag defined as a `StringP` type is retrieved via the `GetString()` function, a flag defined as a `StringSliceP` is retrieved by the `GetStringSlice()` function, and an `IntP` type is retrieved using the `GetInt()` function.

Listing 12.10 Implementing the `Run` field of our `managerCmd`

```
Run: func(cmd *cobra.Command, args []string) {
        host, _ := cmd.Flags().GetString("host")
        port, _ := cmd.Flags().GetInt("port")
        workers, _ := cmd.Flags().GetStringSlice("workers")
        scheduler, _ := cmd.Flags().GetString("scheduler")
        dbType, _ := cmd.Flags().GetString("dbType")
```

Finally, we create the manager and its API and then start it up. This should look familiar, as we're simply performing the same calls as we did in our old `main.go` program.

Listing 12.11 Starting up the manager with the same calls as the old `main.go` program

```
log.Println("Starting manager.")
        m := manager.New(workers, scheduler, dbType)
        api := manager.Api{Address: host, Port: port, Manager: m}
        go m.ProcessTasks()
        go m.UpdateTasks()
        go m.DoHealthChecks()
        go m.UpdateNodeStats()
        log.Printf("Starting manager API on http://%s:%d", host, port)
        api.Start()
    },
}
```

Now let's start up the manager:

```
$ go run main.go manager -w 'localhost:5556,localhost:5557,localhost:5558'
2023/04/29 15:03:40 Starting manager.
2023/04/29 15:03:40 Starting manager API on http://0.0.0.0:5555
2023/04/29 15:03:40 Checking for task updates from workers
2023/04/29 15:03:40 Checking worker localhost:5556 for task updates
2023/04/29 15:03:40 Processing any tasks in the queue
2023/04/29 15:03:40 No work in the queue
2023/04/29 15:03:40 Sleeping for 10 seconds
2023/04/29 15:03:40 Collecting stats for node localhost:5556
2023/04/29 15:03:40 Performing task health check
2023/04/29 15:03:40 Task health checks completed
2023/04/29 15:03:40 Sleeping for 60 seconds
2023/04/29 15:03:40 Checking worker localhost:5557 for task updates
2023/04/29 15:03:40 Collecting stats for node localhost:5557
2023/04/29 15:03:40 Checking worker localhost:5558 for task updates
2023/04/29 15:03:40 Task updates completed
2023/04/29 15:03:40 Sleeping for 15 seconds
```

And voila! At this point, we have replaced our old `main.go` program from previous chapters with individual commands to start the worker and manager independently.

12.8 *Implementing the run command*

We have replaced our `main.go` program with separate commands to start up our manager and worker components. But let's not congratulate ourselves just yet. There is more we can do to make our orchestration system feel more real.

If you recall, in past chapters, we have started and stopped tasks by manually calling the manager's API using the `curl` command. In case you've forgotten, this is how we have been starting tasks:

```
$ curl -X POST localhost:5555/tasks -d @task1.json
```

And here is how we have been stopping them:

```
$ curl -X DELETE localhost:5555/tasks/bb1d59ef-9fc1-4e4b-a44d-db571eeed203
```

There is nothing technically wrong with the way we have been starting and stopping tasks up to now. It has gotten the job done. If, however, we think about existing orchestration systems like Kubernetes or Nomad, we know we don't start and stop tasks by calling their APIs using `curl`. Instead, we use a command-line tool like `kubectl` or `nomad`.

So let's create a command that will allow us to start a task. For our purposes, we'll call this command `run`. Create the skeleton for it by using the `cobra-cli add` command:

```
$ cobra-cli add run
run created at /home/t/workspace/personal/manning/code/ch12-experimental
```

Afterward, you should see the new file in the `cmd` directory:

```
$ tree cmd/
cmd/
├── manager.go
├── root.go
├── run.go
└── worker.go
```

Again, we have a skeleton to start from:

```
/*
Copyright © 2023 NAME HERE <EMAIL ADDRESS>

*/
package cmd

import (
    "fmt"

    "github.com/spf13/cobra"
)

// runCmd represents the run command
var runCmd = &cobra.Command{
    Use:   "run",
```

```
        Short: "A brief description of your command",
        Long: `A longer description that spans multiple lines and likely
➥ contains examples
and usage of using your command. For example:

Cobra is a CLI library for Go that empowers applications.
This application is a tool to generate the needed files
to quickly create a Cobra application.`,
        Run: func(cmd *cobra.Command, args []string) {
            fmt.Println("run called")
        },
}

func init() {
    rootCmd.AddCommand(runCmd)

    // Here you will define your flags and configuration settings.

    // Cobra supports Persistent Flags which will work for this command
    // and all subcommands, e.g.:
    // runCmd.PersistentFlags().String("foo", "", "A help for foo")

    // Cobra supports local flags which will only run when this command
    // is called directly, e.g.:
    // runCmd.Flags().BoolP("toggle", "t", false, "Help message for toggle")
}
```

By now, the skeleton and framework should be familiar to us, so we're going to move a little faster.

To start, let's define two flags in our `init` function. The first flag is named `manager`, and it will allow a user to specify the manager to talk to. We provide a default value of `localhost:5555` since that is what we have been using. The second flag is named `filename`, and this flag allows the user to specify the name of the file containing the task definition.

Listing 12.12 The Run command defines the `manager` and `filename` flags

```
package cmd

import (
    "bytes"
    "errors"
    "fmt"
    "io/fs"
    "log"
    "net/http"
    "os"
    "path/filepath"

    "github.com/spf13/cobra"
)
```

```
func init() {
    rootCmd.AddCommand(runCmd)
    runCmd.Flags().StringP("manager", "m", "localhost:5555", "Manager to
    ➥ talk to")
    runCmd.Flags().StringP("filename", "f", "task.json", "Task specification
    ➥ file")
}
```

So we allow a user to specify a filename holding their task definition. What happens, however, if that file doesn't exist? Let's create the `fileExists` function in listing 12.13 to check that a file actually exists before we attempt to read it. To do this, we call the `Stat` function in the `os` package, passing it the name of the file. We discard the value returned and only store any errors. Then we use the `errors.Is` function to check whether the `err` returned from the call to `Stat` is of type `fs.ErrNotExist`. We use the `!` (not) operator to return `true` when `errors.Is` returns false, and `false` when it returns `true`.

Listing 12.13   The `fileExists` function

```
func fileExists(filename string) bool {
    _, err := os.Stat(filename)

    return !errors.Is(err, fs.ErrNotExist)
}
```

Now on to the meat of our new command, `runCmd`. Replace the skeleton values for the `Use`, `Short`, and `Long` fields, as seen in the following listing.

Listing 12.14   Updating the text used in the command's help message

```
var runCmd = &cobra.Command{
    Use:   "run",
    Short: "Run a new task.",
    Long: `cube run command.

The run command starts a new task.`,
```

If we run the command with the `--help` flag at this point, we will see the following:

```
$ go run main.go run --help
cube run command.

The run command starts a new task.

Usage:
  cube run [flags]

Flags:
  -f, --filename string   Task specification file (default "task.json")
  -h, --help              help for run
  -m, --manager string    Manager to talk to (default "localhost:5555")
```

The last bit of the command to implement is the `Run` field. As with the `worker` and `manager` commands, we start by getting the values from the `manager` and `filename` flags passed on the command line and storing them in variables.

```
Run: func(cmd *cobra.Command, args []string) {
        manager, _ := cmd.Flags().GetString("manager")
        filename, _ := cmd.Flags().GetString("filename")
```

Once we have the `manager` and `filename` variables defined, we move on and check that the file specified by `filename` actually exists. We do this by first getting the absolute path of the filename using the `Abs` function from the `filepath` package. Then we pass the `fullFilePath` to our `fileExists` function, and if the file does not exist, we log a message and exit. Checking for the existence of the task file allows us to do some sanity checking and provide the user with a relevant error message.

```
fullFilePath, err := filepath.Abs(filename)
        if err != nil {
            log.Fatal(err)
        }

        if !fileExists(fullFilePath) {
            log.Fatalf("File %s does not exist.", filename)
        }
```

Having confirmed that the `filename` passed into the command exists, we can move on and start the task. We'll use the following process:

- Log helpful messages about the manager and absolute file path.
- Read the contents of the task definition file, printing out another log message.
- Call the manager's API (the equivalent of `curl -X POST localhost:5555/tasks`).
- Handle any errors.

The bulk of the `Run` field's function deals with calling the manager's API and handling any errors.

```
log.Printf("Using manager: %v\n", manager)      <─┐
        log.Printf("Using file: %v\n", fullFilePath)
```

Logs helpful errors that tell a user the manager being used and the path to the task file

```
    data, err := os.ReadFile(filename)        ◁──── Reads the contents
    if err != nil {                                  of the task file and
        log.Fatalf("Unable to read file: %v", filename)   checks for errors
    }
    log.Printf("Data: %v\n", string(data))

    url := fmt.Sprintf("http://%s/tasks", manager)    Calls the manager's
    resp, err := http.Post(url, "application/json",   API via the POST
    ⇒ bytes.NewBuffer(data))                   ◁──── method and passes
    if err != nil {                                   the task in the
        log.Panic(err)                                request body
    }

    if resp.StatusCode != http.StatusCreated {        ◁───────────┐
        log.Printf("Error sending request: %v", resp.StatusCode)  │
    }                                                              │
                                                                   │
    defer resp.Body.Close()                                        │
    log.Println("Successfully sent task request to manager")       │
    },                                                             │
}
                              Checks that the request was ─────────┘
                              successful and the task was created
```

With this code, we're ready to start a task! If you stopped your workers and manager from the previous sections, start them back up. Then run the run command:

```
$ go run main.go run --filename task1.json
2023/04/30 15:51:40 Using manager: localhost:5555
2023/04/30 15:51:40 Using file:
⇒ /home/t/workspace/personal/manning/code/ch12-experimental/task1.json
2023/04/30 15:51:40 Data: {
    "ID": "a7aa1d44-08f6-443e-9378-f5884311019e",
    "State": 2,
    "Task": {
        "State": 1,
        "ID": "bb1d59ef-9fc1-4e4b-a44d-db571eeed203",
        "Name": "test-chapter-9.1",
        "Image": "timboring/echo-server:latest",
        "ExposedPorts": {
            "7777/tcp": {}
        },
        "PortBindings": {
            "7777/tcp": "7777"
        },
        "HealthCheck": "/health"
    }
}

2023/04/30 15:51:40 Successfully sent task request to manager
```

Watching the output from the manager, you should see it start up the task. And you can confirm it by running docker ps:

```
$ docker ps
CONTAINER ID   IMAGE                           CREATED         STATUS
99b32646ef35   timboring/echo-server:latest    1 second ago    Up 1 second
```

We can also query the manager's API directly to verify the task is running:

```
$ curl localhost:5555/tasks|jq
[
  {
    "ID": "bb1d59ef-9fc1-4e4b-a44d-db571eeed203",
    "ContainerID":
    ➥ "99b32646ef35ed3819196b0b890bebd94ae6d9085dce7914e742e133c8a86fdd",
    "Name": "test-chapter-9.1",
    "State": 2,
    "Image": "timboring/echo-server:latest",

    // output truncated
  }
]
```

Nice! But let's not stop here. Now that we've created a command to start tasks, let's create one to stop them.

12.9 Implementing the stop command

By now, you should know what's coming next. We start by creating a skeleton:

```
$ cobra-cli add stop
stop created at /home/t/workspace/personal/manning/code/ch12-experimental

$ tree cmd
cmd/
├── manager.go
├── root.go
├── run.go
├── stop.go
└── worker.go
```

Next, we add our flags to the skeleton in the `cmd/stop.go` file. We only need a single flag, `manager`, for the `Stop` command.

> **Listing 12.18 Using the `manager` flag for the `Stop` command**

```
package cmd

import (
    "fmt"
    "log"
    "net/http"

    "github.com/spf13/cobra"
)

func init() {
    rootCmd.AddCommand(stopCmd)
    stopCmd.Flags().StringP("manager", "m", "localhost:5555", "Manager to
    ➥ talk to")
}
```

With our flags defined, we replace the boilerplate usage strings generated by the `cobra-cli add` command with more relevant ones:

```
var stopCmd = &cobra.Command{
    Use:   "stop",
    Short: "Stop a running task.",
    Long: `cube stop command.

The stop command stops a running task.`,
```

At this point, we can run our command with the `--help` flag and verify that our command works:

```
$ go run main.go stop --help
cube stop command.

The stop command stops a running task.

Usage:
  cube stop [flags]

Flags:
  -h, --help              help for stop
  -m, --manager string    Manager to talk to (default "localhost:5555")
```

With our `stop` command, notice that we did not define a flag to specify the task we want to stop. Instead, the user will pass the task as an argument to the command. Here is what this will look like:

```
$ go run main.go stop bb1d59ef-9fc1-4e4b-a44d-db571eeed203
```

To read the argument, we define the `Args` field on our `stopCmd` variable. We give this variable a value of `cobra.MinimumNArgs(1)` to say that we expect the user to pass one argument to our command. The `Run` field should look familiar at this point. We're performing the equivalent of calling `curl -X DELETE localhost:5555/tasks/{taskID}`.

Listing 12.19 The `Stop` command using arguments in addition to flags

```
Args: cobra.MinimumNArgs(1),
    Run: func(cmd *cobra.Command, args []string) {
        manager, _ := cmd.Flags().GetString("manager")
        url := fmt.Sprintf("http://%s/tasks/%s", manager, args[0])
        client := &http.Client{}                              ⟵ Creates
        req, err := http.NewRequest("DELETE", url, nil)   ⟵      an HTTP
        if err != nil {                                          client
            log.Printf("Error creating request %v: %v", url, err)
        }
```

**Creates a request with the method set to
DELETE. This is necessary because the client
itself only has methods for Post() and Get().**

```
    resp, err := client.Do(req)                          ◁─── Makes the
    if err != nil {                                            request by
        log.Printf("Error connecting to %v: %v", url, err)    calling the
    }                                                          client's Do(req)
                                                               method, passing
    if resp.StatusCode != http.StatusNoContent {    ◁───       in the request
        log.Printf("Error sending request: %v", err)
        return                                              Checks whether
    }                                                       the request was
                                                            successful
    log.Printf("Task %v has been stopped.", args[0])
},
}
```

Let's try to stop the task we started using our new `stop` command:

```
$ go run main.go stop bb1d59ef-9fc1-4e4b-a44d-db571eeed203
2023/04/30 16:13:44 Task bb1d59ef-9fc1-4e4b-a44d-db571eeed203 has been
⮕ stopped.
```

Now let's verify it stopped our task by checking the output of `docker ps`:

```
$ docker ps
```

Nice! With our `stop` command, we have successfully replaced the manual processes we had been using in previous chapters. Now we can perform everything by the way of commands: starting the worker(s), starting the manager, and starting and stopping tasks.

12.10 Implementing the status command

As long as we're already in the headspace of our command-line tool, let's create two more commands. The first will be the `status` command. If you recall, throughout this book, we have used the `docker ps` command to get a list of our running Docker containers after starting tasks:

```
$ docker ps
CONTAINER ID   IMAGE                         CREATED          STATUS
a4a7028e5463   timboring/echo-server:latest  19 seconds ago   Up 18 seconds
92462d09ee98   timboring/echo-server:latest  50 seconds ago   Up 49 seconds
e29a26176fcb   timboring/echo-server:latest  15 minutes ago   Up 15 minutes
```

For our purposes, we want output similar to `docker ps`, but we want it to contain information about our tasks instead of our containers. That is, we want the output to come from the source of truth for our orchestration system (i.e., our manager).

So let's create the skeleton for our `status` command using the `cobra-cli add` command:

```
$ cobra-cli add status
status created at /home/t/workspace/personal/manning/code/ch12-experimental
```

```
$ tree cmd
cmd
├── manager.go
├── root.go
├── run.go
├── status.go
├── stop.go
└── worker.go
```

With our skeleton created, we can start our customization by defining our flags in its init function. In this case, we are only defining a single flag, manager, to tell the command the address of the manager from which it will get the status of our tasks.

Listing 12.20   Defining the manager flag in the init method

```
package cmd

import (
    "cube/task"
    "encoding/json"
    "fmt"
    "io"
    "log"
    "net/http"
    "os"
    "text/tabwriter"
    "time"

    "github.com/docker/go-units"
    "github.com/spf13/cobra"
)

func init() {
    rootCmd.AddCommand(statusCmd)
    statusCmd.Flags().StringP("manager", "m", "localhost:5555",
➥     "Manager to talk to")
}
```

Next, let's customize our help output to make it more useful:

```
var StatusCmd = &cobra.Command{
    Use:   "status",
    Short: "Status command to list tasks.",
    Long: `cube status command.

The status command allows a user to get the status of tasks from
➥ the Cube manager.`,
```

And as we've seen before, we can now run the command with the --help flag:

```
$ go run main.go status --help
cube status command.
```

The status command allows a user to get the status of tasks from the Cube
➥ manager.

Usage:
  cube status [flags]

Flags:
  -h, --help   help for status
  -m, --manager string   Manager to talk to (default "localhost:5555")

Last, but not least, we can implement the function for our `Run` field. The function will
perform the following operations:

- Retrieves the manager address passed on the command line
- Uses the manager address to build the URL for the manager's API
- Makes a GET request to the manager's API to retrieve all tasks
- Unmarshals the JSON body sent in the response and converts it to a slice of
  pointers to `task.Task`
- Prints out a portion of each task's info in a formatted table (similar to the out-
  put of `docker ps`)

The `Run` field's function is responsible for calling the manager's API and printing out
the response in a readable format. One thing to note is that we use the `tabwriter`
(https://pkg.go.dev/text/tabwriter) package from Go's standard library to create
our output.

Listing 12.21 The `Run` function

```
Run: func(cmd *cobra.Command, args []string) {
      manager, _ := cmd.Flags().GetString("manager")

      url := fmt.Sprintf("http://%s/tasks", manager)
      resp, _ := http.Get(url)
      body, err := io.ReadAll(resp.Body)
      if err != nil {
          log.Fatal(err)
      }
      defer resp.Body.Close()

      var tasks []*task.Task
      err = json.Unmarshal(body, &tasks)
      if err != nil {
          log.Fatal(err)
      }

      w := tabwriter.NewWriter(os.Stdout, 0, 0, 5, ' ',
  tabwriter.TabIndent)
      fmt.Fprintln(w, "ID\tNAME\tCREATED\tSTATE\tCONTAINERNAME\tIMAGE\t")
      for _, task := range tasks {
          var start string
          if task.StartTime.IsZero() {
```

```
                    start = fmt.Sprintf("%s ago",
        ➥   units.HumanDuration(time.Now().UTC().Sub(time.Now().UTC())))
                } else {
                    start = fmt.Sprintf("%s ago",
        ➥   units.HumanDuration(time.Now().UTC().Sub(task.StartTime)))
                }

                state := task.State.String()[task.State]
                fmt.Fprintf(w, "%s\t%s\t%s\t%s\t%s\t%s\t\n", task.ID, task.Name,
        ➥   start, state, task.Name, task.Image)
            }
            w.Flush()
        },
    }
```

With that, we can run the status command in figure 12.3.

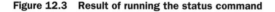

```
t@spot:~/workspace/personal/manning/code/ch12$ go run main.go status
ID                                   NAME            CREATED                STATE     CONTAINERNAME    IMAGE
bb1d59ef-9fc1-4e4b-a44d-db571eeed203 test-chapter-9.1 Less than a second ago Running   test-chapter-9.1 timboring/echo-server:latest
21b23589-5d2d-4731-b5c9-a97e9832d021 test-chapter-9.2 Less than a second ago Running   test-chapter-9.2 timboring/echo-server:latest
95fbe134-7f19-496a-acfc-c7853e5b4cd2 test-chapter-9.3 Less than a second ago Running   test-chapter-9.3 timboring/echo-server:latest
```

Figure 12.3   Result of running the status command

12.11 *Implementing the node command*

The last command we'll implement is the node command. The purpose of this command is to provide a summary of the nodes in our orchestration system. It will list the following:

- Node name
- Memory
- Disk
- Role
- Number of tasks

Now, technically, we don't really need this command. Like the status command, we can use the manager's API and query the /nodes endpoint directly. Here's what it looks like using the curl command and piping the output to jq to make it more readable:

```
$ curl localhost:5555/nodes|jq
[
  {
    "Name": "localhost:5556",
    "Ip": "",
    "Api": "http://localhost:5556",
    "Memory": 32793076,
    "MemoryAllocated": 0,
    "Disk": 20411170816,
    "DiskAllocated": 0,
```

```
    "Stats": {
      "MemStats": {...},
      "DiskStats": {...},
      "CpuStats": {...},
      "LoadStats": {...},
      "TaskCount": 0
    },
    "Role": "worker",
    "TaskCount": 0
  }
]
```

This output should look familiar to you. It's a list of `Node` types, which we implemented in chapter 10 while working on the scheduler. Notice that there is a single node in the list of nodes and that it has the `Stats` field, which should also look familiar, as it is the `Stats` type we implemented in chapter 6.

While we can get information about the nodes in our system using `curl` to query the manager's `/nodes` endpoint, it's not the easiest on the eyes. This is why we're going to implement the `node` command. We'll condense the information down to the most essential and output it in a more readable manner.

Again, we'll use the `cobra-cli add` command to create our skeleton:

```
$ cobra-cli add node
node created at /home/t/workspace/personal/manning/code/ch12-experimental

$ tree cmd
cmd
├── manager.go
├── node.go
├── root.go
├── run.go
├── status.go
├── stop.go
└── worker.go
```

Like the `status` command we implemented, the `node` command will have only a single flag.

> **Listing 12.22 The `node` command defining a single flag of type `StringP`**

```
package cmd

import (
    "cube/node"
    "encoding/json"
    "fmt"
    "io"
    "net/http"
    "os"
    "text/tabwriter"
```

```
        "github.com/spf13/cobra"
)

func init() {
    rootCmd.AddCommand(nodeCmd)
    nodeCmd.Flags().StringP("manager", "m", "localhost:5555", "Manager to
⇒  talk to")
}
```

Next, let's update the Use, Short, and Long fields on our nodeCmd struct. nodeCmd provides information about the nodes in the orchestration system.

Listing 12.23   The nodeCmd struct

```
var NodeCmd = &cobra.Command{
    Use:   "node",
    Short: "Node command to list nodes.",
    Long: `cube node command.

The node command allows a user to get the information about the nodes in the
⇒  cluster.`,
```

At this point, we should have a working command, which we can once again confirm by running the command with the --help flag:

```
$ go run main.go node --help
cube node command.

The node command allows a user to get the information about the nodes in the
⇒  cluster.

Usage:
  cube node [flags]

Flags:
  -h, --help              help for node
  -m, --manager string    Manager to talk to (default "localhost:5555")
```

Finally, we'll implement the Run field. Again, this process should look familiar, as it's similar to the status command:

- Retrieves the manager address passed on the command line
- Uses the manager address to build the URL for the manager's API
- Makes a GET request to the manager's /nodes endpoint to retrieve all nodes
- Unmarshals the JSON body sent in the response and converts it to a slice of pointers to node.Node
- Prints out a portion of each node's info in a formatted table (similar to the output of docker ps)

Like the status command, the node command talks to the manager's API and formats the response in a concise manner that is easy to read.

Listing 12.24   The `node` command

```
Run: func(cmd *cobra.Command, args []string) {
        manager, _ := cmd.Flags().GetString("manager")

        url := fmt.Sprintf("http://%s/nodes", manager)
        resp, _ := http.Get(url)
        defer resp.Body.Close()
        body, _ := io.ReadAll(resp.Body)
        var nodes []*node.Node
        json.Unmarshal(body, &nodes)
        w := tabwriter.NewWriter(os.Stdout, 0, 0, 5, ' ',
            ➥ tabwriter.TabIndent)
        fmt.Fprintln(w, "NAME\tMEMORY (MiB)\tDISK (GiB)\tROLE\tTASKS\t")
        for _, node := range nodes {
            fmt.Fprintf(w, "%s\t%d\t%d\t%s\t%d\t\n", node.Name,
                ➥ node.Memory/1000,
                ➥ node.Disk/1000/1000/1000, node.Role, node.TaskCount)
        }
        w.Flush()
    },
}
```

Let's give it a try!

```
$ go run main.go node
NAME               MEMORY (MiB)     DISK (GiB)      ROLE        TASKS
localhost:5556     32793            20              worker      0
localhost:5557     32793            20              worker      0
localhost:5558     32793            20              worker      0
```

Nice! As you can see, I have three nodes running. Since I'm running all three workers on the same machine, the MEMORY and DISK fields will be the same. Now let's start up the same three tasks that we've used in past chapters and see how the output of the node command changes:

```
$ go run main.go node
NAME               MEMORY (MiB)     DISK (GiB)      ROLE        TASKS
localhost:5556     32793            20              worker      1
localhost:5557     32793            20              worker      1
localhost:5558     32793            20              worker      1
```

As expected, the output of the node command has changed after starting three tasks, with each node running one of those tasks. With that, we have implemented all of our commands.

Summary

- The Cobra framework helps build CLIs by providing standardized components, similar to web frameworks.
- Cobra provides its own CLI, `cobra-cli`, that allows developers to initialize a new command-line project and to add commands to an existing one.
- Commands follow the pattern of `APPNAME COMMAND ARG --FLAG`.
- Commands provide built-in help.
- We replaced the old `main.go` program with the new `worker` and `manager` commands, giving us more flexibility to start the worker and manager components independently.
- We created additional commands that made it easier to interact with our orchestration system. Instead of starting, stopping, and getting the status of tasks by calling the manager's API using `curl`, we provided the commands `run`, `stop`, and `status`. We also provided the `node` command, which gives a user an overview of the current state of the nodes in the cluster.

Now what?

Chapter 12 concluded our work to build the Cube orchestrator. Let's review what we've accomplished:

1 We designed and implemented the worker component.

2 We designed and implemented the manager component.

3 We created a Storage interface that allowed us to implement in-memory and persistent data stores for storing tasks and events. This interface is then used by both the worker and manager components.

4 We built a Scheduler interface and then refactored our original round-robin implementation to adhere to this interface. We also wrote a more sophisticated scheduler, called E-PVM.

5 Finally, we replaced our crude main.go program with a proper command-line interface (CLI). This CLI allowed us to run the worker and manager components independently, even on different machines. The CLI also provides us with the ability to perform management operations: we can start and stop tasks, query the state of tasks, and get an overview of the state of each node in the orchestration system.

While this is all "neat," so what? What can we do with the knowledge that we've gained? Well, a theoretical answer to these questions would be that we can write a new production-quality orchestrator, something to compete with or replace the likes of Kubernetes or Nomad. Personally, I find this answer unrealistic. Kubernetes has a strong foothold in the industry, and Nomad is a reasonable alternative if, for some reason, you or your company doesn't want to use Kubernetes. There are, however, more practical answers.

13.1   Working on Kubernetes and related tooling

While you may not write your own general-purpose orchestrator, you could contribute to Kubernetes. Remember, the Kubernetes project is open source, and it's also written in Go. As of this writing, there have been more than 3,500 contributors to its codebase. Similarly, maybe you're interested in contributing to the K3s project. Packaged as a single binary, K3s advertises itself as a lightweight version of Kubernetes targeted to edge, IoT, development, and other smaller types of deployments (i.e., those that are not "web scale"). K3s is also written in Go.

Or maybe you want to work on tools for Kubernetes or Nomad. With your knowledge of how orchestration systems work, you could contribute to projects like K9s (https://github.com/derailed/k9s) or Wander (https://github.com/robinovitch61/wander). Both K9s and Wander provide terminal UIs (or TUIs) for managing and working with Kubernetes (K9s) and Nomad (Wander) clusters.

Why would you want to contribute to any of these projects? What would you get out of it? Perhaps you have a need that these projects don't currently meet. By contributing to the project, you can have your individual need satisfied as well as help others who might also find your contribution useful. Or perhaps you simply want to contribute to an open source project. There is satisfaction in seeing your name listed as one of the contributors on a project's repo.

13.2   Manager–worker pattern and workflow systems

Kubernetes and Nomad are examples of general-purpose orchestration systems, and they make use of what is sometimes called the manager–worker pattern. As we saw in our implementation of the Cube orchestrator, the manager–worker pattern has a `manager` component that manages a pool of `workers` for the purpose of running `tasks`. In the case of Cube (and Kubernetes and Nomad), those tasks just happen to be applications that can be used to build complex distributed systems. There are, however, other types of systems that also use this manager–worker pattern.

One of these other types of systems is the workflow system. A workflow system provides a programmatic way for users to define and run a sequence of tasks. While this sounds similar to an orchestration system, workflow systems are more specialized, focusing on automating the steps in a well-defined process. One popular workflow system is Apache Airflow (https://github.com/apache/airflow).

If you work on a DevOps or site reliability engineering (SRE) team, you are likely already using one or more workflow systems. Your team may be responsible for managing many services that provide the infrastructure to your development teams, who are writing code for user-facing products. The infrastructure services may be things like databases, virtual machines, Kubernetes or Nomad clusters, build tools, and more. All of these services have processes for managing them. And those processes almost certainly are broken down into discrete steps that can be automated. So one option to help you automate the management of these services could be to write your own special-purpose workflow system.

13.3 Manager–worker pattern and integration systems

There are other places where knowledge of the manager–worker pattern can be used. For example, on my current team, we realized that the original version of our integration service was brittle and difficult to extend to meet the company's needs as we looked into the near future. This integration service is pretty straightforward: it needs to ingest data from IoT devices, apply some transformations to that data, and then forward the data on to other destinations (databases, monitoring systems, financial systems, etc.). Our original implementation supported only a few hard-coded transformations. Moreover, we built it into our monolithic backend system and did not provide any reasonable means for scaling it over time.

Thus, we started down the path of designing a new integration service. While working on the design for this new service, I realized that what I was describing was, in fact, a service that could use the manager–worker pattern. Instead of tasks, as in a general-purpose orchestration system, the subject of our integration system was workflows. We have a worker component that is responsible for performing the individual steps of each workflow. And we have a manager component that is responsible for administrative tasks, like creating, updating, and deleting workflows in the system, as well as dispatching incoming requests from devices to individual workers.

With this new design, we have much more flexibility in how we operate our integration system. We can run it inside our existing monolith, choosing to rip out the original integration service and replace it with this new one. We can run it as a separate microservice with all of the components running in a single process on a single machine (great for development purposes). Or we can run individual components of the system as separate processes, either on a single or separate machines. This is great for production and allows us to scale as necessary.

13.4 In closing

The previous examples are just a few ways in which you can take the knowledge you've gained from this book and apply it in real-world situations. Thus, the time you spent writing the Cube orchestrator was not simply an academic exercise.

At the end of the day, I hope you also had fun!

Here is a review of what we have covered:

- To organize code into Go types based on a mental model, see chapter 2.
- To use the Docker API to start and stop containers, see chapter 3.
- To manage the state of tasks over the course of their lifetime, see chapter 4.
- To write an HTTP API using the `chi` router, see chapters 5 and 8.
- To schedule tasks onto a pool of workers, see chapters 7 and 10.
- To store tasks in a key-value datastore using the BoltDB library, see chapter 11.
- To write a command-line application using the Cobra library, see chapter 12.

appendix
Environment setup

A.1 Installing Go

Installing a version of Go is as easy as downloading it and untarring it. The latest version can be downloaded from https://go.dev/doc/install.

The Go language spec is currently at version 1. In general, "programs written to the Go 1 specification will continue to compile and run correctly, unchanged, over the lifetime of that specification" (https://tip.golang.org/doc/go1compat). This means that any version of Go should work.

The code in this book has been tested with the following versions:

- 1.20
- 1.19
- 1.16

A.1.1 Installing on Linux

The default instructions for installing Go recommend removing previous installations. If you want to work with multiple versions of Go, see the doc "Managing Go Installations" (https://go.dev/doc/manage-install).

> **Listing A.1 Installing a version of Go on Linux**

```
$ curl -L -O https://go.dev/dl/go1.21.6.linux-amd64.tar.gz

# Remove previous Go installations
$ rm -rf /usr/local/go && tar -C /usr/local -xzf go1.21.6.linux-amd64.tar.gz

# Add /usr/local/go/bin to your $PATH
$ export PATH=$PATH:/usr/local/go/bin

# check version
$ go version
```

A.2   *Project structure and initialization*

Create a directory to hold the source code and other files for your work.

Listing A.2   Creating a directory named `cube` for our project

```
$ cd $HOME
$ mkdir cube
```

Once you have created your project directory, change into it and initialize the module:

```
$ cd $HOME/cube
$ go mod init cube
go: creating new go.mod: module cube
```

Once initialized, you should see a single file in the root of the project:

```
$ ls
go.mod
```

Next, to save some time while working through the book, you can install the dependencies we'll use:

```
$ go get \
github.com/boltdb/bolt \
github.com/c9s/goprocinfo/linux \
github.com/docker/go-connections \
github.com/go-chi/chi/v5 \
github.com/golang-collections/collections \
github.com/google/go-cmp \
github.com/google/uuid \
github.com/moby/moby \
github.com/docker/docker/api/types \
github.com/docker/docker/api/types/container \
github.com/docker/docker/client \
github.com/docker/go-units \
github.com/spf13/cobra
```

index

Symbols

! (not) operator 238

Numerics

404 status code 79

A

Abs function 239
Action field 43
add command 227, 233
Address field 76, 126
AddTask method 62, 68, 114, 126
agent 12
AIX (proprietary Unix OS) 7
An Introduction to High Availability Computing: Concepts and Theory (Siewiorek) 20
API (application programming interface) 71
  exposing metrics on 98–99
  manager API
    API struct 126–128
    handling requests 126–128
    putting together 131–136
    refactorings 129–131
    serving 129–131
  starting, stopping, and inspecting containers
    from Docker API 40–41
  worker
    API struct 76–80
    handling requests 77–80
    serving worker API 80–81
API Security in Action (Mittal) 21

API struct 80–81, 126, 201
Api type 186
append function 170
Args field 242

B

BoltDB 16, 207–212
BoltDB library 217
bolt.DB type 208
bolt.Tx type 210
Borglet 11
BorgMaster 11, 106
Bucket field 208
buckets 208

C

calculateCpuUsage function 180–182, 185
calculateLoad function 180, 182
candidates variable 171
cgroups (control groups) 6
checkTaskHealth method 150
chi 16
chi.URLParam 79
CLI (command-line interface) 26, 221–222, 224, 251
  building
    implementing worker command 227–232
    run command 236–241
  Cobra, setting up application 224
  cobra-cli add command 227, 236, 242–243, 247
  cobra-cli init command 225
  Cobra framework 223–224

CLI (command-line interface) *(continued)*
  defined 11–13
  implementing manager command 233–235
  implementing node command 246–249
  implementing worker command 227–232
  main.go file 224–226
    root.go file 225–226
  setting up 224
  status command 243–246
  stop command 241–243
client 13
Client field 43
Close() function 213
Close method 209
clusters 11
cmd directory 236
cmd package 225
cobra.Command type 225
Cobra framework 223–224
CollectStats() method 28, 30, 98, 116
comma, ok 193
Command type 226
Completed state 24, 63, 65, 151
composition 59
Config field 43
Config struct 42, 45
Config type 45
"Consensus: Reaching Agreement" 20
container.Config type 45
ContainerCreateCreatedBody type 46
ContainerCreate method 41, 45–47
Container field 146
container.HostConfig type 45
ContainerId field 43
ContainerInspect() method 146–147
ContainerInspect API call 146
ContainerLogs method 47
ContainerRemove method 48
container.Resources type 45
container.RestartPolicy type 45
containers 5–7
  overview of 6–7
  starting, stopping, and inspecting from command line 37–39
  starting, stopping, and inspecting from Docker API 40–41
ContainerStart method 41, 46–47
ContainerStop method 48
Contains function 65
Content-Type header 78, 98
context.Context 45
continue statement 198

control groups (cgroups) 6
control plane 12, 107
Count() function 213
count counter 184
Count method 194, 209, 212
CpuStats field 93, 96
CPUStat type 93, 95
CreateBucket() function 213
CreateBucket method 210–211
createContainer() function 48–50
createResult.Error 50
createResult variable 50
Cube 13–16
  tools and libraries 15–16
CUBE_HOST environment variable 110, 119, 131
CUBE_MANAGER_HOST environment variable 131
CUBE_MANAGER_PORT environment variable 131
cube orchestrator, manager–worker pattern 252
CUBE_PORT environment variable 110, 119, 131
CUBE_WORKER_HOST environment variable 131
CUBE_WORKER_PORT environment variable 131
curl command 4, 40–41, 83–84, 120, 156, 236, 246
CurrentState column 64

D

data format, requests, and responses 74–76
data plane 107
DBA (database administrator) 5
DB (database)
  counting tasks 60
  implementing worker's methods 60–67
    RunTask method 66–67
    StartTask method 61–62
    StopTask method 60–61
    task state 63–65
Db field 27–28, 60, 63, 67, 79, 208
DbFile field 208
Db type 201
dbType argument 196
dbType flag 229, 233
dbType variable 197
Delete method 190
DELETE request 85, 124
Dequeue() method 67
Designing Data-Intensive Applications (Kleppmann) 18
Designing Distributed Systems (Brendan Burns) 18

Disk attribute 26
Disk field 42, 249
DiskFree method 94
DiskStats field 93, 96
DiskTotal method 94
Disk type 93–94
DiskUsed method 94
distributed computing 18
Docker
    starting, stopping, and inspecting containers
        from API 40–41
    tasks and 58–59
docker binary 48
docker command 120
docker inspect command 39–40
docker inspect cube-book command 39
DockerInspectResponse struct 146–147
Docker object 62
docker ps command 69, 136, 147, 243
DockerResult struct 43–44, 61
DockerResult type 46
docker rm command 48
docker run command 38, 48
docker stop command 48, 158
docker stop cube-book command 39
Docker struct 43, 58, 60–62, 68, 146–148
dockerTask variable 50
Docker type 148
DoHealthChecks method 152–153, 155

E

Effective Go (Pike) 31
embedded datastores 207
empty interface 191
Encode method 78
Env field 42, 45
E-PVM (Enhanced PVM) scheduler 10, 178–183,
    186–187
    in practice 179–183
    theory 178
Epvm struct 179
Error field 43, 67, 146
errors.Is function 238
err value 198
err variable 44, 46, 48, 198
Event column 64
Event DB 107
EventDb field 196–197
EventDb store 200
eventDb variable 115, 196
EventsDB database 112

EventStore store 217
EventStore struct 212
Execute command 226
ExposedPorts attribute 26

F

Failed state 24, 63–65, 151
failure scenarios 139–142
    application bugs 140
    application startup failure 139–140
    manager failures 142
    task failures due to Docker daemon crashes and
        restarts 141
    task failures due to machine crashes and
        restarts 141
    task startup failures due to resource issues
        140–141
    worker failures 141–142
feasibility phase 15
FIFO (first-in, first-out) 27
fileExists function 238–239
FileMode field 208
filename flag 237, 239
filename variable 216, 239
filepath package 239
FinishTime field 26
flag package 223
fmt package 229
fmt.Sprintf function 81
ForEach method 209
for loop 4, 184, 199
framework 12
fullFilePath 239

G

Get() function 214
GET call 183
GetDiskInfo() function 97
getHostPort method 150–151
GetInt() function 234
GetInt method 231
Get method 113, 193, 198, 200–201, 203, 205, 209,
    211–212
getNodeStats function 182–185
Get Programming with Go (Nathan Youngman) 15
GET request 85, 124–125
GetStats() function 96, 98
GetStatsHandler method 98
GetStats helper 186
GetStats method 185

GetString() function 234
GetString method 231
GetTasks() function 127
GetTasks() method 75, 78, 127, 199, 202
GetTasksHandler method 77–78
github.com/google/uuid package 60
go keyword 116, 132
golang-collections package 33
goprocinfo library 16, 93, 96–97
    collecting metrics with 93–97
goroutines 81

H

HA (high availability) 11
handlers 72, 123
handlers.go file 126
HealthCheck field 149
health checks 145–153
    and restarts 149–153
    implementing task updates on workers
        148–149
    inspecting tasks on workers 146–148
    putting together 153–159
/health endpoint 154
/healthfail endpoint 154
- -help flag 222, 228, 230, 234, 238, 242, 244
high availability (HA) 11, 19–20
host flag 229, 233
http package 77, 81, 173
http.ReponseWriter type 77
http.Request type 77
HTTPWithRetry helper function 184–185

I

Image attribute 26
Image field 42
ImagePull method 41, 44–46
ImagePull operation 47
init command 224
init function 226–227, 233, 237, 244
initRouter() method 80–81
In-memory Store 189
in-memory stores, for task events 195–201
    refactoring manager to use new in-memory
        stores 196–201
InMemoryTaskStore 192, 208
Inspect method 147–148
InspectTaskHandler 205
InspectTask method 148–149
integration systems 253

interfaces. *See* scheduler interface
IntP method 229
io.Copy function 44
io package 44
io.ReadCloser interface 44

J

jobs, defined 9–10
jq command 41
json.Encoder object 78
json.Encoder type 78
JSON (Javascript Object Notation) 74
json.NewEncoder() method 78
json package 211

K

kubeadm 221
kubectl 221
kubelet 12, 221
Kubernetes, contributing to 152
    and concept of job 9
    architecture 13
    manager-worker pattern and integration
        systems 253
    manager–worker pattern and workflow
        systems 252
    scheduler interface 165–166
    terminology 12
Kubernetes objects 12

L

leader 20
Learn Amazon Web Services in a Month of Lunches
    (Butler) 20
List() method 194, 199, 209, 212, 214
ListenAndServe function 73, 81
LoadAvg type 93
load balancing 20–21
LoadStats field 93, 96
Long field 226, 230, 238, 248
lowestScore variable 182

M

main() function 49, 70
main.go file 48–49, 224–226
    root.go file 225–226
main.go program 48
make() function 196

manager 105–121
  Cube manager 106–108
    components that make up 107–108
  defined 10
  manager skeleton 29–30
  Manager struct 108–115
    implementing methods 109–115
  putting it all together 116–120
  serving API 129–131
manager API 122–137
  API struct 126–128
  data format 124–125
  handling requests 126–128
  overview of 123–125
  putting together 131–136
  requests 124–125
  responses 124–125
  routes 124
manager command 233–235, 239
Manager component 23, 29, 51, 106
manager directory 126
manager failures 142–145
Manager field 126
manager flag 237, 239, 241
manager.go file 29, 126
Manager struct 29–30, 108–115, 130, 166,
    196, 201
  adding new fields to 169
  implementing methods 109–115
    SelectWorker method 109–110
    SendWork method 110–111
    UpdateTasks method 112–114
Manager type 196–197
manager variable 239
manager–worker pattern 252–253
map type 188, 207
marginal_cost 178
Marshal function 211
master 12
maxJobs variable 180
MemAvailableKb method 94
MemAvailable method 94
MemInfo type 93
Memory attribute 26
MEMORY field 42, 249
memory storage 229
MemStats field 93–94, 96
MemStats.MemTotal field 94
MemTotalKb method 94
MemUsedKb method 94
MemUsedPercent method 94
Message struct 139

metrics 88–101
  collecting 89–90
  collecting with goprocinfo 93–97
  exposing on API 98–99
  putting together 99–100
multiplexer (mux) 77, 123
Mux object 80

N

Name attribute 25
Name field 42, 173
name flag 229
namespaces 6
nat package 33
net/http package 111, 113, 184
networking argument 46
network.NetworkingConfig type 45
// new code comment 174
NewEventStore() function 212, 215
New function 115, 176, 186, 196–197, 206,
    215–217
New helper function 202
  modifying 170–173
NewInMemoryTaskEventStore function
    197
NewInMemoryTaskStore function 197
NewInMemoryTaskStore function call
    202
NewInMemoryTaskStore helper function
    192
NewNode function 170
NewRequest function 173
NewTaskStore function 215–216
NewTaskStore helper 208–209
newWorker variable 168
NextState column 64
Node, completing implementation
    183–186
NodeCmd struct 248
node command 246–249
node.GetStats method 185
node.go file 185
node.NewNode function 170
node.Node type 170, 183, 185
node/ package directory 185
nodeScores variable 167, 180
/nodes endpoint 246–247
Node struct 32
Node type 183, 185, 247
node variable 183
nomad binary 222

O

Open function 209
orchestration system
  creating skeletons
    other 31–32
    testing 32–35
  starting, stopping, and inspecting containers
    from Docker API 40–41
orchestrator 3–21, 251–254
  building command-line interface, run
    command 236–241
  components of 8–13
    clusters 11
    command-line interface 11–13
    jobs 9–10
    managers 10
    schedulers 10
    tasks 8
  containers 6–7
    overview of 6–7
    starting, stopping, and inspecting from com-
      mand line 37–39
  containers, starting, stopping, and inspecting
    from command line 37–39
  Cube 13–16
    tools and libraries 15–16
  environment setup, project structure and
    initialization 256
  exposing metrics on API 98–99
  failure scenarios 138–142
    application bugs 140
    application startup failure 139–140
    manager failures 142
    overview of new scenario 139
    task failures due to Docker daemon crashes
      and restarts 141
    task failures due to machine crashes and
      restarts 141
    task startup failures due to resource
      issues 140–141
    worker failures 141–142
  from mental model to skeleton code, scheduler
    skeleton 30–31
  hardware 16–21
  health checks, putting together 153–159
  history of 4–5
  implementing health checks 145–153
    health checks and restarts 149–153
    implementing task updates on workers
      148–149
    inspecting tasks on workers 146–148

implementing more sophisticated scheduler
  adapting round-robin scheduler to scheduler
    interface 166–169
  putting it all together 175–178
implementing persistent storage for tasks
  implementing in-memory store for task
    events 195–201
  switching out in-memory stores for perma-
    nent ones 215–216
manager skeleton 29–30
not implementing or discussing 18–21
  distributed computing 18
  high availability 19–20
  load balancing 20–21
  security 21
  service discovery 18–19
recovery options 142–145
  recovering from environmental failures
    142–144
  recovering from manager failures 145
  recovering from worker failures 144–145
  recovery from application failures 142
starting, stopping, and inspecting containers
  from command line 37–39
task configuration 42–51
  starting and stopping tasks 43–51
task skeleton 36–37
worker API
  API struct 76–80
  handling requests 77–80
workers 10
  tasks and Docker 58–59
os.FileMode type 208
os package 238
OSPF (Open Shortest Path First) 107

P

parameterized routes 72
Paxos Made Simple (Lamport) 20
pending field 29
Pending queue 174, 190, 200
Pending state 24, 63, 65, 151
persistent case 215
persistent storage 229
persistent storage for tasks
  implementing persistent task store 208–212
  introducing BoltDB 207–212
  putting it all together 205–207
Persistent Store 189
pFlag library 223, 229
picking phase 15

Pick method 168–169, 177, 182–183
platform argument 46
PortBindings attribute 26
Port field 76, 126, 175
- -port flag 229, 232–233
Post function 111
POSTGRES_PASSWORD environment variable 38
POSTGRES_USER environment variable 38
POST request 85, 124–125, 152
POST /tasks route 84
practice, E-PVM scheduler 179–183
ProcessTasks method 131–132
/proc filesystem 93
project structure and initialization 256
proprietary Unix OS (AIX) 7
psql command-line client 38
PublishAllPorts field 45
Put() function 214
Put method 190–192, 199–201, 203–204, 209, 211
PVM (Parallel Virtual Machine) 178

Q

queue, role of 59
Queue field 27, 59, 62–63, 67
Queue implementation 33
Quick Introduction to Load Balancing and Load Balancers (Bonte) 21

R

ReadDisk() method 93
reader variable 44
ReadLoadAvg() method 93
ReadMemInfo() method 93
ReadStat() method 93
recovery options 142–145
    recovering from environmental failures 142–144
    recovering from manager failures 145
    recovering from worker failures 144–145
    recovery from application failures 142
refactoring, workers 201–205
Remove method 190
Remove operation 190
request router 77
requests
    handling 77–80
    manager API 124–125
responses, manager API 124–125
resp variable 46–47
RestartCount field 149, 152, 159

- -restart flag 143
restart policy 8
RestartPolicy attribute 26
RestartPolicy field 42
restartTask method 152, 200
REST (representational state transfer) 74
Result field 43
result variable 67, 198
RetryCount field 158
retry.go file 184
rootCmd 225
rootCmd.AddCommand method 227
rootCmd variable 226
root.go file 225–226
RoundRobin scheduler 167, 178
round-robin scheduler, adapting to scheduler interface 166–169
RoundRobin struct 166
RoundRobin type 170
router 72
Router field 76, 80, 126
routes 72, 123
    manager API 124
rp variable 45
Run() method 41, 48, 62
runCmd command 238
run command 236, 240–241
Run field 226–227, 231, 234, 239, 242, 248
Run method 43–45, 48, 62
Running state 24, 63–65, 151, 158
runTask method 28, 60, 63–64, 66–68, 129, 202–203
runTasks function 116, 129, 132
RunTasks method 129, 131–132
runTasks method 100, 129
r variable 45

S

scalability 11
Scheduled state 24, 63–65, 67, 151
scheduler 163–187
    bug in 173–174
    completing Node implementation 183–186
    implementing more sophisticated
        putting it all together 175–178
    interface 169–173
        adding new fields to Manager struct 169
        modifying New helper function 170–173
    scheduling problem 163–164
Scheduler field 170, 196
scheduler flag 233

scheduler.go file 185
scheduler interface 169–173, 175, 183, 189, 251
    adapting round-robin scheduler to 166–169
    adding new fields to Manager struct 169
    modifying New helper function 170–173
Scheduler.Pick method 171
schedulers
    defined 10
    E-PVM scheduler 178–183, 186–187
        in practice 179–183
        theory 178
scheduler.Scheduler interface 169
Scheduler.Score method 171
Scheduler.SelectCandidateNodes method 171
scheduler skeleton 30–31
schedulerType argument 196
schedulerType parameter 170
Score method 167–168, 177, 179
scoring phase 15
security 21
Security by Design (Mittal) 21
SelectCandidateNodes method 167–168, 171, 177,
    179
selectedNode 171
SelectWorker method 30, 109–110, 167, 171, 173,
    177
SendWork method 110–111, 117, 131, 172–174,
    190, 200–201
separation of concerns 106
server 13
service discovery 18–19
Service Discovery in a Microservices Architecture 19
Short field 226, 230, 238, 248
skeleton code 22–35
    task skeleton 24–27
    worker skeleton 27–29
skeletons
    other 31–32
    testing 32–35
specs.Platform type 45
SQL (Structured Query Language) 207
SRE (site reliability engineering) 253
Start() method 81, 116, 129, 132
StartTaskHandler 126
StartTaskHandler method 77
StartTask method 28, 60–62, 67, 74, 203–204
StartTime field 26
State field 25, 146, 158
StateString struct 147
State struct 147
stateTransitionMap type 65
State type 24

Stat function 238
/stats endpoint 183–184
Stats field 247
stats.go file 93
/stats route 99
stats.Stats type 183
Stats struct 93
Stats type 93–94, 96, 247
status command 243–248
stdcopy.StdCopy(os.stdout, os.stderr, out)
    call 47
Stdout 44
Stop() method 60
stopCmd variable 242
stop command 241–243
stopContainer function 49
Stop method 48, 62
StopTaskHandler 128, 205
StopTaskHandler method 77, 79, 201
StopTask method 28, 60–62, 67, 173–174, 204
storage, persistent
    for tasks, storage problem 189
    refactoring workers 201–205
    Store interface 189–191
    switching out in-memory stores for permanent
        ones 215–216
Storage interface 251
Store interface 189–191, 197–199, 201, 203, 205,
    208–211
stores, in-memory, for task events 195–201
    refactoring manager to use new in-memory
        stores 196–201
store.Store interface 196, 201, 217
map 208
StringP method 229
StringSliceP function 234
StringSliceP method 233
struct_literal 196
switch statement 170, 186, 197, 215
syscall package 93, 97

T

tabwriter package 245
t argument 148, 150
task 152
task1.json file 156
task.Completed state 79–80
task component 23
Task concept 51
task configuration 42–51
    starting and stopping tasks 43–51

TaskCount field 32, 60, 98
taskCount value 210
TaskDb 107, 112, 115, 151
TaskDb datastore 152
TaskDb field 196–197
TaskDb map 200–201
TaskDb store 198
taskDbType argument 202
taskDb variable 196
task.DockerResult type 61
TaskEvent 152
task events, implementing in-memory store
    for 195–201
  refactoring manager to use new in-memory
      stores 196–201
task event store, implementing persistent
    212–215
TaskEvent struct 27, 29
task.go file 42–43
taskID 124
taskID argument 173
task.ID field 152
Task implementation 51
task-level failures 143–144
task package 60
taskPersisted.State state 67
taskPersisted variable 199
Task Queue 108
taskQueued.State state 67
task runtime 15
tasks 58–59
  counting 60
  defined 8
  health checks and restarts 149–153
  implementing updates on workers
    148–149
  inspecting on workers 146–148
  persistent storage, Store interface 189–191
  persistent storage for
    implementing persistent task store
      208–212
    introducing BoltDB 207–212
    putting it all together 205–207
    storage problem 189
  role of queue 59
/tasks endpoint 134, 156
task skeleton 24–27
Tasks struct 149
task starting and stopping 43–51
task startup failures 140–141
task state 63–65
Task Storage layer 15

TaskStore 208
task stores, in-memory store for tasks
    191–194
TaskStore store 217
TaskStore struct 208–209
Task struct 25–27, 29, 58, 68, 90, 149
task.TaskEvent 152
task.TaskEvent type 74, 77, 190, 195, 200, 212
*task.Task type 208
task.Task type 66–67, 74, 80, 148, 150, 195, 199,
    211–212
task templates, implementing persistent storage
    for 212–215
TaskWorkerMap 29, 150, 152
taskWorkerMap map 115
templates, implementing persistent task event
    store 212–215
The Go Programming Language (Donovan and
    Kernighan) 15
The Raft Consensus Algorithm (Ongaro and
    Ousterhout) 20
tmux 18
ts variable 197
tx.Bucket function 211
type assertion 193
types.ContainerJSON struct 146
types.ContainerStartOptions 47
Types of Load Balancing Algorithms (Bonte) 21

U

- -unix-socket flag 41
Unmarshal function 211
Update function 210–211
UpdateTasks method 30, 112–114, 118–119,
    130, 132, 148, 155
updateTasks method 130, 148–149, 197–198,
    204
uptime command 95
URLParam function 79
Use field 226, 230, 238, 248
utils directory 184
UUID package 33
uuid.Parse() method 79
UUID (universally unique identifier) 25
uuid.UUID type 79

V

ValidStateTransition function 65, 67
View function 210–211
VMs (virtual machines) 5–6

W

Web Application Security (Gupta) 21
worker API 71–87
  API struct 76–80
  data format, requests, and responses 74–76
  handling requests 77–80
  overview of 72–76
  putting together 81–86
  serving 80–81
worker argument 173
worker command 227, 230–232, 239
Worker component 27, 29, 51, 105
worker component 23
worker failures 141–145
Worker field 76, 80, 126
WorkerNodes field 169–170
Worker object 129
worker package 202
workers 55–70
  DB (database)
    counting tasks 60
    implementing worker's methods 60–67

defined 10
health checks and restarts
    149–153
implementing task updates on
    148–149
inspecting tasks on 146–148
overview of 56–57
putting together 67–70
refactoring 201–205
tasks and Docker, role of queue
    59
Workers field 109
workers field 29
workers flag 233
worker skeleton 27–29
Workers subcomponent 108
Worker struct 27–28, 59–60
worker subdirectory 27
WorkerTaskMap field 29
workerTaskMap map 115
Worker type 80
wport variable 175